GUIDELINES FOR

WORLD EVANGELISM

BY

George P. Gurganus
C. Philip Slate
Stan Shewmaker
Wendell Broom
Dan Coker

Ed Mathews
B. E. Davis
Glover Shipp
Joyce Hardin
Dan Hardin

Bob Douglas

With a Foreword By JOHN C. STEVENS

GEORGE P. GURGANUS
EDITOR

106576

Published By
BIBLICAL RESEARCH PRESS
774 East North 15th Street
Abilene, Texas
79601

GUIDELINES FOR
WORLD EVANGELISM

Edited by GEORGE P. GURGANUS

COPYRIGHT © 1976
BIBLICAL RESEARCH PRESS

◇

LIBRARY OF CONGRESS CATALOG CARD No. 76-56592
I. S. B. N. 0-89112-040-8

◇

FOREWORD

For a good many years, it has seemed to me that many of us who are Christians have been more concerned with analyzing our own shortcomings than with evangelizing the world.

Now surely there is nothing wrong with self-examination—we learn that lesson from the scriptures; furthermore, we are taught to confess our sins and to exhort one another day by day. But it is also true that one needs to get outside one's self and take the gospel to others. We acknowledge our own imperfections; but we are not seeking to convert people to ourselves. We preach Christ and Him crucified—and this is the message the world desperately needs.

So I am thankful that evangelism is back on the track. I see a growing determination in the church to take the message of Christ to humanity. We want to lead mankind to the kingdom of God.

It is essential that we utilize all of the knowledge and wisdom available to us in accomplishing this great—this seemingly impossible—task.

The authors of the chapters in this volume are eminently qualified to discuss the topics undertaken. They have studied principles of world evangelism and missions and have put their teachings into practice. From hard experience they have learned of things that will not work as well as principles that are successful.

I commend this volume because, first of all, it is dealing with the most important subject confronting Christians today; secondly, it has been written by people who are qualified to challenge our thinking; and thirdly, it is our fervent hope and prayer that it will help to stimulate us to more productive achievement.

John C. Stevens, President
ABILENE CHRISTIAN UNIVERSITY

CONTENTS

INTRODUCTION

GEORGE P. GURGANUS

It is incredible to think that the church of Jesus Christ can forget or minimize its prime function—that of witness bearing. Yet, many churches that claim Jesus as Lord do appear to act as though Missions is an option. A large congregation was given a test of Bible knowledge and the results indicated that the members generally understood and accepted the fact that God desires the reconciling of all men of all races to Christ and that this was God's principal goal for His Church. Yet, when asked to make choices relating to the ongoing program and the uses of funds of the church, these same people placed a greater importance upon parking lots, expansion of classroom facilities and other self-serving tools, than upon direct evangelism at home or abroad. In fact, the latter was curtailed in order to expand local services. Thank God that this is not true of all congregations. *The church that is truly the body of Christ will place priority on the "discipling of the nations"* in word and in deed.

This book offers *Guidelines for World Evangelism* for Christians involved in supporting outreach from the home base and for the men engaged in evangelism on the field. To place the study in historical perspective, a review will now be made of some key periods in the Protestant world outreach from the seventeenth century to the present. It is wise to learn from history and not to repeat the mistakes of others.

The Period of the Pioneers

In what we have termed the first period of critical reevaluation of the missionary enterprise, Dr. C. H. Carpenter, a Northern Baptist, wrote a book entitled *Self-Support, Illustrated in the History of the Bassien-Karen Mission from 1840 to 1880,* which was published by Rand Avery and Company, Boston, in 1883. In this book Dr. Carpenter explained the reasons for a change from the "subsidy system" to the self-support policy and described the process of the changeover and the rapid growth of the Karen church after the change of policy. The fact that the Karen church in Burma has taken roots and has grown as few other churches, appears to support Dr. Carpenter's contention that the change in missionary methods made the difference. Some have questioned this conclusion, however, pointing to local factors, such as the inferior position of the Karens in Burma and their animistic faith, as providing possible favorable circumstances for mass conversion. [1] The Buddhist Burmese, they point out, were not very responsive to the message of this particular missionary. Their different type of religion may account for this fact. This work points up the need for further study in order to determine whether methods do make a difference.

The views of Dr. Carpenter were not popular in his day. According to a contemporary missionary to China:

> ... the Northern Baptist Board had sedulously kept the knowledge of the self-support movement in Burma from the people during all these forty years. They decapitated Dr. Carpenter for publishing the work. [2]

Dr. T. P. Crawford was sent to China as a missionary by the Southern Baptist Missionary Society in 1952. He soon became dissatisfied with what he called the "subsidy system" practiced by his mission and decided that a change of policy was needed. He began to agitate for a standard worldwide policy on the part of his mission board. But he, like Carpenter, ran into opposition, and his name was dropped from the roll of missionaries of the Southern Baptist Church. Dr. Crawford operated as an independent missionary in the latter days of his life. A book of his papers, entitled *Evolution in my Mission Views,* was published posthumously by a friend, J. A. Scarboro of Fulton, Kentucky, in 1903.

The policy advocated by Dr. Crawford and later put into practice in China by him after he became an independent consisted of three principles:

---

[1] Charles Iglehart, *A Century of Protestant Christianity in Japan* (Rutland, Vermont: Charles E. Tuttle Company, 1959), p. 343.

[2] T. P. Crawford, *Evolution in My Mission Views* (Fulton, Kentucky: J. A. Scarboro, publisher, 1903), p. 41.

First—the gospel of Christ as the power of God unto salvation in every mission field, unaccompanied by any kind of pecuniary inducement to the people; or, in other words, through native support everywhere.

Second—the churches of Christ should, as organized bodies, singly or in cooperating groups, do their own mission work without the intervention of any outside convention, association, or board.

Third—self-denying labors for Christ's sake, both by the churches at home, and by the missionaries abroad.

A Gospel Mission Band of twelve persons, eight men and four women, was organized by Dr. Crawford to carry out his plans by following the principles that he advocated. They worked together from 1894 to 1900 and reported some success. Their labors were interrupted by the Boxer Rebellion, and the group was forced to flee the country. Dr. Crawford was unable to return to his work due to failing health and eventual death in 1902.

Dr. Crawford was unable to test adequately his theories of missionary methods in actual practice. No method seems to have been very successful in China.[3] Some might claim that this was due to the fact that the Chinese were adherents of great world religions and not animists, as were the Karen Burmese. Hendrik Kraemer explains the lack of acceptance of Christianity in China as due, among other things, to a confused message from the West and to "faith in science and in modern humanism, which are rightly felt by their inherent relativism and pragmatism to be akin to Chinese mind patterns . . . "[4]

Dr. John L. Nevius was also a missionary in China, but he represented the Presbyterian Church. His principal contribution was a series of articles that appeared in the

---

[3] *World Christian Handbook* (London: World Dominion Press, 1962), p. 149.

[4] Hendrik Kraemer, *The Christian Message in a Non-Christian World* (Grand Rapids: Kregel Publications, 3rd ed., 1956), p. 249.

Chinese Recorder in 1885. These were later published in book form and came into the hands of a group of missionaries in Korea, who were in the early stages of the development of the mission program of the Presbyterians.

The Nevius Plan, as reiterated by a Korean Presbyterian missionary,[5] may be summarized briefly as including:

1. *A policy of native self-support.* The native Christians must provide their own schools with only small mission subsidies to be expected in the early stages of the program.

2. *A policy of self-propagation.* Every believer to be both a learner from someone who knows more than he does and a teacher of someone who knows less. Lay preachers and other church leaders must support themselves and teach until the native church can assume the burden of their support.

3. *A policy of self-government.* Every church must be under its own self-chosen unpaid leaders. A pastor should be chosen when the church is able to support him.

4. *A policy of wide itineration on the part of the missionary.*

5. *A policy of strict church discipline.*

6. *A policy of benevolence by the native Christians.*

The Nevius Plan contains other provisions, but the ones mentioned are basic. Clark felt that the fundamental idea of the Plan was self-support. A mission historian gives the following account of the adoption of the Nevius Methods:

> Mr. Underwood was interested in these methods with a view to applying them to the work of the Mission. Aside from this also, he felt the need of advice and guidance from some of our older missionaries in China and "had repeatedly written that some one of experience might be sent." It was a determining factor in the history of the Mission therefore, when Dr. and Mrs. Nevius came from

---

[5]C. A. Clark, *The Nevius Plan of Mission Work in Korea* (Seoul, Korea: Christian Literature Society, 1937), p. 32.

Chefoo, China, in June 1890, and spent two weeks in Seoul with the seven members of the Mission. The result was, as Mr. Underwood states, "After careful and prayerful consideration, we were led in the main, to adopt these (the Nevius Methods)."[6]

The progress of the Presbyterian Church in Korea was slow at first but growth mushroomed after the first few years. In less than fifty years there were about half a million Protestants in Korea with nearly three-fourths of them Presbyterians.[7] Rhodes, the mission historian, notes this phenomenal growth but does not affirm that the Nevius Methods were a dominant influence on the growth. He writes: "Whether the church flourishes because of the system or the system is possible because of the flourishing condition of the church is a question that might be argued." And it was argued. Latourette claims that "the reasons for the rapid advance after 1895 and especially between 1906 and 1910 appear to have been mixed."[8]

One could not deny that the reasons for the rapid advance were mixed, but in this instance, where missionaries were dealing with people of the great religions, and where the Presbyterians, who were practicing the Nevius Plan, far outstripped all other denominations, including the Catholics, in growth, the evidence seems to support the methods as having had a definite bearing on the success of the mission project.

Dr. Roland Allen was the last of the great pioneer advocates of the indigenous church, and perhaps the most effective in stating the principles involved and in publicizing the concept. He was a prolific writer. The World Dominion Press in London published his two major books: *Missionary Methods: St. Paul's or Ours* in 1912 (it has gone into a

---

[6]Harry A. Rhodes (ed.), *History of the Korean Mission Presbyterian Church,* U. S. A., 1884-1934 (Seoul, Korea: Chosen Mission Presbyterian Church U. S. A., 1934), p. 86.

[7]Clark, *op. cit.*

[8]Clark, *op. cit.*, p. 426.

number of editions and is presently published in paperback by Wm. B. Eerdmans Publishing Company of Grand Rapids, Michigan) and *The Spontaneous Expansion of the Church* (in 1960 it was in its fourth edition). In addition to these books, Roland Allen also wrote a great deal for the missionary magazine *World Dominion,* which has since changed its name to *Frontier.*

Roland Allen recommended that missionaries adopt the methods of the Apostle Paul in doing mission work. These methods he set forth as:

1. Begin the work in strategic centers of population and influence.

2. Do not aim at any particular class.

3. Do not take money from the people to whom you are ministering at the time.

4. Don't take money from other churches to give to the mission church.

5. Do not administer local church funds.

6. Make the churches self-supporting from their inception.

7. Preach a simple doctrine as Paul did.

8. Organize the churches in a simple New Testament pattern.

9. Encourage self-discipline on the part of the new churches.

The contribution of Roland Allen was principally that of widely publicizing the concepts advocated by earlier missionaries. He did not demonstrate the effectiveness of the principles but he popularized them.

The Period of the Social Gospel

In the year 1928, the Jerusalem Missionary Conference was held. According to Harold Lindsell, the trend of this meeting was toward "the social gospel, the ethnic concept of religion in which Christianity was denominated as differing in degree rather than in kind from other religions."[9] This was

---

[9]*A Christian Philosophy of Missions* (Wheaton, Illinois: The Van Kampen Press, 1949), p. 24.

consistent with the generally accepted philosophy of history—the idea of progress. The current conviction associated with this idea was that of believing that one had only to be true to his conscience or to live up to the light he had. It was in this theological climate that the next major investigation of missionary methods and motives took place.

Rethinking Missions is the report provided by the Laymen's Committee that was financed by John D. Rockefeller, Jr., for the purpose of studying mission work and recommending future policy and methods. The motive for this project evolved from the conviction of the promoters of the importance of the work and the fact that the Missions were facing difficult times. The preface includes a statement to this effect:

> It is doubtful whether any enterprise dependent entirely on continuous giving has so long sustained the interest of so many people as has the foreign mission . . . There is a growing conviction that the missionary enterprise is at a fork in the road, and that momentous decisions are called for.[10]

William Earnest Hocking, an outstanding philosopher and professor of Harvard University, was chosen to be chairman of the committee. He also served as co-editor of the report. These researchers worked independently of the large mission boards, but received helpful cooperation from them in carrying out their investigation. Countries chosen for investigation were India, Burma, China, and Japan. Groups were sent into each of these countries to study mission programs and collect data.

The Laymen's Report stated that ideally the first missionaries should have planted indigenous churches, as did the Apostle Paul, and permitted them to develop on their own. Since this was not the case, the group recommended

---

[10](New York: Harper and Brothers, 1932), p. IX.

certain changes for specific places and situations; but on the whole, the general policies suggested were:

1. An eventual transfer of all authority in the churches and the institutions from the missionaries to the natives.
2. Non-Christian religions should not be debated by missionaries.
3. A positive presentation of Christian principles should be made.
4. A sharing should take place between Christianity and non-Christian religions. Each should adopt the good points of the other.
5. Ultimately, the missionary should become an advisor or minister in the service of the native church.

No little stir was created by the release of this report. There were many outcries, as evidenced by the following statement in the *Christian Century:*

It is true, of course, that the report has burst like a thunderclap on a great portion of the American church. It is true that mission boards and other forms of institutionalized religion are having a bad time trying to find some way of dealing with it. It is true that the assumptions on which the report is based as well as its specific contents, bring not only the missionary enterprise but the whole Christian church to a parting of the ways. The Presbyterian general council has already flatly said that the commission which wrote this report does not know what Christianity is—a statement that drives as sharp a line of demarcation as ever Luther drove between himself and the pope.[11]

Some objections to the Laymen's Report were as follows:

1. The Holy Spirit and His work were not mentioned in the publication.[12]

---

[11]Paul Hutchinson, Review of *Rethinking Missions,* ed. W. E. Hocking, *Christian Century,* Dec. 21, 1932, pp. 1577-78.

[12]Harold Lindsell, *Missionary Principles and Practices* (New York: Fleming H. Revell Company, 1955), p. 332.

2. The group was directed by a philosopher, not a missionary or a theologian.[13]

3. The attitude of appreciation of non-Christian faiths and synthesis sharing among faiths is extreme.[14]

4. The report is basically a presentation of the philosophy of William Ernest Hocking, as stated in his book, *Living Religions and a World Faith.*[15]

5. The group represented the most liberal Protestant denominations and had only Western Christians investigating Western missions.[16]

6. The Laymen's Report failed to recognize the fact that God sent Jesus Christ into the world as the Way, the Truth, and the Life.[17]

The Laymen's Committee and Report served a good purpose in the judgment of this writer. It opened up the field of missionary endeavor to critical inspection. Such a development could be very significant as the barriers preventing progress could be recognized and steps could be taken toward the eventual elimination of these barriers.

Lindsell characterized *Rethinking Missions* as "theologically-arrived-at conclusions of the hour."[18] To him it appeared that Hocking and his assistants had pronounced the death sentence on Missions. Others shared the same views and by the time of the Madras Ecumenical Conference of 1938, a shift of sentiment had taken place. The convention attacked "the social gospel."

---

[13]Lamott, *op. cit.,* pp. 145-46.

[14]*Ibid.,* p. 145.

[15]Lamott, *op. cit.,* p. 145.

[16]Frederick B. Fisher, "Rethinking Missions," *Christian Century,* Dec. 14, 1932, p. 1538.

[17]Kraemer, *op. cit.,* p. 49.

[18]*A Christian Philosophy of Missions,* p. 28.

The Neo-Orthodox Period

Dr. Hendrik Kraemer of the University of Leiden in Holland was asked by the International Missionary Council to prepare a book on the approach to the task of world evangelism and to "state the fundamental position of the Christian church as a witness-bearing body in the modern world."[19] This book served as a keynote to the Madras World Missionary Conference in 1938.

In essence it might be said that the Laymen's Report tried to take the Holy Spirit out of Missions and Kraemer tried to put it back in. The Laymen's Report had equated the Church to the great faiths while Kraemer pointed up the uniqueness of the Church and of salvation through Christ. These points are made clear in Kraemer's summation:

> The conclusion that we have in view is that the only valid motive and purpose of missions is and alone can be to call men and peoples to confront themselves with God's acts of revelation and salvation for man and the world as presented in Biblical realism, and to build up a community of those who have surrendered themselves to faith in and loving service of Jesus Christ.[20]

The Anthropological Period

The World Missionary Conference at Madras was also characterized by a new emphasis—a study of the relationship between Missions and the cultural context and the role of missionaries as carriers of culture. This led to the development of intensive research in cultural anthropology. In 1945 J. Merle Davis, a second generation missionary to Japan, published an anthropological study of Missions entitled *New Buildings on Old Foundations.*[21] This work introduced a

---

[19]*Op. cit.,* p. v.

[20]*Ibid.,* p. 292.

[21] (New York: International Missionary Council, 1945).

new dimension to Missions theory and research and since then cultural anthropology has become the science of the missionary. So much so that Harold Lindsell said in 1955:

> It may be said dogmatically that the best missionaries have been good anthropologists. Perhaps they knew little or nothing about the formal side of the science, but they had an intuitive grasp of the science without formal training in it.[22]

The Church Growth Period

A natural outgrowth of the anthropological approach to a study of Missions is the present Church Growth philosophy. This school of thought centers around the person and ideas of Donald A. McGavran, the founder of the School of World Missions and Institute of Church Growth of Fuller Theological Seminary. It may be said that this period began in 1955 with the publication by McGavran of *The Bridges of God.*[23] The basic premise of the Church Growth school of thought is its affirmation that the goal of Missions is church planting. The claim is that God wants church growth. This being true, the work of the student of Missions is set. He needs to be able to determine *how churches grow* and how to discover *ripe fields.* Cultural anthropology and sociology are indispensable tools in the process of seeking answers to both of these questions.[24] McGavran's school of thought still dominates in Missions and his influence has reached all denominations, even the Roman Catholic Church.

---

[22]*Missionary Principles and Practices* (New York: Fleming H. Revell Company, 1955), p. 278.

[23](New York: Friendship Press, 1955).

[24]Randy Becton, "A Study of the Theological Basis of the Church Growth Philosophy of Missions" (unpublished Master's thesis, Abilene Christian University), p. 265.

The question may be raised, "What does all this have to do with churches of Christ today?" First of all, it puts a study of Missions in perspective and offers valuable data that can be helpful in avoiding the mistakes of others in the past and in planning a strategy for world evangelism for the present and the future.

In structuring *Guidelines for World Evangelism,* the areas of most vital concern for the understanding of present day Missions and the planning of a strategy for successful church planting were decided upon. Then a quest was made to find the most capable persons available to write on the topics relating to these areas, in which each had both practical experience and academic competence. Such a team was put together and the succeeding chapters which they have written are dedicated to the Lord Jesus Christ and to the planting of His church worldwide.

THE BIBLICAL IMPERATIVE
C. PHILIP SLATE

A few years ago an elder in a midwestern church was reported to have said, "This missionary business is just a fad which will pass off before long." I did not believe then, nor do I now, that most of our world evangelism is a product of a fad. Most of the workers I knew had reasonably good motives, even if they shared with me an inadequate preparation for their task. But there is a tragic truth reflected in the elder's comment, a truth greater than he apparently knew: *work done for the Lord can have an insufficient foundation.*

In the nineteenth century when Europeans were sailing the seas and establishing colonies, it was very easy for "missionaries" to go to those colonies. They were privileged and had easy access to the "heathen". A whole set of circumstances made it easy for one to follow the flag carrying the cross.[1] It was easy to be interested in foreign evangelism during "The Great Century." But when circumstances changed—war interrupted peace, colonies wanted independence, economic conditions changed, etc.—it was easy to forget "missions". The churches were influenced by the world in which they lived.

In our own case there was a great surge forward in world evangelism just after World War II. Why? There were several causes, including the availability of funds, comparative peace in the country and in the church, and a new interest in the world which came from former military people who had traveled and seen world conditions, and from the general national interest in helping other countries.[2] The national posture influenced the church's attitude.

---

[1] Kenneth S. Latourette, *The Great Century: Europe and the United States,* vol. 4: *A History of the Expansion of Christianity* (CEP edition; Grand Rapids: Zondervan Publishing House, 1970), chapter I.

[2] For a useful analysis see Philip W. Elkins, *Church-Sponsored Missions: An Evaluation of Churches of Christ* (Austin, Texas: Firm Foundation Publishing House, 1974), pp. 4-7.

The story has been repeated many times. When the circumstances are favorable, the church pushes forward with evangelism. But there is a corresponding danger in letting interest in evangelism be conditioned so much by the political and economic climate of the country in which we live that we do not evangelize *out of principle*. Fad becomes more important than faith! There seems to be no way to escape this fadism in evangelism other than through grounding our evangelistic thinking and action in the Scriptures.

Evangelism: Life of the Church

1. Old Testament Background. From Genesis through Revelation there is a concern for man's relationship with God. In this sense the whole of Scripture is related to the evangelistic task. Although a creature of God, man was separated from God through sin[3] and became a worshipper of creatures rather than the Creator.[4] The task of bringing mankind back to the fellowship with God was not an easy one because of the power of sin in man's life. So God began by working through the few (the Jews) in order that He might ultimately reach and regain all. The promise to Abraham shows both God's choice to use the Jews and an ultimate desire to bless all his creatures.[5]

The Jews, as God's blessed people, were to be "a light to the nations" (Gentiles),[6] the means by which God shows something of Himself to all mankind. God was concerned about the Gentiles. Their idolatry produced a senselessness for which God did not make His creatures.[7] But while the

---

[3]Gen. 1:26-27; Ps. 8:5-8; Gen. 3:22-4; Isa. 59:1-2.

[4]Rom. 1:24-5: cf. Everett Ferguson, "The Pagan," in *World Evangelism*, Abilene Christian College Annual Bible Lectures (Abilene: Abilene Christian College Book Store, 1971) pp. 151-161.

[5]Gen. 12:1-2; cf. Acts 3:24-6.

[6]Isa. 42:6; 49:6.

[7]Ps. 115:1-8.

prophets denounced idolatry[8] and extolled the living God, there was in the Old Testament nothing like an evangelistic enterprise. Moses' speaking to Israel as God's envoy[9] and Jonah's preaching on Nineveh[10] are not real cases of evangelization.

Even though there was no proper evangelism in the Old Testament, there was a keen expectation for a time when "the nations" (Gentiles) would bow before their Creator:[11]

> All nations thou has made shall come
> and bow down before thee, O Lord,
> and shall glorify thy name.

Some marvelous time was coming when the nations would go to Jerusalem and learn of the Lord.[12] Thus, in the Old Testament the tragic plight of idolatrous mankind is portrayed, and along with it there is the promise that something wonderful is yet to come which will rescue man. The road out of Eden is clearly visible at the end of the Old Testament. But there is a promise of something better.

2. Jesus and the "Hinge of History." During his ministry Jesus had declared that something new was happening: "The kingdom of heaven is at hand." But he sent his disciples only to "the lost sheep of the house of Israel" during his ministry on earth.[13] It was not until after his death and resurrection that the Old Testament expectations burst forth into a new

---

[8] E.G., Isa. 44:9-20; Jer. 10:1-16.

[9] Ex. 3:7-12.

[10] Although exceptional for the Old Testament, only two verses relate the message preached (Jonah 3:4-5). The design of the book is more to show God's mercy (3:10; 4:2, 9-11) than to record evangelization by a Jew.

[11] Ps. 86:9; cf. Ps. 96:1-9; Jer. 16:19-20; Zech. 8:20-23.

[12] Isa. 2:1-4; Mic. 4:1-4.

[13] Matt. 10:5-6. For a discussion of Jesus' dealings with the Gentiles see Joachim Jeremias, *Jesus' Promise to the Nations* (London: S C M Press, 1958), pp. 19ff.

era. Before his victorious ascension on high[14] Jesus appeared in Galilee to the eleven. There he made such claims for himself ("all authority"), gave his disciples such a charge ("all nations"), and made such a reference to time ("to the close of the age") that one realizes he was announcing the dawning of a new era.[15] The Old Testament hopes were now to be fulfilled. The Gentiles were to receive God's favor. The long Jewish era had come to the point in time for which it had prepared. This new era is sandwiched between two important events: the ascension and the final appearing of Jesus. The events in Jerusalem (death and resurrection) and Jesus' commission in Galilee constituted a "hinge of history", the ushering in of and the era in which the church of Jesus' promise[16] came into existence.

3. Evangelism: the Church's Life-blood. In the new era the church comes into being by the gospel. It is ideally composed of people "from every tribe and tongue and people and nation," who exist to praise God,[17] who have accepted and live under the gospel. But the message which brings the church into existence is the message the church is to proclaim. A part of its life-blood is to proclaim to others that which it has come to enjoy.

> If your faith in the Saviour has bro't its reward,
>   If a strength you have found in the strength
>   of your Lord,
> If the hope of a rest in His palace is sweet,
>   O will you not, brother, the story repeat?

---

[14]I Tim. 3:16; Eph. 4:8; Col. 2:15; cf. Ps. 24:7-10.

[15]For an interesting discussion of this text (Matt. 28:16-20) see Johannes Blauw, *The Missionary Nature of the Church* (New York: McGraw-Hill Book Co., Inc., 1962) pp. 83ff.; cf. C. Philip Slate, "World Evangelism", in *What the Bible Teaches*, 1972 Lectureship of Harding Graduate School of Religion (Nashville: Gospel Advocate Book Co., 1972), pp. 161-178.

[16]Matt. 16:18.

[17]Rev. 5:9-10.

This evangelizing ("gospel-izing") is to be a characteristic feature of Jesus' people "to the close of the age." From ascension to second coming evangelism is a part of the church's affirmation of its own faith in Jesus as Lord. In George Rawson's hymn ("By Christ Redeemed") we are reminded that the Lord's supper is a chain from betrayal night to last advent:

> And thus that dark betrayal night,
> With the last advent we unite,
> By one bright chain of living rite,
> Until He come.

Similarly, between the "days of his flesh" and his last appearing those who are Jesus' disciples are to make disciples among others. Churches that live this way live near the heart of God and are less prone to "evangelize because it is a fad." Failure to evangelize is a kind of denial of one's own faith!

Something wonderful happens when a church gives prominence to world-wide evangelization, along with its otherwise balanced program of work. A few years ago Frank Pack reminded us of the 2,106-member Park Street (Congregational) Church in Boston which supported "one hundred twenty-three missionaries on the field" and that sixty-one of them were from its own membership. Over half of its budget was sent to the evangelistic enterprise. It was a conservative church which developed a passion for spreading its faith.[18]

Similar stories are heard of other churches, and they need not be large. I know a fine church which for years used over fifty percent of its contribution to evangelize; but when a building program markedly reduced that percentage, one of its elders told me that they had a "bad conscience" about it. Not until they restored that evangelistic emphasis did they regain something of their former spirit. We must beware of

---

[18]Frank Pack, "Why Couldn't This Happen Among Us?" *Gospel Advocate* (Nov. 5, 1959): 705., 714.

"one-factor" analysis, be careful about trying to use any *one* thing to build up the church. But the evidence is rather convincing that when a church catches a glimpse of how through evangelism it can be a part of God's world-wide work, something wonderful happens to its faith, its work, and its peace.

Goals

The history of evangelistic work, ours and others', indicates that unless the general terms "evangelism" and "mission work" are defined in terms of goals it is possible to waste much effort and money. Many of the specific and short-range goals will be determined by local conditions in a "ripe" or "unripe" area. But it is of considerable importance for the church to understand those broad goals God has set for his people:

1. Universalize the Message. Jesus specified that the gospel is for "all nations," the "whole creation," "to the end of the earth."[19] The Creator God who gives "life and breath" to all men is also concerned about their relationship with himself. The person who is at the remotest point on earth from us is one for whom Jesus died, whom God loves as much as he does me, and who is capable of "becoming" a child of God.[20] The God of the universe who cares more for people than for sparrows, sees redeemable creatures throughout the world. Potentially, he has many people who do not yet know him.[21] The gospel needs to go to all precisely because it is addressed to all. The Lord's people are charged with that difficult and rewarding task.

---

[19]Matt. 28:19; Lk. 24:47; Mk. 16:15; Acts 1:7.

[20]John 1:112. Note the change in the Corinthians (I Cor. 6:9-11).

[21]If the Lord viewed Corinth, of all cities, in that light (Acts 18:9-10), how must he view people today?

A marvelous truth lies back of two frequently misused texts in Colossians. When Paul affirmed that the gospel was bearing fruit in "the whole world" and had been "preached to every creature under heaven,"[22] he was evidently not meaning to say that every single creature of the globe had heard the message since several areas of even the Roman Empire apparently did not receive the gospel until later.[23] We wish to take nothing from our first-century brothers whose accomplishments still baffle the historian! But there is back of this Colossian situation a precious truth which need not elude us. Paul's purpose is to stabilize a group of Christians in the Lycus Valley whose faith is being challenged by those who sought to undermine it by suggesting that something besides the gospel is needed.[24] Paul counteracts the teaching by showing Christ to be pre-eminent in everything, creator and sustainer,[25] in whom alone one has fullness of life.[26] Accordingly, it was not within Paul's purpose to rehearse church growth statistics as such. Rather, he was saying, "What you have received has been received by all kinds of people throughout the world. Indeed, this has to be for the whole world, not just for Judea and your little valley, because it is the gospel of the Christ of the universe. You are a part of God's world-wide work." Precisely because the gospel is good news about Christ, it must be universalized in its proclamation. Failure to do so today may suggest that it is indeed a Western religion rather than a part of God's world-wide work.

---

[22]Col. 1:6, 23.

[23]See Michael Green, *The Evangelism of the Early Church* (Grand Rapids: Wm. B. Eerdmans Pub. Co., 1970), chapter 10.

[24]Col. 2:8-23. Note the emphasis on angels, fasting, and visions (verses 16-18).

[25]Note 1:15-20 in which Christ is presented in terms of the universe, not just as the Son of God who lived, died and was resurrected in Judea.

[26]Col. 2:9-10. Completeness in him renders unnecessary and futile any other effort to obtain salvation. The exclusiveness of Christianity is at once a point of confidence for Christians and an irritant to the non-Christian religions. But the emphasis arises from the nature of Christ himself. See John 14:6; I. Tim. 2:5; Acts 4:12; 17:30-31.

Paul made a similar point in a paragraph to the Corinthian Church. Because the new age had come, in which God was seeking to do something for all mankind in Christ, it was necessary for Paul and others to make that message known to as many people as possible.[27] Perhaps one of the surest ways of knowing that the gospel is taken seriously is to observe the extent to which it is made known to all for whom it is intended. The new song of the saints, which John heard in a vision, should be worked for by the church:[28]

Worthy art thou to take the scroll
    and to open its seals,
for thou was slain and by thy blood
    didst ransom men for God
from every tribe and tongue and
    people and nation,
and hast made them a kingdom and
    priests to our God.

In their praying and planning local churches should seek to get the gospel to unreached peoples, those who have never heard the message. Universalizing the message is a part of God's plan.

2. Work for Valid Decision. Whatever is necessary in making people feel the real impact of the gospel must be done. It does no good to drop gospel literature from an airplane to people who cannot read. The use of interpreters, choice of message elements, and the actions of the workers have a part in making men see God's plan for the ages.[29] The goal is so to communicate the message that people will be able to decide validly whether or not they will follow Jesus Christ. While there is no biblical evidence that we will ever

---

[27] II Cor. 6:1-10.

[28] Rev. 5:9-10.

[29] Eph. 3:8-10.

"win the world for Christ," there must be the desire to "win obedience" as far as possible.[30] It is known that people can say "yes" (by outward acts like baptism and the Lord's supper) to our efforts without responding to the gospel itself. On the other hand, people have said "no" (refused baptism, etc.), not so much to the gospel itself as to its crude handling by the messengers. In both cases we ought to be dissatisfied. There are cases in the New Testament where people said "no" to the apostolic message without blame being placed on the messengers.[31] It is upsetting when people clearly understand the gospel and refuse to accept Jesus as Lord, but they deserve to know who he is and what he has done for them. It is much more pleasant when men hear, understand clearly and receive the word. Jesus described these positions in his parable of the sower.

The matter of importance here is that Christians must do all possible to make the message understandable. Whatever is necessary to that task must be done. Paul referred to it, in his own case, as becoming all things to all men so he could save them.[32] Preparation in language and culture studies, as well as in biblical studies, would seem clearly to be implied in the necessity of working for valid decision.

3. Strive for Persistence of Faith. Jesus constantly warned his disciples about falling away and becoming faithless, and the same emphasis is found in the Epistles. It is clear that in God's purposes Jesus does not want three-month disciples, but people who will have faith to the end, even if it brings physical death.[33] The object is for men to live so as to praise God. The kind of work done by the messengers has something to do with the stability, the persistence in faith, of the new converts.

---

[30]Rom. 15:18.

[31]There are no less than fourteen cases of non-conversion in Acts, among them 5:33; 7:54ff.; 9:28-9; 14:2, 19; 17:32.

[32]I Cor. 9:19-22.

[33]Rev. 2:10.

In some areas the best that can be done is to win individuals, sometimes in very isolated conditions. In other cases it is possible to win family units or even villages.[34] But in either case every effort needs to be made to weld people into groups or assemblies. Paul had real concern for new converts and went to them in order to "strengthen" them.[35] Most of his Epistles were written with that in view. But Paul and others characteristically formed those new converts into groups called churches or assemblies. The size of those assemblies is not always indicated, but is obviously varied. Local churches were referred to as "bodies" to denote, among other things, the inter-relationship of the members.[36] There is in the New Testament such a pattern of Christians' functioning in groups that we must conclude that it was a part of apostolic strategy to start churches. Nor is it surprising that they did start churches when one notices what those groups did for their members.

What Christians were to do for "one another" pre-supposes some regular interchange of life. In fact, the "one-another-ness" of any church is one yardstick for measuring its strength. They were to comfort, encourage, prefer, forbear, forgive, edify, exhort, confess to, and be hospitable toward "one another."[37] Where an isolated Christian lacks this kind of help it is hard for him to hold on. Perhaps we all know cases where a distant, isolated Christian did not remain faithful.

All of this suggests that "evangelizing in general" may not focus our energies on the church-planting activity by which persistence in faith is encouraged. The local church is the cutting-edge of the kingdom, abroad as at home. Thus a

---

[34]Acts 16:15, 29-34; 9:32-35. On this point see Donald A. McGavran, *The Bridges of God* (New York: Friendship Press, 1955).

[35]Acts 14:22 and 16:36.

[36]Rom. 12:3-8; I Cor. 12:11-27. Local churches are in view.

[37]I Thess. 4:18; 5:11; Heb. 10:25; Rom. 12:10; Eph. 4:2, 32; Jas. 5:16; I Pet. 4:9.

major criterion for measuring evangelistic effort is the number and vitality of local churches which have resulted from the work.

The biblical mandates seem clear enough: the church of Christ is to spread the gospel message all over the world with such clarity that people can make a valid decision about Jesus Christ, and start viable churches so the new Christians will persist in their faith. But what will impel the church to do this kind of evangelism? What encouragements are there to carry through?

Motives

It is at the motive level that faith and fad in evangelism are most clearly to be seen. Bandwagon evangelism ceases when the wagon bogs down. But individuals and churches who evangelize because of their heavenly citizenship will evangelize when it is not fashionable to do so.

Since there are several ways of listing the biblical motives for evangelism[38] the following group is purely functional. But it is felt that these call attention to the major areas of motives.

Although Peter refers to the Lord's command to "preach to the people", and Paul and Barnabas mention the Lord's command to go to the Gentiles,[39] there is surprisingly little evidence that the command of Jesus was the decisive motivation for evangelism in the first century. It may have been a more important factor than we can detect. However that may be, it is important to notice the other motives which impelled the early Christians to evangelize far and wide in spite of difficulty.

---

[38]Useful discussions are found in Ferdinand Hahn, *Mission in the New Testament* (Naperville, Ill.: Alec R. Allenson, Inc., 1965); Donald G. Miller, "Pauline Motives for the Christian Mission", in *The Theology of the Christian Mission,* ed. Gerald H. Anderson (New York: McGraw-Hill Book Co. Inc., 1961), pp. 72-84; Michael Green, *Evangelism in the Early Church,* chapter 9.

[39]Acts 10:42; 13:47.

1. Time Motives. Unlike the Mosaic period, which looked forward to another era of blessings and opportunities,[40] the present era will terminate in a decisive judgment following the appearing of Jesus.[41] This expectation served time and again to urge Christians to evangelize while they had a chance. If one feels, as do Hindus, that each person goes through a series of incarnations, there is no real urgency to teach a religious message. There will be other chances. But when one believes, as Scripture teaches, that after death comes judgment, that after a general resurrection there will be a universal judgment, the incentive to teach is different.[42] It was partially in view of man's ultimate standing before the judgment seat of Christ that Paul persuaded men concerning the gospel.[43] If the church firmly holds the view of history set out in Scripture, it will busy itself preparing as many as possible for the final appearing of Jesus, both to avoid earned destruction and to prepare a host to meet the King. Michael Green is likely right in saying, "It is not too much to say that without a coherent eschatology it is not possible to do effective evangelism."[44]

2. Man Motives. The person who himself has been rescued from sin and comes to enjoy life in the Son may well think of the plight of those still estranged from God. Paul's deep feeling for Israel is a case in point: "For I could wish that I myself were accursed and cut off from Christ for the sake of my brethren, my kinsmen by race."[45] He felt himself

---

[40] Jer. 31:31ff.; Isa. 66:18-23.

[41] I Cor. 15:23; II Thess. 1:7-10.

[42] Heb. 9:27; Acts 24:25.

[43] II Cor. 5:10-11.

[44] Green, *Evangelism in the Early Church*, p. 277.

[45] Rom. 9:3.

to be debtor to men who were ignorant of Christ.[46] Gerhard Kromminga has argued forcefully that the New Testament injunction for Christians to love their neighbors is sufficient authority for them to teach the gospel to their neighbors.[47] This dimension of love is important to consider. Seeking the best for one's neighbor must certainly involve his spiritual as well as his physical welfare. Love for sinners is God-like; that is what God does for us, and we should extend it to others.[48]

3. God Motives. Several motives found among the early Christians were rooted in their consideration for the nature and activity of God. John explained that "we love because he first loved us"; what he did for us causes us to extend the same kind of concern to others.[49] It is hard to see how this would exclude the proclamation to others of the good news which originally came from God. Jessie Brown Pounds embodied the idea in the hymn, "Will You Not Tell It Today."

There was also the desire that God be recognized for what he really is, the one true God, Lord of heaven and earth.[50] Anyone who loves God can identify with Paul's agony of soul when he saw the city of Athens given to idolatry.[51] However, merely being enraged at the foolishness of idolatry does not produce praise for God; nor does the mere destruction of the physical idols themselves. Idolatry must be removed from the hearts of men so they can see "the light of the gospel of the glory of Christ," and live no longer for themselves (or any other God) but for him who for their

---

[46]Rom. 1:14; I Cor. 9:16-17.

[47]Carl G. Kromminga, *The Communication of the Gospel Through Neighboring* (Franeker: T. Wever, 1964).

[48]Rom. 5:6-11.

[49]I John 4:19, 7-12.

[50]Isa. 45:21ff.; Acts 17:23-4.

[51]Acts 17:16.

sakes died and rose again.[52] To that end Paul and others engaged in a divine warfare by which they sought to "destroy arguments and every proud obstacle to the knowledge of God, and take every thought captive to obey Christ."[53] This is evangelistic work.

To this day there is something thrilling in the awareness each Lord's day that because of someone's evangelism throughout the world, there are former idolaters of all sorts who "keep the feast." Paul claimed that the Godhead initiated salvation in order that saved people might live "to the praise of his glory."[54] It is a source of joy to see former Animists, Communists, Hindus and Secularists now living to the praise of God's grace. Since Christians exist to praise God, the desire to increase the number of "God-praisers" in the world is a wonderful motive for evangelizing. Paul demonstrated this to the Corinthians. "Why should we apostles endure all of this affliction, perplexity, and persecution as a consequence of our preaching?" he asked them. Why, "it is all for your sake, so that as grace extends to more and more people it may increase thanksgiving, to the glory of God."[55] He evangelized in order to increase the number of "God-praisers" in the world. When Christians are eager for others to glorify God, to live in gratitude before him, singing "Praise God from whom all blessings flow", their evangelism will increase in both quantity and quality.

Another way of regarding one's evangelism is found in Paul's attitude toward his work among the Gentiles. He knew that Christ's "service" was so designed that "the Gentiles might glorify God for his mercy."[56] Christ also worked

---

[52]II Cor. 4:4; 5:15.

[53]II Cor. 10:3-6.

[54]Eph. 1:6, 12, 14; cf. I Pet. 2:9-10.

[55]II Cor. 5:8-15.

[56]Rom. 15:8-9.

through him "to win obedience from the Gentiles."[57] Those whom Paul evangelized and brought to obedience he regarded as an "offering" to God as an act of his "priestly service of the gospel of God."[58] Churches who support and workers who go for such service can think of themselves as rescuing people from evil and offering them to God. This can give an added significance to reports about baptisms. When through evangelizing, people are brought to confess Jesus as God's Son and their Lord, and put him on in baptism, they may be regarded as an offering to God.

These God-oriented motives seem to lift up workers to a higher level of work than they would have by evangelizing primarily to save their own souls or to carry out the commission of Jesus as a rather cold commandment. To the Christian, God is to be the center of everything. Evangelism is his work done through his people.

Conclusion

We live in the era marked off by the ascension and final appearing of the "Lord of Glory." What he set in motion by his life, death, resurrection, and directives, his church is to carry out to the end of the era. Man's reconciliation to his Maker and Sustainer, and the praise of God by his creatures, are involved in the evangelistic enterprise. Its faithful and aggressive execution will depend significantly on the dimensions of faith found in local congregations.

The door is open for churches of Christ to have "partnership in the gospel" as the Philippian church had with Paul. By supporting him through gifts of love and prayer, deliberately identifying themselves with his evangelistic work, they were fellow-partakers with him of God's grace.[59] Paul did not seek their gifts of love, but they were regarded as "a

---

[57]Rom. 15:18.

[58]Rom. 15:16.

fragrant offering, a sacrifice acceptable and pleasing to God."[60] Because of their motives in helping Paul and his work, the gifts were somehow fruit which increased to their credit.[61]

Wonderful things happen in local churches when elders, preachers, and teachers direct the body in this course of life.

SUGGESTED READINGS

ANDERSON, Gerald H. (ed)., *The Theology of the Christian Mission.* New York: McGraw-Hill Book Company. 1961.

BEYERHAUS, Peter, *Shaken Foundations.* Grand Rapids: Zondervan Publishing House. 1972.

BLAUW, Johannes, *The Missionary Nature of the Church.* New York: McGraw-Hill Book Company. 1962.

BOER, Harry R., *Pentecost and Missions.* Grand Rapids: William B. Eerdmans Publishing Company. 1961.

HAHN, Ferdinand, *Missions in the New Testament.* London: S.C.M. Press. 1965.

LINDSELL, Harold, *An Evangelical Theology of Missions.* Grand Rapids: Zondervan Publishing House. 1970.

PETERS, George W., *A Biblical Theology of Missions.* Chicago: Moody Press.. 1972.

TRUEBLOOD, Elton, *The Validity of the Christian Mission.* New York: Harper and Row Publishers.

VICEDOM, George F., *The Mission of God.* Translated by Gilbert A. Thiele and Dennie Hilgendorf. St. Louis: Concordia Publishing House. 1965.

CULTURE AND COMMUNICATION

GEORGE P. GURGANUS

No two concepts are more vitally related to the purposes of the religion of Jesus Christ than culture and communication. Neither are there two concepts more closely intertwined with each other. In fact, it has been affirmed that culture is communication.[1] The spiritually impelled foreign missionary will excel in his ministry to the extent that he understands culture and can free himself from cultural prejudices so that he can function unhindered in a foreign culture. That is why so many top students of culture and linguistics are missionaries. It is also the reason for calling cultural anthropology the science of the missionary.

"Communication is a process of inducing others to interpret an event, fact, opinion, or situation in accordance with the intent of the speaker," according to Robert T. Oliver.[2] The speaker comes up with an idea in his head that he wishes to communicate to another person or persons. He encodes this concept in words from his vocabulary and verbalizes his messages by agitating the airwaves.[3] The receiver feels the sensation in his ears and decodes the symbols and supplies the meaning from his own background of experiences. This process is complex enough by itself but is further complicated by the fact that there are countless other cues that contribute to the message conveyed to the receiver such as gestures, facial expression, and numerous other possibilities associated with the speech situation. Communication takes place within a culture and people can

---

[1] Edward T. Hall, *The Silent Language,* Fawcett Premier Book, New York, 1966, p. 93.

[2] *Communicative Speech,* New York: The Dryden Press, 1955, p. 5.

[3] See K. S. Sitaram, "What is Intercultural Communication?" *Intercultural Communication: A Reader.* (Belmont, California: Wadsworth Publishing Company, Inc., 1972), p. 20.

only communicate effectively if they share a common culture. Culture largely predetermines the form that the communicative process will take and from the total cultural context the meaning is decoded by the receiver. The Apostle Paul was bi-cultural. When speaking to the Jews, he followed the Jewish custom of recounting God's dealings with Israel throughout history and tied his messages into God's plans for Israel. To the Greeks on Mars Hill, Paul utilized the channel of Greek rhetoric which was customary with them to communicate God's plan for all men. Paul did not here quote the Jewish Bible but used Greek sources to support his claims. To have done otherwise would have been a mistake.

Culture has been defined in many ways. In broad general terms it may be said that culture constitutes the unique way of life of a people or their total design for living. When a group of individual human beings are together long enough to begin to work together for the accomplishment of common goals they form a society. This society then develops a unique culture by sharing common goals, behavioral patterns and meanings. Culture is learned as all habits are formed. Hunger, sexual desire, self-preservation and other basic drives impel cooperative action. These actions encounter success or failure. Successes are repeated and habits are formed. Multi-individual habits or customs are called cultural traits. The cultural trait is the basic unit of culture.

As previously stated, culture has been defined as a system of shared meanings. Only man is able to symbolize; to establish arbitrary meanings. Only man creates a culture. Man gives meaning within a specific culture to artifact, mentifacts and sociofacts;[4] however, the meaning given in one culture does not necessarily hold true in another. In U. S. culture the automobile has many meanings and functions. On the other hand, if a group of isolated Australian aborigines in the outback wilderness were to come upon an American auto in the desert, they could not possibly share common meaning or understanding of functions with the Americans or European

---

[4]Physical creations, mental constructs and social relationships.

Australians. When people share life together they develop common behavioral patterns and establish a system of shared meanings.

The person who is totally monocultural in his orientation cannot possibly understand or appreciate peoples of other cultures and is likely unaware that he is blind to the forces that are determining his course within his own culture. Ruth Benedict indicates that the principal benefit of studying other cultures is the insight that one gains of his own.[5] In world missions a knowledge of the nature of culture and of one's self as a participant in culture is essential to success.

The Nature of Culture

Any approach to a study of culture is necessarily limited and must be an oversimplification. Cultural anthropology is not an exact science. On the other hand, a map is an oversimplification. It is hoped that this study will be as helpful as a map is to one who is traveling over a territory. Some important characteristics of culture are as follows:

1. *Culture is learned.* When a human baby is born, it has no culture. As the baby grows physically it is learning culture at the same time. This process of growing up in a culture and becoming a part of it is called enculturation. Humans learn culture from their parents and others of the same generation and pass it on to future generations.

2. *Culture is shared.* It is this aspect of culture that makes effective cooperation and communication possible. To a Texan, a firm and enthusiastic handshake accompanied by a smiling face and friendly talk constitutes a proper form of greeting. Everyone knows this and the nonconformists are disapproved. On the other side of the world, such a behavioral pattern might be meaningless or foolishness to a Japanese. He feels right about a greeting if it is properly done by bowing in the correct manner. All individuals within a

---

[5]*Patterns of Culture* (Boston: Houghton, Mifflin Company, 1959).

culture who fail to abide by the customary rules of behavior are highly suspect. They are the "bad guys" of the group and often not to be trusted fully.

3. *Culture is a dynamic adaptive system.* There are opposing forces in culture. One is to resist change and the other to change. Change comes inevitably but with varying degrees of rapidity. Primitive societies tend to promote continuity in culture and teach their children to be true to the old ways. The people of the U. S. promote discontinuity and teach their children to leave the old ways and go on to new and supposedly better ways. This leads to extremely rapid cultural change. Alvin Toffler dramatized this rapid rate of change in Western culture in the creation of the term "future shock."[6] According to Toffler, U. S. culture is changing at such a fast pace that one only has to wait a few years and he is in a quite different culture. In this way he suffers culture shock; therefore, Americans must learn to live in a future oriented society. When a missionary goes to a foreign country and falls victim to culture shock he can get relief by coming home. There is no escape from future shock.

Changes in culture are not often destructive but in harmony with the total context of the culture. It is a system in moving equilibrium like a cloud in the sky. The cloud is constantly changing its shape but remains a unique whole. When the missionary comes to realize the adaptive nature of culture, he is able to see the behavior of the nationals in a different light. Cultural traits are not ridiculous if they are seen in the context of the whole culture and as an attempt by the people to cope with their environment in a way to provide for basic needs. The Eskimo has some strange practices but seen in the context of his environment and the adaptation that he has so effectively made to it, each cultural trait appears more understandable. At least it can be said that the Eskimo has maintained his culture intact over a longer period than most peoples.

---

[6]*Future Shock* (New York: Bantam Books, Inc., 1971).

4. *Culture is patterned.* It is an integrated whole. Culture is not composed of a randomly arranged group of cultural traits but is structured with each element related directly or indirectly with every other element of the culture. Each cultural element has its function as a part of an "organic" whole. Culture is interrelated in all of its parts. Affect one and it affects all other aspects of the culture to some degree. Remove one element of culture and you have affected all others to some degree.

An anthropologist in Zambia told the missionary team there that the daily beer drinking custom of the villages was going to be a tremendous problem to them in bringing the village people to Christ. This custom was tied into other aspects of their culture. It involved their recreation, economics and to a lesser degree every other aspect of their village life. The missionaries were told that they were going to have to recognize this practice as Christian or supply a functional substitute. To eliminate it without a replacement could throw the culture so out of balance that the people would be destroyed. This type of thing was reported to have happened in New Guinea when missionaries introduced steel axes into a primitive culture. Prior to that, the men owned the stone axes as a symbol of their authority. When women and children were given the superior steel axes the result was chaos. The tribe disappeared.[7]

A similar example of the interrelation of beer to other aspects of culture was found among the Tarahumara Indians of Mexico.[8] A man with beer could have a party. In appreciation his neighbors would help him clear land on which he could plant more corn. More corn resulted in more beer. Corn could also be fed to the cows. The cows produced fertilizer which produced more corn and so on.

---

[7]Yehudi A. Cohen, *Man in Adaptation: The Cultural Present* (Chicago: The Aldine Publishing Company, 1968), p. 821.

[8]Eugene A. Nida, *Customs and Culture* (New York: Harper & Row, 1954), p. 45.

Interrelationship Between Cultural Elements

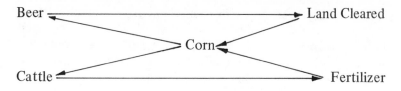

5. *Culture may be oriented in many different directions.*
Early students of culture pointed out the nature of culture as
a total design or as a "Configuration."[9] Other terms used to
describe this integrated wholeness of culture were "Soul" or
"Ethos." Sumner used the term "Ethos" to indicate "the
dominant set or direction of a culture."[10] Opler later
indicated that there were several interrelated "themes" in a
culture and not just one unified "theme" for the whole
culture.[11]

Ruth Benedict emphasized the overall unity of a culture
and yet in her book *Chrysanthemum and the Sword*[12]
revealed two seemingly contradictory aspects of the Japanese
people. They were gentle, artistic, polite and non-violent on
one side of the coin and belligerent, cruel and destructive on
the other. The Japanese were a real enigma to the Americans
in World War II. Ruth Benedict unravelled the mystery of the
Japanese cultural pattern so that Americans could have a

---

[9] Robert B. Taylor, *Introduction to Cultural Anthropology* (Boston: Allyn
and Bacon, Inc. 1973), p. 44.

[10] Felix M. Keesing, *Cultural Anthropology* (New York: Holt, Rhinehart, and
Winston, Inc. 1966), p. 56. Also see Roger M. Keesing and Felix M. Keesing, *New
Perspectives in Cultural Anthropology* (Same publisher, 1971) , pp. 391-395 for an
updating.

[11] Morris Edward Opler, "Themes as Dynamic Forces in Culture," *American
Journal of Sociology*, 1945, 51:198-206.

[12] (Boston: Houghton Mifflin Company, 1946).

much better understanding of their behavior and be more able to predict what they would do under certain circumstances and why they behaved as they did generally. Before the work of Benedict, the U. S. didn't even know how to fight the Japanese properly. Their behavior didn't make sense to the Americans.

The following diagram of culture is given as an aid to understanding the nature of culture.

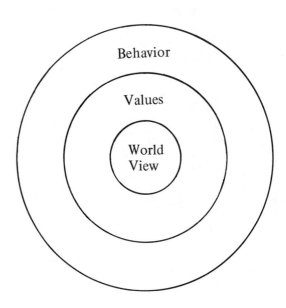

1. The core of culture is the *world view* or very basic assumption about what is real and what is true in the world. This involves the mythology and religion of the people.

People are monists, dualists or pluralists depending on whether or not they believe that reality is composed of one, two or more substances. These positions may be represented as here indicated.

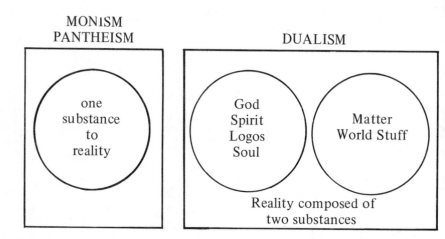

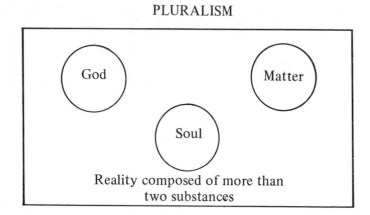

Reality Composed of many substances

Hindus, Buddhists and Animists are for the most part monists. They believe that reality is one and that everything that exists is a functioning part of that whole which is spirit. Western man for the most part may be called a monist also as he believes that God is dead and matter is the only substance to reality. Bible believing Christians would be pluralists.

2. Values of a culture arise out of the world view. The Sawi of New Guinea traditionally placed a high value on treachery until the missionary came to tell them of the *Peace Child*.[13] The people of the U. S. place high value on money, work and individual freedom among other things.

3. Behavior is the observable level of culture. These patterns emerge out of the World View, and Values of the culture. Americans couldn't understand why the Japanese in WWII preferred death to capture until Ruth Benedict revealed the profile of Japanese culture. The Japanese soldier had two honorable alternatives. He could die and have his soul enshrined as a god in the military cemetery in Tokyo where his wife, children, other family and descendants would worship him or he could come home victorious. The surrender of a Japanese soldier was not an option to them. He could never come home again, because he was a traitor to his people. This explains why Japanese soldiers have hid out for decades before being captured.

A serious problem in missions is the missionary who operates in a foreign culture but never goes deeper than the behavioral level. He has to maintain an American colony environment. Inquiry was made into the work of a foreign missionary. "Isn't he a great missionary," the question was asked. "No," came the reply from a fellow missionary. "The problem with him is that he never got out of Texas." This is a common problem. The missionary lives in another culture

---

[13] Don Richardson, *Peace Child,* (Glendale, Calif.: Regal Books Division, G/L Publications, 1974).

but he still thinks, reacts and interprets the behavior and other cues of the nationals as he did at home.

Comparison of Culture

Suppose that an American missionary goes to serve among Hindus in India. How broad will the cultural gap be? Here is a comparison of the basic assumptions of the two peoples.

CHRISTIAN WORLD VIEW

REALITY
    Pluralists
        1. GOD
        2. Soul
        3. Matter

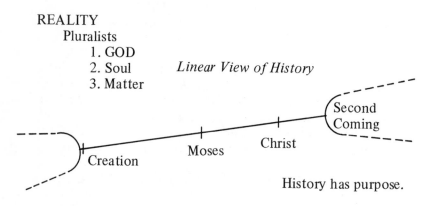

Linear View of History

History has purpose.

HINDU WORLD VIEW

REALITY
    Monist
        1. Spirit

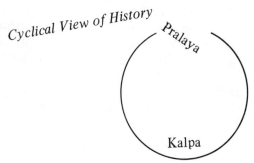

Cyclical View of History

Kalpa = Period of Created Being
Pralaya = Period of Sleep (Suspended Animation)

CULTURAL DIFFERENCES

U. S. CHRISTIAN	*HINDU INDIAN*
1. One life and then eternity.	1. Reincarnation
2. Goal is heaven	2. Goal is extinction of personality and merging with great all-Soul.
3. History important	3. History unimportant.
4. Time is steady progression. A moment gone is gone forever. Each new event is different.	4. Time is cyclical. Everything has happened before and will happen again. Anything that has not happened will never happen.
5. Truth is absolute. A fact is either true or false. What is true for one is true for all.	5. Truth is relative. There are many kinds of truth.
6. God can and will forgive.	6. What you sow in this life *you must* reap in the next.

The Hindu culture of India and the U. S. Christian culture are poles apart. The task of bridging this gap is truly great. What about the Hindu who believes that the ideal life is the renunciation of the world and a life as a hermit or holy man in ashes and rags? How is he going to view the U. S. missionary who lives in a substantial home, drives an automobile, wears nice clothes and seems to have plenty of money. The American claims to be a religious teacher but he is enmeshed and enslaved to materialism. The American cannot be a reliable religious teacher. The holy men of India are the ones like Mahatma Gandhi who have renounced material things and who live in austerity. Gandhi wore robes similar to those of Jesus. These are the ideals of Indian people—the holy men. Jacob Loewen describes the "conflict of missionaries' words as holy men over against the way they are perceived by the Hindu of India."[14]

* Holy men wear one dirty, yellow robe.	* Missionaries have a wardrobe of stylish clothes.
* Holy men have a begging bowl for a living.	* Missionaries have bank accounts and endless foreign income.
* Holy men are celibate.	* Missionaries indulge in sex.
* Holy men are totally dedicated to the gods.	* Missionaries say so too, but they have cars and go on furloughs.

Another cultural gap that the U. S. Christian must face up to in his own country is with the majority of the population—the secular masses. These people have a different world view and value system. Christians need an understanding of culture and communication in order to evangelize in their own country. This evangelism must involve principles of cross-cultural communication in the same way that evangelism to the Hindu in India does.

WORLD VIEW OF THE SECULAR AMERICAN

REALITY
    Monist
        1. Matter is only
           substance

Linear view of history

Now

Man

Life

Origin

Evolutionary Theory

---

[14]Jacob A. Loewen, "Roles: Relating to an Alien Social Structure," *Missiology*, IV, 2, April, 1976, p. 221.

The Individual and Culture

The individual and his native culture.

The personality of the individual develops as he grows up in his native culture. Although there are anomic persons (rebels) and well-adjusted people within a culture, most tend to accept the world view, value system and behavioral patterns of the society. The individual as he grows is conditioned to intuitively accept certain attitudes and stereotypes as well as physical responses. One not brought up in a supermarket culture will put out his hand automatically as he approaches a supermarket door. This unthinking response also occurs when greeting or shaking hands with another person.

Human groups seem to have a compulsion to feel superior to others. The Pharisee in his prayer was not in the minority of humans when he thanked God that he was "not like the rest of men."[15] People are ethnocentric (group centered)[16] and this is glaringly evident to anyone who listens to human conversation. Expressions like "Mexicans are lazy", "Texas is the greatest", "American food is the world's best", "Orientals are tricky", and "the English are fifty years behind the times" are simple examples of this tendency. Put a Harvard graduate and a rough and ready illiterate cowboy together on a dude ranch in the Southwest and each will consider himself superior and will talk about the other to his friends in a disparaging manner. No problem is greater in missions than this one of ethnocentrism—the superiority attitude and the tendency to look down on peoples who are culturally different. This attitude must go if the church is to spread as it should.

The individual in a foreign culture.

When an American who is monocultural goes to China or India, he literally finds himself in another world where the

---

[15] Luke 18:11.
[16] People are ethnocentric who judge persons of other cultures by using their own values and customs as the standard of judgment.

people have a different way of thinking and even a different way of seeing and interpreting reality. He is a square peg in a round hole. All of the conditioning that made him able to respond in an acceptable way in his own society are no longer valid. He doesn't know how to behave nor how to interpret the behavior of the local people. Nevertheless, he interprets anyway and has to act anyway. When he does either, he is wrong about 100% of the time. All of the familiar cues that made life so understandable and smooth at home have suddenly become invalid. Working within one's own culture, a person is able to get along very well since his stereotypes fit fairly accurately the general stereotypes of the society. He seems to know what to do and how to interpret intuitively. These same stereotypes are not only useless in dealing cross-culturally, they are generally a downright hindrance. "Lazy Mexicans" might not be too popular a phrase in Mexico. The same is true of Polish jokes in Poland. The attitudes that lead to the creation of such jokes may be an even greater problem to cross-cultural acceptance.

Sometimes the common things done in one culture become offensive in others. The Japanese are offended when people walk into certain homes and buildings without removing shoes. In situations like this, one can act like a good American and still make enemies. An American G. I. married a Japanese girl in a church ceremony in Tokyo. At the conclusion of the service, the G. I. wanted to claim his bride with the kiss. The bride suddenly realized what was about to happen and was filled with embarrassment. Such a public display of affection was taboo in Japanese culture. The Japanese bride thought of the reaction of all of her friends and relatives in the audience and froze. She resisted the bridegroom's embrace. Now it was time for the G. I. to be red faced. Not understanding the situation he interpreted the bride's action as personal. His next move was to lunge at his bride and grasp her in a bear hug. Needless to say, confusion reigned in this conflict of cultures.

When a person becomes immersed in a strange and foreign culture, the first reaction is usually one of *fascination.* This is the tourist level of contact with another culture. In this stage of exposure the novice is usually guided around by a bicultural native or fellow countryman. However, this arrangement is only temporary. Eventually, the newcomer must venture out on his own and encounter the strange ways and thinking of the people. This is when he discovers that all of the familiar cues and symbols have lost their meaning for him and that he is a "babe in the woods." Helpless in this situation, he becomes more and more frustrated. His attempts to deal with the natives seem to always lead to his own failure. They appear to want to cheat him. He can't trust anyone. All appear to be "bad guys" since they never do as he thinks they should. This frustration leads to culture shock. The anxiety associated with culture shock can't go on and on or it will lead to a physical or mental breakdown. Some adjustment must be made.

The following are some adjustments that missionaries make in relationship to the new culture. The first three are unhealthy adjustments. The final one is preferred.

1. *Go home.* Quick relief can be found by going back to familiar surroundings. The person again knows what is expected of him and how to predict the behavior of others. Life is made easy and simple again. The problem is found in the fact that the person who goes home often does not know what happened to him. He has a reinforced ethnocentrism and a sense of failure.

2. *Go native.* Going native is a maladjustment because it is motivated by neurotic or psychotic tendencies. Often the missionary feels rejected at home or by his own colleagues in the foreign colony. Feeling a deep need for acceptance and security he attempts to join a people that he often considers inferior. "Surely these people will be proud to accept me because I am an American," he thinks. The problem lies in the fact that he is blindly accepting these people and their culture with neither a respect for them nor an understanding of them. This becomes apparent to the local people and they resent the person who goes native. The American tourist girl in Japan sees the lovely kimonos and desires one. She parades before the Japanese in her lovely new kimono in which she looks ridiculous to them. She often wears the wrong shades

and designs for her age and class, she walks clumsily, she doesn't know how to tie the belt and puts it on crudely This display isn't attractive to the Japanese even though the girl tourist feels that she is complimenting the Japanese by expressing an appreciation for their clothing. This explains how the person who goes native without an appreciation for and understanding of a culture will actually appear ridiculous to the natives.

3. *Go colonial.* In reaction to cultural jolts in a new country a missionary often draws himself more and more back into his ethnocentric shell of culturally acquired beliefs, attitudes and behaviors. He settles in his own American colony with others of his home country residing in the area, his mission station family, or his own home and family. He contacts the local culture and people through native helpers or interpreters. To the local people he is continually extolling the virtues of his home country. "At home," he says over and over, "we have bigger buildings, cleaner streets, better sports, more efficient and honest government, etc., etc." The longer such a missionary stays the more reinforcement he gets for his feeling of superiority over the natives. Such a paternalist, however, often does much more harm than good to the cause of Christ. He maintains the cooperation of the natives only by paying them for services rendered.

4. *Identify with the local people and culture.* The Apostle Paul "became all things to all men" in order to win them to Christ.[7] Identification is a healthy process of learning and appreciating the people and the culture so as to be able to communicate effectively with them within their own frame of reference. Eugene Nida says that the steps to proper identification are: 1) know yourself, 2) know the people, 3) participate in the lives of the people not as a benefactor but as a co-laborer, 4) be willing for the people to

---

[7] I Cor. 9:19-24.

truly know you, and 5) love the people.[18] This process is as vital to the success of the missionary as it was to the Apostle to the Gentiles. The next chapter of this book will deal with identification in far greater detail.

God, Christ and Culture

God's attitude toward cultures is best expressed by Peter when he preached to Cornelius. "And Peter opened his mouth and said: Truly I perceive that God shows no partiality, but in every nation any one who fears Him and does what is right is acceptable to Him'."[19] God sits in judgment of all cultures. He is interested in the men and women in all cultures. In a sense He works through the cultures of men to accomplish His purposes but at the same time He is in continual conflict with certain aspects of every culture. "Do not be conformed to this world but be transformed by the renewal of your mind, that you may prove what is the will of God, what is good and acceptable and perfect."[20] Jesus also reveals how the customs and traditions of men's cultures could replace God's commandments.

> Then Pharisees and scribes came to Jesus from Jerusalem and said, "Why do your disciples transgress the tradition of the elders? For they do not wash their hands when they eat.' He answered them, 'And why do you transgress the commandment of God for the sake of your tradition? For God commanded, 'Honor your father and your mother,' and 'He who speaks evil of father or mother let him surely die.' But you say, 'If any one tells his father or his mother, What you would have gained from me is given to God, he need not honor his father.' So for the sake of your tradition, you have made void the word of God. You hypocrites! Well did Isaiah prophesy of you when he said: 'This people honors me with their lips, but their heart is far from me; in vain do they worship me, teaching as doctrines the precepts of men.'[21]

---

[18] Eugene A. Nida, *Message and Mission* (New York: Harper & Row, 1960), p. 1684.

[19] Acts 10: 34-5, RSV.

[20] Romans 12:2, RSV.

[21] Matt. 15:1-9, RSV.

God's people are constantly at war with the traditions of men. The Jews were God's chosen people not because of their merits but because of His grace. Yet the Jews interpreted this choice as an indication of their superiority and God through his prophets and through His Son reprimanded them over and over again for their false pride and hypocrisy. He charged them with being a "proud and stiffnecked people."[22] The prayer of the Pharisees "who trusted in themselves that they were righteous and despised others" and thanked God for the fact that they were "not like other men" represents generally the attitude of Israel through history and peoples in general.[23] Grassi notes the prayer in the synagogue which reflects this attitude.[24]

> Blessed be thou O Lord our God . . .
> Who hast not made me a Gentile . . .
> Who hast not made me a slave; . . .
> Who hast not made me a woman!

Ethnocentrism is the culprit. C. S. Lewis in *Mere Christianity* says that there is a Great Sin.[25]

> There is one vice of which no man in the world is free; which everyone loathes when he sees it in someone else; and of which hardly any people, except Christians, ever imagine that they are guilty of themselves.

Lewis goes on to reveal this sin.

> It is Pride which has been the chief cause of misery in every nation and in every family since the world began. Other vices may sometimes bring people together: you may

---

[22]Deut. 9:6, RSV.

[23]Luke 18:9, RSV.

[24]Joseph A. Grassi, *A World to Win* (Maryknoll, New York: Maryknoll Publications, 1965), p. 124.

[25]C. S. Lewis, *Mere Christianity*, (New York: Macmillan Co., 1952), p. 96.

find good fellowship and friendliness among drunken people or unchaste people. But Pride always means enmity—it *is* enmity.

It appears that Israel tended toward this type of group pride that is so characteristic of peoples of the earth. Even Christians have a serious problem in this area. At least Peter L. Berger believes so.[26]

.... an objective observer is hard put to tell the difference (at least in terms of values affirmed) between the Church members and those who maintain an "unchurched" status. Usually the most that can be said is that church members hold the same values as everybody else, but with more exact solemnity. Thus church membership in no way means adherence to a set of values at variance with those of the general society; rather it means a stronger and more explicitly religious affirmation of the same values held by the community at large.

Even if Jews and Christians are guilty of ethnocentric exclusivism and pride, God does not intend for it to be so. If one begins with Genesis of the Old Testament and reads through the entire Bible, this message that God loves all men equally and that He disdains personal or group arrogance stands out clearly. Look to Exodus 22:21, the second book of the Bible: "You shall not wrong a stranger or oppress him, for you were strangers in the land of Egypt."

Next turn to the third book of the Bible, Leviticus 19:18: "You shall love your neighbor as yourself." Wait a minute! Wasn't Jesus the first one to say this? Evidently not, since here it is in the early part of the Scriptures. But you

[26]Peter L. Berger, *The Noise of Solemn Assemblies* (Garden City: Doubleday Co., 1961), p. 41.

say, this only refers to another Israelite as a neighbor. Is this the case? Look on down to verse 33 of the same chapter: "When a stranger sojourns with you in your land, you shall not do him wrong. The stranger that sojourns with you shall be to you as the native among you, and you shall love him as yourself; for you were strangers in the land of Egypt."

Jesus made this principle of God's concern for all men plain in many ways but strikingly so in the story of the Good Samaritan. Jesus broke down all walls of prejudice that separate men from each other. To Jesus the first priority was to love God and then one has the basis and power to love his neighbor as himself.[27] Neighbor for Jesus included every human being.

The solution to the problem of man is conversion. "If any man will be my disciple," Jesus said, "let him deny himself and take up his cross and follow me."[28] This will get rid of pride and ethnocentrism. As the missionary goes out to help others understand the gospel, he must free himself from the kind of pride in self or in country that makes him look down upon or be disdainful of others. Paul tells us the way to eliminate the barriers that separate people.

> Now if your experience of Christ's encouragement and love means anything to you, if you have known something of the fellowship of His spirit and all that it means in kindness and deep sympathy, do make my best hopes for you come true! Live together in harmony, live together in love, as though you had only one mind and one spirit between you. Never act from motives of rivalry or personal vanity, but in humility think more of one another than you do of yourselves. None of you should think only of his own affairs, but each should see things from other people's point-of-view.[29]

---

[27]Matt. 22:37-40, RSV.

[28]Matt. 16:24, RSV.

[29]Phil. 2:1-4, (Phillips).

Summary

The concept of culture presents a real enigma for the missionary candidate who is monocultural. His very provincialism almost guarantees that his ethnocentrism will blind him to the need for cultural study prior to going to the field; therefore, he will end up on the foreign field where he will suffer severe culture shock or worse. The percentage of failures who return home during their first tour abroad because of lack of training is unbelievably high. Some churches with little or no training lose more than fifty percent of their missionary force during the first tour. Wycliffe Bible Translators, with adequate training, lose three percent.

This chapter is an attempt to explain generally the concepts of culture and communication and to communicate the need for prefield training for the foreign worker. A foreign missionary needs to understand his own culture, himself as a participant in culture, the nature of culture, and the language and culture of his host country or ethnic group. He would be wise to master all but the language and culture of his field of labor prior to his departure from home. The people who promote and oversee the missionary enterprise from the home base also vitally need an understanding of culture and of themselves as participants in culture.

> Given the almost infinite variety of human cultures it is a most remarkable fact that the Christian Good News of God's redemption has been preached successfully to so many societies ... Paul affirmed that in Christ there can be neither Greek nor Jew, circumcision nor uncircumcision, Barbarian, Scythian, slave nor free, but Christ is all and in all (Col. 3:11). Scythians were nomads from Russia who were the epitome of savagery in the ancient world: they tatooed themselves, took scalps from their captives, and smoked hemp ... !
>
> Rightly understood and rightly preached Christ is the hope of glory for every man (Col. 1:27, 28), whatever his culture, his kindred, people, tongue, or nation. (Rev. 5:9). [30]

---

[30] Edwin M. Yamauchi, "Christianity and Cultural Difference," *Christianity Today,* June 23, 1972.

SUGGESTED READINGS ON CULTURE
AND COMMUNICATION

Arensberg, Conrad M. and Niehoff, Arthur H. *Introducing Social Change.* Chicago: Aldine-Atherton, 1971.

Hall, Edward T. *The Silent Language.* Greenwich, Conn.: Fawcett Publications, Inc., 1961.

Luzbetak, Louis J. *The Church and Culture.* Techny, Ill.: Divine Word Publications, 1970.

Mayers, Marvin K. *Christianity Confronts Culture.* Grand Rapids, Mich.: Zondervan Publishing House, 1971.

Nida, Eugene A. *Customs and Culture.* New York: Harper & Row, Publishers, 1954.

Nida, Eugene A. *Message and Mission.* New York: Harper & Row, Publishers, 1960.

Perry, Bert M. *Missionary Know Thyself.* Winona, Miss.: J. C. Choate Publications, 1973.

Richardson, Don. *Peace Child.* Glendale, Calif.:G/L Publications, 1974.

Shewmaker, Stan. *Tonga Christianity.* South Pasadena, Calif.: William Carey Library, 1970.

IDENTIFICATION

STAN SHEWMAKER

Introduction

"You know, I can tell you anything that is in my heart and I know that you will understand and not be angry with me. And . . . it doesn't matter whether I tell you in your language or mine, because I know you will hear every word."

"I feel the same way about you, brother . . ." was all the missionary could say before choking up with emotion.

In darkness of that small room an African and an American had reached the level of communication where their deepest feelings and values could be shared. Their conversation was honest, genuine, intimate. No phoniness. No pretension.

Every missionary who earnestly desires to share the Good News of love, peace and salvation in Jesus Christ should aim for this type of relationship with the people he wants to serve, a relationship based upon sincere *identification.*

Identification is an extremely complex concept because it involves the totality of human relationships. Far from being merely an imitation of people in another culture, identification means, not being someone else, but being more than oneself.[1] It is a purposeful participation in the lives of others.

For the missionary, identification should not mean stooping to the level of the host people but rather an under-

---

[1] Eugene A. Nida, *Message and Mission* (New York: Harper and Row, 1960), p. 162.

standing and acceptance of the validity of another culture's style of life, different though it may be. True identification is never a vertical condescension, but a horizontal cultural shift.

A missionary among the Quiche Indians of Latin America defines identification as

> ... the establishment of a relationship between two or more parties so that there may be a free and honest interchange of ideas, attitudes, and emotions. It is the establishment of such a relationship of equality so that either party may feel free to express his true opinions and positions.[2]

Commissioned by the Lord Jesus Christ to make disciples of the peoples[3] and entrusted with delivering the message of reconciliation,[4] missionaries cannot be satisfied with a superficial adjustment to other cultures. Their message and mission is far too important to allow selfishness and pride to hinder full participation in the lives of people who are culturally different from them. Their mission in the world demands more than being just "good friends." It involves being all things to all men,[5] emptying themselves of the ways most natural to them[6] and truly becoming one with their adopted people. The local people should be able to say of their missionary, "He is one of us."[7]

---

[2] Pat Hile, "A Study of the Nature and Importance of Physical Identification on the Part of the World Evangelist" (unpublished Master's thesis, Harding Graduate School, Memphis, Tennessee, 1968), p. 34.

[3] Matthew 28.19.

[4] II Corinthians 5.18.

[5] I Corinthians 9.22.

[6] Philippians 2.6-7.

[7] Louis J. Luzbetak, *The Church and Cultures* (Techny, Illinois: Divine Word Publications, 1963), pp. 95-96.

As important as identification is to the missionary, however, it should never become an end in itself. His task is not
complete merely because he has managed to adapt to the
ways of the people. Identification may be convincing or it
may become a sham. It may be romantic or dull. It must
always be regarded as only the vehicle for communicating the
message—not the message itself.

Of the numerous problems confronting missionaries
today, probably the two greatest are identification and
communication. So interdependent are these two problems
that one cannot be resolved without the other, nor can one
be properly understood except as it relates to the other.[9]
Those who seek to teach the truths of God's word without
first establishing a broad base of rapport, trust, and mutual
respect with the listeners are destined for intense personal
frustration and possibly the rejection of their message.

Types of Identification

With the decline of "the mission-station approach" to
missions and a new emphasis upon closer contact with the
host people, many missionaries are necessarily having to
reexamine their living standards within and attitudes toward
the native culture. In their attempts to grapple with the
implications of real identification and its effect upon
communication of the Gospel, missionaries are generally
moving in one of two directions: they identify with the
people either *psychologically* or *physically*. And a few have
successfully combined the two.[10]

Psychological, or inner identification, involves the
missionary's attitudes—his understanding of, his empathy

---

[8] William D. Reyburn, "Identification in the Missionary Task," *Practical Anthropology*, Vol. 7, No. 1. Tarrytown, New York, p. 3.

[9] Eugene A. Nida, "Identification, a Major Problem of Modern Missions," *Practical Anthropology*, Vol. 2, No. 4. Tarrytown, New York, p. 90.

[10] Hile, *op cit*, p. 31.

with, his appreciation for the native culture, his respect for the people and their values, his desire to truly understand them, and his willingness to know and to be known by them. To achieve this inner identification one must be aware of other people's ideas, understand their viewpoints, and empathize with their struggle for self-expression, however unfamiliar its forms.[11] Psychological identification does not mean that the total value system of the local people must be adopted, but it must be taken very seriously.

Physical identification, on the other hand, means adopting native ways and values[12] in such areas as housing, dress, food, transportation, income, customs and general standard of living. Many missionaries, though, react negatively to an all-out physical identification, equating it with "going native" and denying that it guarantees achieving psychological identification. They feel it is impossible for a missionary family to completely adopt local standards— especially housing, food and income—for an extended period of time without suffering serious psychological damage.

William Muldrow warns that physical identification can become superficial, a "pious display to cover over the real fact of a person's inability to relate on a more personal basis."[13] Each family, then, must work out its own living situation individually, hopefully to reflect a genuine love for the people rather than a concern about the personal possessions sacrificed for the sake of identification.

The relationship of physical to psychological identification is best defined by an African church leader who explained that the comparative wealth of missionaries to

---

[11] Nida, *Message and Mission*, p. 164.

[12] Luzbetak, *The Church and Cultures*, p. 96.

[13] William F. Muldrow, "Identification and the Role of the Missionary," *Practical Anthropology*, Vol. 18, No. 5, Tarrytown, New York, p. 210.

natives is no real problem to the African as long as the missionary's "heart is right." [14] By this he means that when the attitude of the missionary is one of love, understanding and acceptance, his standard of living (assuming it is reasonable) does not necessarily constitute a barrier to identification.

It seems safe to conclude that one cannot successfully identify psychologically without some measure of external adaptation to the ways of the local people, but it is possible to identify physically without ever identifying psychologically.

Identification and Communication

It is essential that the Good News of Jesus Christ be communicated in forms that are meaningful to people. Not only must the message have meaning, but it must be carried on the lips and in the lives of its messengers. For these messengers to deliver the message effectively they must become one with the local people. There must be mutual respect and understanding between the receivers of the message and the messengers. Identification, then, is a prerequisite to effective communication.

Missionary identification is the avenue by which the message can penetrate the lives of his hearers. The missionary willing to identify with the local people will find language learning easier, will come to appreciate their cultural values, will discover their needs and aspirations, will become more understanding and empathetic and will begin to experience emotional unity with them.

Language learning. Two Zambian Christian men, one elderly and the other middle-aged, once stood talking with me in their native tongue. During the course of the conver-

---

[14] Jacob A. Loewen, *Culture and Human Values* (South Pasadena: William Carey Library, 1975), p. 28.

sation the middle-aged man reached into his pocket and produced a large ring of keys. Then, looking at me intently he placed the keys in my hand and said, "Citonga is my language, and because you understand and speak my language I give you the keys of my heart. I trust you and therefore I can open the doors of my heart to you." The lesson is overwhelming.

A language cannot be learned in a vacuum. The learning process requires dedicated and persistent participation in the daily activities of the native people. Structure and grammar can be studied in books, but idioms, proverbs, and other "spices" of language come alive only through day-to-day interaction with the native speakers. Identification facilitates language mastery, and fluency makes possible an ever-deepening integration with the people.

Genuine respect for the native culture usually coincides with good language learning.[15]

Appreciation of cultural values. Fluency in the native language is not enough. There must also be a knowledge of native customs and habits which creates a common ground of experience, interest, and feeling on which good communication is based.[16]

It is a universal principle that people are more inclined to accept newcomers who appreciate their way of life and who consider it to be a valid expression of their worth and importance. Involvement in the lives of the national people will enable the missionary to better understand why they do certain things the way they do. As he comprehends and respects their values his frustrations and his tendency to feel superior will diminish. When the missionary appreciates and respects local cultural values, people usually reciprocate by accepting and respecting him.

---

[15]*Ibid.,* p. 31.

[16]Muldrow, *op cit.,* p. 220.

Felt needs and aspirations. Absolutely vital to the missionary is an awareness of the felt needs of the people. Without this knowledge his preaching and teaching will lack relevance and will fail to "scratch where it itches." People who are chronically hungry, for example, find a heaven where there will be no more hunger far more attractive than one where there's only singing. Well-fed missionaries who have never experienced a hungry day in their lives might begin to "feel" why the people conceive of heaven in such "earthy" terms, if they lived in a native home for a few weeks and shared their meager diet. The ability to feel the needs of the people is the one basic positive attitude the missionary should develop.

"In order to know what really lay hidden in the hearts of the Quechua Indians," [17] William Reyburn travelled the Equadorian Andes dressed as an Indian, sleeping in Indian markets, enduring the discomforts of drenching rain and biting pests. As a missionary linguist-anthropologist he sought to discover the real longings of their hearts so that he could better minister the Good News to those needs. He wanted to find out what it was that drunkenness seemed to satisfy. Why was the Indian so resistant to inner change? What were his anxieties and what did he talk about when he gathered with other Indians at night in the security of his little group? Reyburn sought to discover "the roots that lay behind the outward symbols which could respond to the claims of Christ." [18]

The missionary who is unwilling to enter eagerly and unreservedly into the deeper dimensions of life where the needs, anxieties, and aspirations are expressed will never effectively communicate the message he is verily pouring out his life to proclaim.

If the Good News of Jesus Christ has anything at all to offer, it is precisely in the areas of felt human need, anxiety, and hopelessness.

---

[17]Reyburn, *op cit.,* p. 2.

[18]*Ibid.,* p. 3.

Barriers to Identification

Missionaries sometimes find their ministries unfruitful, unsatisfying and frustrating. They feel completely thwarted and cut off from the people they have come to serve. To them the nationals are more often than not "ignorant," "lazy," "untrustworthy," "dirty." Along with the frustrations comes an increasing bitterness toward the host people and a withdrawal from them. In spite of his attempts to conceal his feelings from the local people, they will probably have sensed them before he has become conscious of them himself.

Ethnocentrism. Perhaps no attitude presents a more formidable barrier to identification for missionaries from the "advanced" West than does ethnocentrism. Ethnocentrism is the belief that one's own pattern of behavior is the best, most natural, most beautiful, most correct, or most important.[19] Not only does this kind of missionary regard his own culture as the best, but he generally despises another culture because in it one lives differently, lives by inhuman, irrational, or unnatural standards.

Ethnocentrism can desensitize a missionary to the realities of his adopted environment. He may have absolutely no idea of what is happening around him, what the local people are saying, thinking or feeling. After all, to him "they are all ignorant anyway."

A typical ethnocentric statement was once made to me by a Roman Catholic missionary stationed near where I was living and ministering. He suggested that the people who lived in a village across the valley from his mission-station had to be the "most ignorant, depraved, deceitful bunch of drunkards anywhere around." Since—in his mission philosophy—it would require 400 years to fully transform such people, all he could do was conduct mass for the

---

[19] John Friedl, *Cultural Anthropology* (New York: Harper and Row, 1976), pp. 88-89.

faithful half-dozen who met in his mission chapel. He was not aware, though, that the largest body of Christians in the immediate area met regularly for worship under a tree in that very village!

Withdrawal and isolation. When a missionary begins his ministry in a radically different culture and is expected to participate in that culture, what was his former frame of reference for living is suddenly stripped away. Trusted guidelines and reference points for behavior are changed. Responses of the local people cannot be predicted or relied upon. [20]

Faced with the insecurity and frustration brought on by this cultural confrontation, the missionary must move in one of two directions: either he must identify with the local people and their patterns of culture, or he must withdraw and isolate himself in an attempt to relieve his frustrations. The latter course of action is too often followed by missionaries unprepared for culture shock or unwilling to go through the identification process.

Sometimes a group of missionaries working in an area will form a self-enclosed "missionary culture" which seals them off from the unfamiliar culture around them, isolating themselves geographically and emotionally from the local population.

---

[20]Muldrow, *op cit.,* p. 213.

Luzbetak has graphically diagrammed the emotional changes which sooner or later occur in every missionary's experience. Withdrawal and isolation often reinforce the missionary's anti-native feelings and attitudes, hindering him from empathizing and identifying with the people.

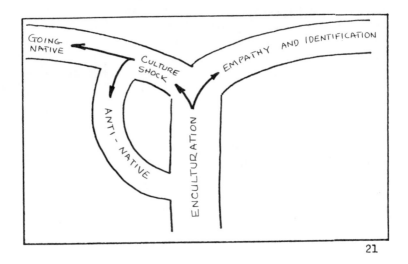

21

Cultural overhang. Another obstacle to effective communication of the Gospel and subsequent growth of indigenous churches is the missionary's inclination to bind American interpretations of Scripture, forms of church life and worship upon native converts. Missionaries tend to continue using methods on mission fields that were successful back home. This is known as "cultural overhang."

Some researchers have discovered that certain evangelistic methods used successfully in America may actually retard church growth on the mission field.[22]

[21]Luzbetak, *op cit.,* p. 97.

[22]Phil Elkins, *Lectures on Mission Work,* 1964, p. 8.

One area in which a missionary's cultural overhang shows first is his preaching. His delivery of a logical and systematic three-point sermon replete with all the appropriate supporting scriptures may leave an African audience unmoved and bored. Whereas, the same sermon preached to a Texas congregation two years earlier had perhaps been tremendously stirring, practical and well-received.

Cultural overhang also manifests itself in the use of "church jargon" or "pew lingo." Missionaries in their conversation and preaching use Christian terms which have little meaning to non-Christians or even to new Christians who have not developed a church vocabulary. Employing esoteric terminology often presents quite a barrier to effective identification and communication.

Ridiculing spiritual phenomena. Missionaries brought up to believe that all spiritual activity ceased in the first century of the Christian era experience tremendous difficulty in coping with non-western beliefs in the spirit world. Because of their scientific and rationalistic background, missionaries distrust their African or Asian fellow-Christians who happen to believe in the realm of spirits and supernatural powers. Their beliefs are therefore ridiculed as superstition, and the naive assumption is that they will grow out of such childish beliefs if given enough education. The result has been that the missionary labels the native view a superstitious mysticism, while the native Christian conceives of the missionary as a secular, materialistic American.

Reyburn is probably rightly convinced that more underlying distrust and lack of confidence has been caused by missionary reaction toward the mysterious than in any other aspect of missionary-African relationships.[23]

Impatience. Westerners, particularly Americans, are very time-conscious. To them time means money, and money equals success. Schedules are planned and fixed,

---

[23]Reyburn, *op cit.*, p. 15.

appointments are firm. They usually feel guilty and irritable when running a few minutes late and lose patience with people who are late for appointments or who do not adhere strictly to a fixed schedule.

Missionaries, who have been reared and educated in a time-conscious and time-honoring culture, experience tremendous pressure when confronted with the "manana" complex. They cannot comprehend why any self-respecting, responsible person would want to put off until tomorrow what "obviously" should be done today. They become so annoyed by this constant clash of cultural values that they frequently become intolerant of and impatient with the local people and categorize them as lazy and irresponsible.

The impatient and insensitive attitudes of a veteran missionary once made in indelible impression upon an African church leader of my acquaintance. He told me that in all the years he had worked with this missionary not once had my friend been able to fully state his case before being interrupted by the missionary. The missionary would hastily say "Mbubo! Mbubo!" ('Alright! Alright!') before the African could explain why he had come.

In societies where time does not have the same value as it does in the western world, a lack of forbearance concerning time constitutes a serious breach of local custom in relating to people. Nothing is more discourteous and impolite than making someone uneasy or rushing him into stating the purpose of his visit before he is fully ready to do so. The sad fact is that the failure of some missionaries to listen patiently, to unhurriedly weigh the facts, and thus to build rapport, has practically nullified the effectiveness of both their individual witness and their elaborate evangelistic programs.

Among societies that are not time-conscious, relationships always take priority over schedules, time-clocks, and programs. Hastiness and intolerance on the part of the missionary grow out of a fundamental misunderstanding of the other person's cultural values and impede progress toward identification.

Imported frills. When missionaries enter into their ministries among other cultures they do not automatically lose interest in Fritos, modern appliances, or Sears-Roebuck catalogues. In fact, sometimes things they often took for granted back home assume an inordinate value. They begin to write letters suggesting that "care" packages would be much appreciated. Loving supporters respond by sending them clothes, canned goods, radios, and a host of other things.

This can be good for the missionaries and their supporters alike, up to a point.

However, when a missionary literally surrounds himself with familiar things from back home he correspondingly decreases his dependence upon the people with whom he is living.

William Scott, describing missionary attitudes in the Philippines, wonders whether it is possible for a missionary to really participate in the beauty of the country or in the friendship of the local people "so long as he is crippled by the weight of a Life-Support-System worthy of sustaining an astronaut on the moon?" [24] He is convinced that missionary reliance upon imported frills prevents them from depending upon and developing significant relationships with the nationals. He believes that:

> Unless he (the missionary—SS) gets out of that space-suit, he will never be able to cry on a Filipino shoulder, lock arms with a Filipino brother on a steep path, or taste the salt of Filipino tears. [25]

---

[24]William Henry Scott, "Rethinking the American Missionary Presence in the Philippines," *International Review of Mission,* Vol. LXII, No. 247, (Geneva, Switzerland), p. 182.

[25]*Ibid.,* p. 182.

Obviously, this list does not cover all of the obstructions to successful identification, but perhaps it will serve to make missionaries and others who are vitally involved in foreign missions aware of some of the attitudes which block the way to an authentic understanding and an emotional oneness.

Ways to Achieve Genuine Identification

Meaningful communication of the Gospel, as has already been emphasized, is predicated upon successful identification. The Good News encounters fewer obstructions and less resistance when it flows naturally and spontaneously from "one of us" to "us" than it does from "us" to "them."

Genuine identification is not merely refraining from participating in certain activities which clash unnecessarily with local customs. Nor is it simply striving to keep oneself from manifesting negative attitudes. Instead, real identification is positive—is rooted in love, the kind of love which proceeds from an all-out commitment to Jesus Christ. It comes from following Christ's example of compassion, empathy and service.

Developing a oneness with the national people requires patient and abiding love. It requires months, sometimes years, of demanding language study, of exhausting culture study, of persistent involvement in the stresses and strains of daily existence, of being laughed at, of being misunderstood and suspected, of sometimes being rejected completely. But whatever price the missionary may be called upon to pay, the mission upon which he is sent requires that the sacrifice be made.

Here let us suggest some positive ways to achieve both psychological and physical identification. Some have to do with attitudes, while others deal more with physical aspects.

Assume the role of a learner. One basic quality a missionary should possess is a continuing willingness to learn. Though he may have prepared himself extensively in general ways before arriving on the field, he must realize that his knowledge is roughly equivalent to that of a child in *this particular* culture.

Once he admits how limited his in-depth comprehension is, he will soon recognize how vital the listening stage is in establishing reciprocity and dialogue. A missionary ought to restrain himself from making authoritative pronouncements in cultural matters about which his specific knowledge is so scanty. Obviously, because he is more likely better-travelled and more academically educated than is the national, the missionary can and should contribute a wider perspective to the dialogue, but, in specific cultural things, the national will always be the expert and the missionary should be willing to assume the attitude of a learner.

Master the language. Language learning takes time and some missionaries are in so much of a hurry to "preach the Gospel" that they will not devote the months and years necessary to master a language. But in actual fact, the history of missions shows conclusively that the missionary who dedicates himself to the important listening stage, to the learning of customs, to the discovery of needs, is not wasting his time. His ministry will be enriched, his preaching and witnessing will have more relevance and impact because they will employ local illustrations instead of foreign proverbs, idioms, and structures.

Language is the channel through which the message of Christ flows to the heart of man. It is far more than the mere mechanical ability to produce acoustical sounds so as to be able to buy, sell, find one's way about, or even to write out and deliver sermons in an intelligible form. It is the process by which the missionary makes vital contacts with a new community, a new manner of life, and a new system of thinking.[26] It enables him to converse with people about their problems, beliefs, fears, desires, aspirations and longings.[27]

---

[26]Eugene A. Nida, *Learning a Foreign Language* (Ann Arbor, Michigan: Friendship Press, 1957), p. 8.

[27]*Ibid.,* p. 7.

In the final analysis, the ability to respond sincerely and spiritually to the deeper problems of the heart is more important than being able to write formal sermons.

Evaluate cultural traits in context. Missionaries who sincerely desire to be empathetic in their approach to the national people should try to see the culture as a whole. Nothing is more insensitive and destructive than for a foreigner to isolate some "strange" custom and render a harsh judgment upon it before considering its relationship to the rest of the culture.

An African puberty ceremony, for example, may seem quite mysterious, immoral, or even cruel to the western missionary. However, after he better understands the local culture and evaluates this particular activity in its context he will discover that it is the vehicle for imparting information concerning sex and the "facts of life." The sex education sessions are conducted by older women for the girls and by adult men for the boys.

In cultures where ceremonial rites of this kind mark the passage of an individual from babyhood to personhood, or from childhood to adulthood, a person does not have to struggle with the problem of who he or she is. The stages of his life are well defined. His culture leaves no doubt as to his position in life. A girl, for instance, who has not had her puberty ceremony knows that she is not a woman yet and is therefore not eligible for marriage. Her duties remain those of a girl and not those of a woman. Identity crises are rare in such societies.

Cultures are entities. They consist of a host of customs and mores and values all of which are interrelated and inter-dependent. It is important therefore for the missionary to understand the relationship of a particular practice or custom to the rest of the culture before condemning it, no matter how immoral and sinful it may appear to him at first. He must be prepared to suggest a *functional* substitute before he would create a cultural void.

Be willing to be known. Most missionaries really want to set a good example for people to emulate. And rightly so. But in seeking to always set the standard of what a Christian should be, they sometimes try to keep their true feelings under cover. They feel that as leaders they cannot afford to make mistakes or reveal their fears and misgivings. Thus they hide behind masks of perfection, and large areas of their lives are never exposed to the nationals.

However, if the missionary really wants to enter into any close relationship with other human beings he must be willing not only to know them, but also to be known by them.[28] A good example of how "removing the mask" opened the way to oneness took place a few months before I left Africa for a period of several years. Mounting daily were the pressures and anxieties of leaving the life and work I enjoyed so much to re-enter the faster pace and competitiveness of life in the United States.

There was an increasing need to share these burdens with someone. Finally, I did what so few missionaries ever do. I shared my deepest fears and anxieties with a native brother. The African Christian listened as I told him in detail about insecurities and uncertainties which awaited my family back in America. At first it seemed almost incredible to the African that anyone would be anxious about going back home to friends and relatives, to the land of his birth. Although he had seen distressed missionaries before, he had yet to see one who was willing to confess his burdens and ask a national brother for help. He offered to pray for me. Within a few days an invitation came by messenger, requesting that my wife and I visit in the home of an old church leader. A group of national Christians had prepared a meal and planned an evening of prayer and singing specifically designed to minister to us. During the course of the evening they all expressed gratitude to us for trusting them enough to let them help us bear our *mapenzi* ('troubles').

---

[28]Loewen, *op cit.*, p. 61.

The result of this meeting proved very interesting. Ignited by my willingness to be known, a renewed sense of body ministry, independence and initiative surged through the entire local native congregation. Members began to take charge of duties which had traditionally been done only by missionaries. No longer were missionaries regarded as superhumans who were not subject to mortal temptations and tribulations. The spirit of brotherhood and of oneness in Christ was given a tremendous boost, simply because the missionary finally took off his mask and exposed his own vulnerability.

Establish one-to-one relationships. In the course of a conversation, an intelligent young African university student once made a startling statement about the lack of spontaneous missionary-national relationships on the mission station where he had attended school. He rather resentfully related how, during the three years he had been enrolled in the Bible School, he had not known of a single instance where a missionary had taken the time to talk with a Bible student one-to-one for just thirty minutes.

He explained that during the day the missionaries would talk with them in the classroom and take part in *group* discussions. But as soon as the sun went down a wall would seem to rise between them. The missionaries would retire into the privacy of their homes and the Africans would visit among themselves. Whatever social relationships that existed during the day were broken when night fell.

Sad as this example may be, it is by no means untypical of missionary-national relationships in many mission areas. This lack of individual and personal dialogue manifests itself not only in personal relationships on the mission field, but also in efforts to evangelize. In one tribe in Africa a survey revealed that over 95 per cent of the converts interviewed had been converted through public preaching. Less than five per cent had been won through personal, one-to-one contact. Practically all of the conversions had taken place at large gatherings. Within that tribe the New Testament pattern of personal witness from house to house and from hut to hut was essentially unknown.

Establishment of meaningful one-to-one relationships has far-reaching implications, not only for opening the way for mutual growth and edification among Christians, but also in restoring the Biblical pattern and dynamic of personal witness to non-Christians.

Some of the most profound changes in the heart and soul occur in the context of one-to-one relationships. People feel less threatened and defensive. Genuine love is given and received. Such is the environment in which the seed of the Kingdom will grow.

Focus upon people instead of upon programs. Westerners are extremely time-conscious and program-oriented. Non-westerners, on the other hand, tend to elevate human relationships above schedules and programs and, in general, are much more people-centered.

Because they are products of western culture, missionaries need to make certain adjustments when they enter a people-centered society. Probably one of the first things missionaries will do is to "structure a program" to carry out their evangelistic plans (and certainly there is nothing inherently wrong with a schedule or program). But in implementing their plans they should always remember that greeting people along the path and inquiring about the health of their children is more important to the nationals than whether or not the sermon begins on time.

If there has been a death in the village the most insensitive thing the missionary could suggest would be that the church leadership-training session go ahead and meet as scheduled. In such a situation it matters little how far the missionary may have travelled to meet with his class, or how much it has cost him. Sitting and listening and sharing the grief are the more appropriate responses. People have feelings, programs do not.

Share meals. Simply because a missionary adapts to the local diet does not in itself guarantee identification, but the sharing of meals can be one of the most effective ways of achieving that goal, because it is a visible sign to the native that the missionary respects and appreciates his way of life.[29] As they partake of the same substance of physical life, it draws them together into a common bond of fellowship and oneness.[30]

Underscoring the importance of sharing meals, Dr. Reyburn cites an interesting instance from West Africa. Intently watching Reyburn indulge in a local dish of roasted caterpillars, a pleased but somewhat surprised, African exclaimed, "White man Kaka is eating caterpillars, he really has a black heart." The experience elicited from Reyburn the observation that, "an emptied pan of caterpillars is more convincing than all the empty metaphors of love which missionaries are prone to expend on the heathen."[31]

Eating food prepared in a native home is another way of saying, "I trust you and I am confident of your ability to sustain my life with your food."

Exchange home visits. As a general rule missionaries have been much more inclined to be entertained in native homes than they are to extend a warm welcome to natives to visit in their own homes. Many missionaries, for example, will make condescending adjustments when they visit in native homes, but few will unselfishly offer the use of their imported double-bed to a tired native visitor and his wife who have arrived late in the evening.

Genuine identification requires the exchange of home visits. It is not enough for the missionary to be willing to spend a couple of nights in a native home. He must also accept visitors with hospitality and share with them the use of his best possessions.

---

[29] Hile, *op cit.,* p. 83.

[30] *Ibid.,* p. 81.

[31] Reyburn, *op cit.,* p. 9.

Adjust standard of living to local conditions. There is no magic formula which when applied to a given situation will guarantee successful identification. However, there are ways to improve one's chances of gaining acceptance and of being integrated into a society. One way is to make whatever modifications are necessary in one's standard of living to bring it in line with local conditions. This involves such things as size and style of house, home furnishings, mode of transportation, clothing and food.

A missionary must adjust his life-style in order for it to be a bridge instead of a barrier in communicating the Gospel. For example, by living on too high an economic level he may discover that his life-style in itself is a drawback to sacrifice in the local church. His comparative economic superiority vitiates his influence as an example of the kind of economic sacrifices which he admonishes local Christians to make in the interest of self-support. [33] His teaching on giving and stewardship falls on deaf ears. He may even wonder why the native brethren always expect him to carry all of the financial load.

One advantage of adaptation to national living standards is that it gives the missionary a deep sense of satisfaction and happiness. Scott emphasizes this point when he says that a foreigner (missionary or otherwise) cannot truly be happy among another people unless he is dependent upon its citizens for companionship and their approval for his well-being, and unless he is submissive to its laws to the point of detention, deportation or death. [34] Interdependence between missionary and nationals is a key ingredient in identification. The local people will always feel closer to the missionary who depends upon them and who is at their disposal than they will to the one who relies exclusively upon his own unlimited financial resources to carry out his programs and plans.

---

[33] Daniel Johnson Fleming, *Living as Comrades* (New York: Agricultural Missions, Inc., 1950), p. 29.

[34] Scott, *op cit.*, p. 181.

Just as there is no formula which produces automatic identification, there also is no single standard of living which applies to all missionaries in all mission fields. Each missionary will have to conscientiously and prayerfully make whatever changes he needs to make. Obviously, an urban missionary working in Vienna will live on a different standard of living than will a village missionary in India. The objective in adapting to the local standard of living is to minimize the economic differences between the missionary and the nationals, and to maximize their interdependence upon each other.

Identification is a prerequisite to communication of the Gospel. Identification is established to a large extent by understanding the local culture, and the local culture is understood best by learning the national language. All of these components work together and reinforce each other to form a complete circle.

Speaking from his extensive experience as both missionary and Bible translator, Dr. Eugene Nida says this concerning identification:

> . . . a close examination of successful missionary work inevitably reveals the correspondingly effective manner in which the missionaries were able to identify themselves with the people . . . Conversely, where missionary work has been singularly unsuccessful, one will always find a failure to resolve the missionary's two great problems: identification and communication.[35]

[35]Eugene A. Nida, *Customs and Cultures* (New York: Harper and Row, 1954), pp. 250-251.

The late Dr. Byang Kato, well-known African church leader and Bible scholar, described the kind of missionary he wants to see come to the African harvest field. He says that

> ... the national church is very much in need of a missionary who, under the guidance of the Holy Spirit, is led to "become all things to all men" (1 Cor. 9.22). We need someone who is coming, not with the sense of superiority in race or education, wealth or culture, but a person coming as his Master came into the world, "not to be served, but to serve" (Mk. 10:45).[36]

As a national Christian who has traveled through most of the countries of Africa, Byang Kato invites missionaries who are willing to identify with the national people and to join in partnership with the native churches to reap the harvests that the Lord has brought to ripeness. He welcomes *partners,* not *bosses.*

SUGGESTED READINGS

Elkins, Phil, *Lectures on Mission Work.* Unpublished. 1964.

Fleming, Daniel Johnson, *Living as Comrades.* New York, Agricultural Missions, Inc. 1950.

Friedl, John, *Cultural Anthropology.* New York, Harper and Row. 1976.

Hile, Pat, "A Study of the Nature and Importance of Physical Identification on the Part of the World Evangelist." Unpublished Master's thesis, Harding Graduate School, Memphis, Tennessee. 1968.

Kato, Byang H., "The National Church: Do They Want Us?" in *Christ the Liberator,* John R. W. Stott, *et al.* Downers Grove, Illinois, Inter-Varsity Press. 1971.

---

[36] Byang H. Kato, "The National Church: Do They Want Us?" in *Christ the Liberator,* by John R. W. Stott, *et al* (Downers Grove, Illinois: Inter-Varsity Press, 1971), p. 167.

Loewen, Jacob A., *Culture and Human Values.* South Pasadena, California, William Carey Library. 1975.

Reyburn, William D., "Identification in the Missionary Task," *Practical Anthropology,* Volume 7, Number 1. Tarrytown, New York. 1960.

Luzbetak, Louis J., *The Church and Cultures.* Techny, Illinois, Divine Word Publications. 1963.

Muldrow, William F., "Identification and the Role of the Missionary," *Practical Anthropology,* Volume 18, Number 5. Tarrytown, New York, 1971.

Nida, Eugene A., *Customs and Cultures.* New York, Harper and Row. 1954.

"Identification, a Major Problem of Modern Missions," *Practical Anthropology,* Volume 2, Number 4. Tarrytown, New York. 1955.

Learning a Foreign Language. Ann Arbor, Michigan, Friendship Press. 1957.

Message and Mission. New York, Harper and Row. 1960.

Scott, William Henry, "Rethinking the American Missionary Presence in the Philippines," *International Review of Mission,* Volume LXII, Number 247. Geneva, Switzerland. 1975.

CHURCH GROWTH PRINCIPLES

WENDELL BROOM

TRYING HARDER OR TRYING DIFFERENTLY

There are grounds for optimism and grounds for pessimism in missions today. What causes some to be optimistic and others pessimistic is not simply "subjective mood." Objective reality in mission experience varies so widely that either optimism or pessimism proves to be required by the facts.

Reuel Lemmons, in his lecture, "Ghosts of Past Failures,"[1] has given chilling examples of tragedy, recounting the examples of missionaries who have labored in foreign fields. The tragedy is that paragraph after paragraph concludes with the phrase " . . . but nothing remains of his work . . . " Some local churches have pulled back or cancelled their missionary support because of disappointing or tragic experiences in mission work done in the past. Some returned missionaries are cynical, disillusioned, or bitter because of their field experiences. Visitors to certain mission fields, for example, are surprised that after two decades of well-publicized missionary work, there is only one church in a capital city, with eight members present on Sunday, seven women and one man, all over sixty years of age.

But missions have another side. The same two decades in another field have produced over five hundred churches, more than 70,000 baptized believers worshipping regularly, with a vitality that has continued to multiply churches, with or without American missionaries present. Protestant, Catholic and independent agencies report that 55,000 people per day are now entering Christianity, and at the present time

---

[1] See bibliography.

1,400 new churches are being planted every week. Stated another way, if we began with a group of 100 Christians and 100 non-Christians in Africa in 1900, the rates of growth would show that the 100 Christians had now grown to 2,900, while the non-Christians would number only 250. Speaking interdenominationally, missions are growing much faster than is the unbelieving world. There is much statistical cause for optimism in world evangelism.[2]

What causes the difference between these statistical evidences for optimism and pessimism? Are some missionaries bad men and others good? Do some try harder and succeed, while the others are lazy and fail?

TRY DIFFERENTLY, NOT JUST HARDER

While the urgency of the Cross demands the best efforts in the work of the kingdom, simply trying harder is not the guaranteed solution. The solution from God may lie in trying differently. Farmers of the 1800's worked desperately hard to scratch out a living, while farmers of today with less effort can produce enough to feed hundreds. The difference is not in the effort, but in the way they farm: better machinery, genetically controlled seeds, fertilizers, weed-killers. We farm differently now, not just harder. So it is in missions.

There are two kinds of n

MISSION A	MISSION B
Preaching is done out of experience and background in American church life.	Strategy is planned and revised on the basis of experience and consultation with the field culture.

---

[2]Wagner, Peter. Article in *Today's Christian,* Fuller Evangelistic Association. Feb.-Apr. 1976. (Box 123, Los Angeles, CA 90053).

A blanket strategy is laid on the supposition that all should hear equally over the years.

Strategy is planned on the evidence of the receptivity of the peoples.

The mission base is established in a permanent "mission station."

Workers are mobility oriented and prepared to leave their foxholes as the battle moves on.

A sense of fatherly superiority demands paternal guidance for the converts and churches.

A realistic sense of cultural difference demands a brotherly relationship with cultural freedom for converts.

Churches are envisioned as a few believers holding on amidst a vast majority of unbelievers.

Churches are intended to liberate the entire society for Christ and move on to the next society.

Decisions depend on subjective needs of the missionary or the home church.

Decisions are geared to objective attainment: to plant churches that will plant churches that will . . . .

Churches started have *terminal* life, (like mules or hybrid corn or seedless grapes).

Churches planted have *germinal* life, (like live rabbits and bermuda grass).

One strategy is set, which continues as official policy, whatever changes occur in the field.

Strategy is reviewed by evaluating growth and receptivity, relative to known opportunities.

The world is viewed as being one place filled with one people — the un-converted.

The world is viewed as a mosaic of varying and distinct homogeneous units of mankind with different degrees of receptivity.

The missions task is measured by the sum total of human forces working within the field: how many men, finances, and resources are available.

The missionary considers sociological forces involved, but seeks for evidences of God's movements or purposes among the nations (famine, revolution, affluence, migrations, people movements, etc.).

Cultural tradition is respected so much that the mission is bound by it (especially the home-land traditions).

Field ministry is consciously free from home cultural ties so that the Spirit can create his people in each cultural unit.

Missionaries and the churches they plant may be in either of the categories above, and still be doctrinally conservative (believe in the inspiration of the Scriptures, the deity of Christ, the person and work of the Holy Spirit, the centrality of the church, the reality of sin, heaven and hell, and the totality of the "faith once for all delivered . . . "). They may agree in the nature of the Christian life (the graces and fruit of the Spirit, the need for social service, love of neighbor, reading and prayer, a pious life). They may agree that all men are lost eternally because of sin, unless they hear the good news of Jesus, and that it is the task of the entire church to carry the good news. They may agree that the power of world evangelism is the power of the Holy Spirit, and that nothing can be accomplished without a certain " . . . power from on high . . . "[3]

While both types of missionaries may be agreed on such solid doctrinal realities, several distinctive points no doubt account for their variation.

---

[3]Luke 24:40.

1. The Lordship of Christ and the stewardship of man demands that churches grow. Non-growing churches can never disciple the whole world. American slow-growth or non-growth has blinded us to the paradox of fishing without catching, empty banquet tables, sowing without reaping, fig trees without fruit, sheep not in the fold, lost and unfound coins, and ripe harvests not reaped. It is not the will of God that churches remain static or gently decline.

2. The church has one irreplaceable task, amidst many good works: to convert and incorporate new believers into churches. Whatever other good things missionaries are doing, if they are not gathering countable new disciples into countable churches, their chief task is not yet done.

3. The task of missions must be biblically identified and repeatedly stated in measurable objectives. This task must be incessantly before the vision of the church. " . . . There is no need for Christians to work under a shadow of doubt as to whether they can really know what God's objective is. Resort to the 'mysterious working of God's Spirit' is often a thinly disguised rationalization of evangelistic failure, couched in pious terms."[4]

4. Strategy is the device of mature and competent servants of God who are seeking the hundred-fold fruit rather than the sixty or thirty-fold. To make plans for the wise utilization of resources to accomplish the greatest possible return to the Lord of talents is both biblical and expedient.

5. The resources of human wisdom should be used to further the purposes of the God of all wisdom. The fields of anthropology, sociology, psychology, and other related social and behavioral sciences can be tested by the word of God and made to contribute to the ultimate desire of God for " . . . all things are yours . . . "[5] In mission strategy, we " . . . prove all

---

[4]Wagner, Peter. Article in *Christianity Today*, December 7, 1973, pp. 12-14 (284).

[5]I Corinthians 3:21.

things . . . hold fast to that which is good . . . "[6] Such valuable principles as people movements,[7] the power encounter,[8] indigeneity,[9] innovation acceptance,[10] and ethnotheology[11] have all been articulated by these behavioral disciplines, and have helped us understand some of the remarkable growth of the church in the New Testament.

6. Research into the facts concerning the mission fields will make possible wise and productive decisions. Promotional, fund-raising, and hopeful success stories can disguise the real facts of which the harvester needs to be aware if the church is to cover the earth. Despite the fund-raising assurances that the fields are ripe unto harvest, if we could see the actual statistics showing that a certain mission field is growing at 583% per decade, while another one is growing at only 87% per decade, we would know where the priority in missionary strength should be used.

These six distinctive viewpoints in missions thinking and activity are crucial for the final results in a field. Highly productive fields and slightly productive fields do not depend entirely on the nature of the soil[12] but partly on the judgments and methods of the human stewards.[13]

---

[6] I Thessalonians 5:21.

[7] McGavran, Donald. *Understanding Church Growth,* (Grand Rapids: Wm. B. Eerdmans, 1970), 296-334.

[8] Tippett, A. R. *Solomon Islands Christianity,* (London: Lutterworth Press, 1967), pp. 100-111.

[9] McGavran. *op. cit.* pp. 335f.

[10] Barnett, Homer. *Innovation: the Basis of Culture Change.* (New York: McGraw Hill. 1953).

[11] Tippett, A. R. (Editor). *God, Man, and Church Growth,* (Grand Rapids: Eerdmans, 1973), pp. 109-126.

[12] Matthew 13.

[13] I Corinthians 3:10-15.

OBJECTIVES OF PRODUCTIVE MISSIONARIES

In the same way the Apostle puts the Christian life into focus by saying that to speak in tongues, have all knowledge, and give one's body to be burned is all nothing without love,[14] so missions have to be put into focus by a clearly stated objective. What is that one thing without which all our admirable projects, commendable social services, and extensive labors will be really nothing?

1. *God wills that we plant churches.* New Testament directives are numerous in assigning individual tasks to believers. "Preach the Word."[15] "Preach the Gospel to every creature . . . "[16] "Go ye therefore, and teach all nations, baptizing them . . . teaching them to observe all things . . . "[17] In modern missions we have utilized social and technological devices, preached sermons, built baptistries, printed tracts, written and distributed correspondence courses, sent out radio sermons, ministered to physical needs, conducted campaigns, and used many other good methods. The pull of all these good ministries has been felt by all of us. Which one good thing should I give myself to? The one ultimate purpose of God, however, is to unite all these good ministries toward one objective: the presence of the living body of Christ among every tribe, tongue and people. Mere fragments of ministry here and there will not suffice. It is inadequate that hundreds have been taught. It is not enough that dozens have been baptized. It falls short if we have only ministered to physical needs. The aim and end of all these is to bring believers into Christ unto eternal life. This necessitates not only conversion, baptism, ministries, but the incorporation of the believers into the living body of Christ. Until they have been made parts of the living organism, with

---

[14]I Corinthians 13.

[15]2 Timothy 4:2.

[16]Mark 16:15.

[17]Matthew 28:19-20.

shepherds to watch for their souls, deacons to minister to their needs, teachers to insure their growth in the word, and opportunity for their faith to bear fruit by others being added to the body—until that life cycle is completed in GROWING CHURCHES, God's will is not satisfied. The planting of churches that plant other churches is the ultimate aim of missions, into which every good ministry fits as contributing parts of the whole.

2. *God wills that we plant churches that plant churches that plant churches that plant . . .*   Ten missionaries can each plant one church each year. If the churches they plant have *terminal* life, after ten years their field will have 100 churches. If the missionaries die or return home, the number of churches remains static, for they do not plant other churches.

The same ten missionaries, by planting churches that have *germinal* life, will in ten years have 5,110 churches in their field. If the missionaries die or return home, the churches will continue to multiply, because they have germinal life.

Terminal life means a unit of life without reproductive power. Mules are hybrid animals incapable of reproduction. Hybrid corn is good to eat, but will not produce a new crop. Seedless grapes are delightful to taste, but like all forms of terminal life, when reproduction is desired, the original source of life must be sought out.

Germinal life means each life unit bears the power of reproduction. Star fish can be cut up, and each piece produces another starfish. Every runner of bermuda grass puts down new root systems and sends out its own runners. A few rabbits imported into Australia for meat production have now over-run the land and the farmers are trying to annihilate them.

These two kinds of churches are described biblically. Paul wrote to Timothy ". . . . what you have heard from me (germination 1) . . . entrust to faithful men (germination 2) . . . who will be able to teach others also" (germination

3)[18] This is germinal life. Paul does not have to teach every man. He teaches Timothy, Timothy teaches others. Timothy teaches others to teach others. Like bermuda grass, star fish, and healthy rabbits, each believer becomes a life-generating source.

Terminal churches are also pictured in Scripture: "For though by this time you ought to be teachers, you need someone to teach you again the first principles of God's word . . ."[19] Here are believers who have not the ability to impart life. If new believers arise, it will not be from these, but because the original teachers came back again to impart spiritual life. Like mules and seedless grapes, a continuing supply must come from the original source.

For world evangelism, it is obvious that terminal missions can never keep up with population growth, much less spread from continent to continent and pole to pole. Germinal missions can. In Acts, it was germinal missions that multiplied so rapidly, for when the believers dispersed at the death of Stephen[20], "those who were scattered went about preaching the word."

Unfortunately, since most American churches are basically terminal, most American missionaries are trained to plant only terminal churches. A vigorous re-training will probably have to take place if American missionaries are ever to be able to plant germinal churches in world evangelism.

4.*God wills that we plan "culture-free" churches.* The American Restoration movement has thrived on the popular slogan that we should be "Christians only." In the American cultural scene, where sectarian division is a major problem,

---

[18] 2 Timothy 2:2.

[19] Hebrews 5:12.

[20] Acts 7 and 8.

this slogan is valid and biblical. However, as one moves into cross-cultural communication of the Gospel, the slogan loses its relevance and becomes an impossibility. Culturally speaking, no one can be a "Christian only." Everyone must be a Christian in some kind of cultural setting. When Jesus came in the flesh, he could not be just "a man." He had to be a Roman or a Greek or a Scythian or a Persian or a Jew —some specific kind of man. To be a Christian requires certain cultural necessities: choice of speech, clothing, gestures, and other incidentals of culture, which are indeed demanded by generic directives of God.

Naturally, the planters of new churches like to see their own familiar cultural incidentals rise up. But the attachment of the culture of the missionary to his message imposes a barrier to those of other cultures who may want admission to the kingdom of the supracultural God. Our comfortable mother tongue may constitute a dreadfully difficult obstacle to Ibibio men, who just can't seem to master it. They have a right to hear God speak in their own tongue, to be Christians in their own cultural setting. They do not need or want "little American churches." Croatian Yugoslavs want Croatian churches. Batak Indonesians want Batak churches. Ibo Nigerians want Ibo churches.

And more important, God wants them to have churches that are culturally comfortable to them. This was the message of Acts 10, 11 and 15. "Peter opened his mouth and said: 'Truly I perceive that God shows no partiality, but in every nation anyone who fears him and does what is right is acceptable to him.' "[21] Despite the efforts of the Jews to demand cultural conformity ("It is necessary to circumcise them, and to charge them to keep the law of Moses"[22]) the final decision was " . . . it has seemed good to the Holy Spirit and to us to lay upon you no greater burden than these necessary things . . . "[23] Gentiles did not have to become Jews

---

[21] Acts 10:34, 35.

[22] Acts 15:5.

[23] Acts 15:28.

to be Christians. Bataks do not have to become Americans to become Christians. God wants Batak churches among Bataks and Ibibio churches among Ibibios. We must plant churches that are culture freê.

4. *God wills that we plant growing churches.* Most American Christians have learned to be content with non-growth or slight-growth patterns of American church life. In the U. S. A., 5% to 10% growth per year is viewed as being an acceptable, and even enviable, growth rate. (Take an hour or so to calculate what the ten-year growth rate of your home congregation may be.) But in world evangelism, there are fields where 50% growth per year is normal. God wants churches to grow, because God wants every possible human being redeemed from sin and prepared for the Wedding Supper of the Lamb. The more souls that are there, the happier God will be. And the process God uses to prepare those souls is life in the body of Christ. God is not content for the church to have twenty or thirty members and remain so for decades, when the possibility exists for there to be two hundred or two thousand.

Does this mean that God wants us to be primarily number-conscious? Are we trying to convert head-hunters into head-counters? Not at all, because growth has more than head-counting dimensions. There are three different aspects of the growing churches God wants:

(1) Quantitative Growth. God wants not only the 144,000, but also the innumerable multitudes in heaven.[24] The ninety and nine were not enough when the shepherd knew there was one more that ought to be in the fold. The Holy Spirit in the book of Acts counted three thousand, then five thousand, and then the disciples were added to and multiplied. The ministry of shepherding (the eldership) demands that those charged with the care of souls know how many souls there are, where they came from and where they went.

---

[24] Rev. 7:4, 9.

(2) Qualitative Growth. Besides the numbers, God wants the church strong in heart and spirit. The disciples are to grow in the fruit of the Spirit (love, joy, peace, etc.)[25] They are to add faith, virtue, knowledge, etc.[26] They are to increase in the grace and knowledge of our Lord,[27] These qualities adorn the church with the beauty that draws men to Christ,[28] and wins the respect of the outsiders[29].This happens when men pray better, know the word better, meditate and commune with God regularly, abound in good works, and reflect the nature and perfect image of Christ.[30]

(3) Organic Growth. God wants the church to have specialized ministries. When cells multiply without specialization, such growth is called a tumor or cancer. But when cells develop into special organs and function in different helpful ways, such organic growth produces a body. It must have eyes, legs, hands, heart, kidneys, etc. The church is the body of Christ.[31] As members of the body grow in their ability to serve in special ways, the church grows organically, and becomes more perfect. Some of these organs of ministry are elders, deacons, teachers, evangelists, servants, those who give, those who visit, those who rule, those who give mercy, those who show hospitality, those who sew, and others as listed in I Peter 4:10, Romans 12:4-8, and 2 Peter 3:15.[32]

---

[25] Gal. 5:22-26.

[26] 2 Peter 1:5-9.

[27] 2 Peter 3:18.

[28] Titus 2:10.

[29] I Thessalonians 4:12.

[30] Ephesians 4:13.

[31] Colossians 2:19, Romans 12, I Corinthians 13, I Corinthians 1:18.

[32] This is dealt with at length in an article, "Gifts and Ministries" in the *Mission Strategy Bulletin*, Vol. 2; No. 6, July-August, 1975.

When we speak of planting growing churches, we thus speak of growth in all three dimensions: quantitative, qualitative, and organic. If any one of these three kinds of growth is lacking, the other kinds will be hindered. God wants all three.

5. *God wills that we should plant indigenous churches.* Banana trees are indigenous to West Africa. They grow and multiply profusely because the climate suits them. Banana trees are not indigenous to West Texas. They will die within the year, unless they are protected by hot-houses, watered and cared for tenderly. Banana trees will never spread like bluebonnets in Texas, for they are not indigenous to the environment.

Churches with brick buildings, English Bibles, college-trained preachers and leaders, bus ministries, parking lots, orphan homes, national radio ministries, and cushioned pews are not indigenous to Third World underdeveloped countries. Churches like these may thrive well enough in "the Bible Belt" of the USA, but only by artificial hothouse care could they survive in Quiche or Quechua villages.

The rule of thumb by which indigenous churches can be most quickly recognized is to ask the three questions:

> Are the churches self-supporting?
> Are they self-governing?
> Are they self-propagating?

If these questions can be answered yes, then the churches will probably spread like bluebonnets in Texas or banana trees in Nigeria. But if the churches have been trained to ways of evangelism that they cannot possibly support financially, or taught to meet in buildings that they could not possibly afford to build, then money must be imported to keep them growing, and they will not multiply quickly or widely.

If churches have been planted in such a way that they are not aware of and confident of the indwelling Holy Spirit

---

[33] Romans 8:1-11.

and His word guiding them and living in them to enable them to make good leadership decisions, to discipline their members, to send out evangelists, and to prepare teachers, then they will not be able to govern themselves. This inability will require importation of "foreign missionary supervisors", and the churches will be able to grow only to the extent that imported, non-indigenous leadership is available.

If churches grow and multiply only when missionary personnel are available to lead or perform the evangelistic duties, then the churches will not be self-propagating. They will be terminal churches. If evangelism, baptisms, new churches, and outreach stop happening while the missionary is on furlough, the church is probably not an indigenous church. It will not spread like dandelions, or like the church in the book of Acts.

Protestant missionary leaders have been conscious of the need of this quality of indigeneity for several generations now. Out of his thirty-two years of experience in China, John Nevius made certain observations about what would keep churches spreading best.[34] Presbyterians began evangelism in Korea on the basis of his guidelines, which included:

(a) Encouraging new converts to continue to earn their living and maintain their own position in life, so that Christianity is seen as a new way of life for ordinary men.

(b) Trusting unpaid leaders to shepherd, teach and watch over the little church groups.

(c) Letting the church meet in homes of members or in meeting places they could afford to rent or build.

(d) Training new converts to evangelize and edify the churches.

(e) Expecting existing churches to plant new churches.[34]

Following these policies, the Presbyterian churches in Korea experienced the most outstanding growth of their

---

[34] Nevius, John L. *The Planting and Developing of Missionary Churches.* (Philadelphia: Reformed and Presbyterian Publishing Co., 1958 reprint), pp. 58, 59.

mission work anywhere in the world. Nevius visited Korea and discussed his missionary methods in 1890. The Presbyterian church grew from 530 members in 1897, to 53,008 in 1912.[35] In 1971, there were 5750 Presbyterian churches with 1,722,500 members. The Methodists were second largest with 300,000 members.[36]

By its nature, the kingdom of God is suited to every kind of human being on our planet. Because the same Creator designed both humankind and the kingdom, it is ideally fitted to meet the needs of all mankind. To keep the church indigenous to man's needs requires only that we keep American culture from becoming a barrier to those who are eager to claim the heritage of God in his kingdom.

6. *God wills that the church should grow infinitely.* The Spirit, speaking through Habakkuk said that the " . . . earth shall be filled with the knowledge of the glory of the Lord, as the waters cover the sea."[37] If the Gospel is to be preached in " . . . all nations . . . "[38] and to " . . . every creature . . . "[39], then the growth pattern of the preaching agency must be capable of infinite reproduction. If we gear the spread of the church to some kind of financial subsidy (e.g. raising foreign money to build church buildings on the mission field, or to support preachers for each new church with funds from abroad) then we put a choker on the growth of the church. If we plan our evangelism so that a missionary ratio of one American to every 10,000 people is necessary, then it will require 300,000 missionaries to reach the unevangelized 3,000,000,000 of the world. If we make literacy a handmaiden of evangelism, then we shall be able to

---

[35] Clark, Charles Allen. *The New Plan for Mission Work, Illustrated in Korea,* (Seoul, Korea: Christian Literature Society, 1937), pp. 13, 15, 84, 189.

[36] Kane, S. Herbert, *A Global View of Missions.* (Grand Rapids: Baker Book House, 1971), p. 274.

[37] Habakkuk 2:14.

[38] Matthew 28:19.

[39] Mark 16:15.

evangelize only in the amount we are able to build schools
and teach literacy to every tribe and tongue.

We must also be aware of the thought pattern that says
"In the beginning of our work we must use some of these
expediencies to get started, but then we shall cast them aside
and grow infinitely." The reality is that once such a marriage
of method and gospel has occurred, the minds of the converts
and their unbelieving neighbors cannot separate the two, and
whether we like it or not, the growth pattern has been
established, along with its built-in limitations.

To summarize:

1. God wills that we plant churches.
2. God wills that we plant churches that plant churches
that plant . . . .
3. God wills that we plant culturally free churches.
4. God wills that we plant indigenous churches.
5. God wills that we plant growing churches.
6. God wills that we plant churches that grow infinitely.

NECESSARY QUALITIES FOR CHURCH PLANTERS

If the planting of such churches were just normally and
naturally the way missionary work proceeds, we would see
many more productive mission fields and ten thousand times
ten thousand more children of God among the nations. Such
church growth is not the result of instinctive missionary
reflexes, any more than good child care is instinctive with
mothers universally. When a nation's infant mortality rate
improves by 300%, it is because mothers have been learning
better hygiene and infant care. If church growth rates
increase from 12% per year to 97% per year, it will be
because missionaries have learned more about how to plant
the kind of churches that God wants.

Some of the qualities in missionaries that will produce
this kind of God-honoring growth are these:

1. *Such church planters must have a strategy.* Spiritually
minded people may hasten to protest: "The Spirit of God

moves where he will, and we cannot tell God what to do with our strategies." Agreeing completely with this objection, we must insist that such strategy as we speak of is completely within the will of God. In fact, it is our objective to find the strategy of God and see where we can fit into it. Where is God's Spirit moving? What can we do to work behind His leadership? How can we harvest where He has ripened? We agree that for us to make plans and expect God to confine himself to the role we assign Him is foolish or even blasphemous. Pity the missionary who reports hysterically that since the Communists have driven all the missionaries out of China, God has no voice nor hand in all of China. While human beings are the messengers of God's grace in Jesus Christ, the hysterical report ignores two realities: (a) not all God's messengers are westerners subject to Communist deportation. There are Chinese believers who remain in service, despite prison, tribulation, and legal prohibition. And (b) God still works in His providence through war, famine, affluence, revolution, conquest and unbelieving kings, just as he did through Pharaoh, Nebuchadnezzar, and Cyrus. God is not awaiting our plan's completion to see where we want Him to be. Our strategy, instead must be to stay spiritually alert to what God is doing where, and then to seek from Him wisdom to know where we can walk behind Him in His footsteps. Good church planters will have a plan, a strategy under God.

2. *Such church planters must be sensitive to receptivity.* The parable of the sower tells us that not all will hear the word the same. To use the Isaiah passage " . . . so shall my word be . . . It shall not return to me empty, but it shall accomplish that which I purpose, and prosper in the thing for which I sent it."[40] To justify a careless selection of fields is to be guilty of twisting the word. God himself says to Isaiah "Say to this people, 'Hear and hear, but do not understand; see and see, but do not perceive' "[41] Jesus says in explaining

---

[40] 55:11.

[41] 6:9.

the sower parable (or as some call it more aptly, the parable of the soils) that God's words to Isaiah are fulfilled in His parables, because some of the word produces nothing when it falls on the wayside heart. There is no biblical assurance that good work done by good men will invariably produce good fruit. Paul, on the contrary states clearly that if a man builds unwisely (even if on the true foundation) his work will be lost, and he shall have no reward.[42]

The obligation is clear, therefore, that church planters must seek the good soil—even the best soil for their labors. In education, the unteachable ones are kept out of schools. In business, sales efforts are not wasted where strong resistance has been clearly demonstrated. In medicine, hospitals for the incurables allow medical talent to be diverted to those for whom there is hope of recovery. Biblically, Paul shook off the dust of his feet when it became clear that they would not hear truth.[43] Jesus clearly instructed his disciples that there were times when they should go to these, not to those.[44]

Since God has a priority for harvesting the ripe when they are ready and leaving the unripe until God has shone upon them and warmed them into readiness, the church planter must be sensitive to this ripeness. More and more data are now becoming available to assist in recognizing receptivity, without the costly "trial and error" measurement. The catalogs of MARC division of World Vision, Inc., may be consulted for this data.

3. *Such church planters must be objective-oriented.* Field labors should not be determined by "where the roads are good," "where I can fly my plane," "where I can find good stamps for my collection," or "where my family will be happy and comfortable." One's choice of ministry must be determined by what God wants. The Scripture is the

---

[42] I Corinthians 3:11-15.

[43] Acts 13:46-49, 14:20, 17:1-10, 18:5-7.

[44] Matthew 10:5-15.

beginning of this quest for the will of God. The system of priorities about what God wants most is clearly laid out in the word. In fact, the failure to recognize these priorities has caused enormous confusion and frustration in making both ethical and ministry decisions.

Once the purpose of God is determined through study and prayer, the servant will be able to clearly state that purpose as the foundation of his ministry. He will also be able to measure his ministry to determine when it is prospering, when it has been completed and the time has come to move on to the next ministry or field. For such objective-oriented men, there will be freedom from fuzzy rationalization and scriptural perversions that try to justify failure. The ministry that is not bearing fruit[45] or producing its reward[46] is a ministry that needs to be passed by in favor of one from which God will have more glory.

4. *Such church planters must be culturally conscious.* This cultural sensitivity can be seen in two ways:

(a) He will learn to see clearly the cultural mosaic present among the people. Nigerians are not one people, but fifty-five different tribes, with customs, languages, and patterns of life distinctly unique from each other. Indonesia has 137 such divisions. They are all Indonesians, but of different cultural systems. Even in our American cities of New York, Los Angeles, or Dallas, there are Chinatowns, little Italys, black ghettoes, and Chicano zones, where the ways of the people are unique. To try to build a middle class, Caucasian, white collar, college level church in a Chinese, semi-literate, agricultural, blue collar community would be to ask for defeat. Church planters who are insensitive to this dimension of human life will waste much valuable time and strength.

---

[45] John 15.

[46] I Corinthians 3.

(b) The church planter must learn what in his religious knowledge is eternally unchangeable, and what is culturally negotiable. He must learn how to separate the eternal gospel from the local and incidentals. The Restoration movement in America proposed a solution to this problem as frontiersmen struggled with what parts of continental religion to leave behind them: "We ought to speak where the Bible speaks and be silent where the Bible is silent." Even here, the problem is not quite solved. Some way must be determined to know what in the Bible is eternally valid and what was temporal and local. Paul urged circumcision on Timothy because he was Jewish by parentage, but forbade circumcision to Titus because he was Gentile. In practice we actually do this by separating certain New Testament practices as not applicable to our time (foot washing, head coverings, the holy kiss, etc.) while insisting upon others as universal and eternal in nature.[47] A new academic discipline, ethnotheology, is just now arising which concentrates on the problem of discerning to what extent our biblical understandings are shaded by our cultural surroundings.[48] The church planter who is unaware of this problem is apt to find himself binding where God has not bound and loosing where God has not loosed.

5. *Such church planters must be able to measure their work.* In terms of the three dimensional growth mentioned above, church planters must be able to know something of how their work is growing quantitatively, qualitatively, and organically. Bankers can measure their business profits and losses very precisely. Farmers can measure their harvest and know how to plant next year. Teachers can measure their pupils' learning and promote them to their next learning stage. Soldiers can know when they have won a battle and can press on to the next victory. To fail to have a means of measurement is to be very soon driven from the enterprise, whatever it be.

---

[47]Unpublished exercise by Mont Smith.

[48]Tippett, *God, Man, and Church Growth.* pp. 109-126.

To be convinced of the validity of this point, read the book of Acts while watching for measurements of growth in quantity, quality, and organic development. Whole new concepts will open to the sensitive church planter in the word of the Spirit. The three thousand soon came to be five thousand. Paul rejoiced in the work of faith, labor of love, and patience of hope among the Thessalonians.[49] Paul marvelled that the Galatians were "so quickly deserting him who called you in the grace of Christ . . . ".[50] Jesus said to the Thyatira believers, "I know your works, your love, and faith and service and patient endurance, and that your latter works exceed your first."[51] But He also said to the Laodiceans, " . . . not knowing that you are wretched, pitiable, poor, blind, and naked."[52] Paul sent Titus to Crete " . . . that you might set in order what was lacking and appoint elders in every town as I directed you . . . "[53] As doctors are sensitive to blood pressure, pulse, respiration and other measurable vital signs as indicators of life processes, so the church planter must cultivate the skills of measuring church vitality.

Church planters will be much more productive workers if they know:

1) How many churches in this nation?

2) How many churches in a homogeneous unit or district? (e.g., in Nebraska, among the Quechuas, among blacks in Los Angeles, among Ibos in Lagos)

3) How large are these congregations? (precise numbers of members, or even whether there are 18 members or 240 members)

---

[49] I Thess. 1:3.

[50] 1:6.

[51] Revelation 2:19.

[52] Revelation 3:17.

[53] Titus 1:5.

4) How many members have come from transferring membership?

   restoring of backsliders?

   baptisms (how many were baptized from the world, and how many were children of members?)

5) How many members have been lost by transferring out to another church?

   death and funeral?

   reversion to the world?

   withdrawn fellowship?

6) What is the net gain or loss each year? [54]

Capable bankers, farmers, teachers, and soldiers know these details about their enterprises. Can faithful stewards in God's kingdom know less about theirs?

6. *Such church planters must review their strategy for ministry periodically.* At pre-determined intervals, the measurements of growth should be studied for signs of receptivity or resistance. Personnel should be reassessed and work commitments adjusted accordingly. Search should be maintained constantly for the cultural bridges from the people where the present work is, over into the neighboring cultural unit. [55]

The missionary should periodically assess every agency, institution, ministry, expenditure, and program by the burning question, "Is this causing the church to grow?" A negative answer should bring corrective adjustments.

Strategy should be re-examined periodically with a sharp eye for revision. Don't be held in the "prison of previous patterns". [56] The decisions by your colleagues before you may have been excellent decisions for their time and circum-

---

[54] McGavran, *Understanding Church Growth,* pp. 83-99.

[55] McGavran's *Bridges of God* discusses these doors God opens from one cultural group into the next one.

[56] McGavran, Donald. *How Churches Grow.* (New York: Friendship Press, 1966), pp. 108-113.

stances, but chances are good that if they were here to see your times and your circumstances they would change their own policies. You should be ready to do the same. The apostle Paul shifted his strategy. In his second journey into Asia Minor, he planned to go one way, then the other, and finally settled on a third. [57] At one phase of his life his strategy was to travel and preach, but later his imprisonment demanded a change of strategy to writing and prayer. Dogged determination to continue in the old plans when the circumstances have changed can spell waste and fruitlessness. Periodic re-examination is essential to valid planning and strategy if the maximum numbers of churches are to be planted.

CONCLUSION

Strong desires are not always enough to insure success. Parents who deeply love their children may see them develop in wrong directions because the parental skills have not been learned. Doctors sometimes have to watch their patients die because the surgical skills required to save life have not been mastered. Christians have sometimes seen souls lost because the "workmanship in the word" (" . . . a workman who has no need to be ashamed, rightly handling the word of truth . . ."[58]) was not adequate to convince and persuade the lost friend.

Strong desires in world evangelism are no substitute for the insights and skills of cross-cultural evangelism. Trying harder will not take the place of trying differently. We must, like Paul, be " . . . skilled master builders . . ."

"Let each man take care how he builds . . .
Now if anyone builds on the foundation with gold, silver, precious stones, wood, hay, stubble—each man's work will become manifest; . . . If the work which any man has built on the foundation survives, he will receive a reward. If any man's work is burned up, he will suffer loss, though he himself will be saved, but only as through fire."[59]

---

[57] Acts 16:6-10.

[58] 2 Timothy 2:15.

[59] I Corinthians 3:10-15.

SUGGESTED READINGS

Barnett, Homer. *Innovation: the Basis of Culture Change.* New York: McGraw-Hill, 1953.

Clark, Charles Allen. *The New Plan for Mission Work, Illustrated in Korea.* Seoul, Korea: Christian Literature Society, 1937.

Kane, J. Herbert. *A Global View of Missions.* Grand Rapids, Michigan: Baker Book House, 1971.

Lemmons, Reuel. *The Ghosts of Past Failures.* (Tape recording of lecture, Abilene Christian University library PTC 266.6, L 54) 1972.

MARC Division of World Vision Inc., 919 West Huntington Drive, Monrovia, CA 91016 (ask for *Directory of Unreached Peoples*).

McGavran, Donald. *Bridges of God.* New York: Friendship Press, 1955. *How Churches Grow.* New York: Friendship Press, 1966. *Understanding Church Growth.* Grand Rapids, Michigan: Eerdmans, 1970.

Mission Strategy Bulletin. Article on "Gifts and Ministries" Vol. 2: No. 6, July-August, 1975.

Nevius, John L. *The Planting and Developing of Missionary Churches.* Philadelphia: Reformed and Presbyterian Publishing Co., 1958 (originally published 1886).

Smith, Mont. "The Culture-Gospel Test." unpublished paper.

Tippett, A. R. *Solomon Islands Christianity.* London: Lutterworth Press, 1967, (editor) *God, Man, and Church Growth.* Grand Rapids, Michigan: Eerdmans, 1973.

Wagner, Peter. Article in *Today's Christian:* Fuller Evangelistic Association, Feb-Apr, 1976. (Box 123, Los Angeles, CA 90053), Article in *Christianity Today.* Dec. 7, 1973. pp. 12-14 (284).

Winter, Ralph. *The Unbelievable Twenty-Five Years.* Pasadena, CA: Wm. Carey Library, 1971.

INSTITUTIONS IN MISSIONS

DAN COKER

Introduction

The missionary's rationale for establishing service institutions, i.e., hospitals, schools, etc., in foreign lands has in the past included two principal considerations: (1) The underdeveloped nations, usually the target for missionary thrusts, are thought to need the modern gadgetry and techniques which can be brought by the missionary. (2) Service institutions provide an entree that often helps to resolve problems related to hard-to-penetrate societal barriers and governmental immigration policies. The entree aspect has occasioned cooperative efforts that otherwise might never have been realized. For example, educational needs have been met through government-church school enterprises in certain emerging African states, especially those once under British rule.

In South America, the early nineteenth century independence movement produced a political climate that facilitated religious change. European Protestants were granted freedom of worship principally because they were seen by the anti-clerical revolutionary leaders as another force against Spanish and Roman Catholic domination. Although not usually interested in becoming Protestants themselves, the new leaders in effect encouraged the growth of Protestantism beyond its original ethnic boundaries by employing the talents of these European immigrants in desperately needed secular services. One such need was schools, to which the Protestants responded with teaching expertise and religious zeal. For example, James Thompson, who worked in Argentina, Chile (invited by Bernardo O'Higgins in 1821) and Peru, not only instituted a series of Lancaster[1] schools, but also was a representative for the

---

[1] A school system designed to facilitate large numbers of students in one building; order was kept and instruction effected by the tutelage of a corps of monitors working under the schoolmaster.

British and Foreign Bible Society, for which he distributed Protestant literature. These activities constituted the first phase in the ,Protestant missionary thrust among the South Americans.

Subsequently, the Protestants began to engage in proselyting efforts and sought help from foreign mission boards. The United States mission boards took the lead in these efforts, about which a one-time Methodist missionary to South America has written:

> Activity by the foreign mission boards represents the second phase of Protestant growth. It was accompanied in many cases by social service projects, for often the sponsorship of such projects was the only formal non-Roman religious activity permitted among the public at large. A number of what have come to be outstanding schools were begun in this way, a most noteworthy example being the American Institute in La Paz.[2]

This "second phase" identified by Carter provides an unusually good background for this study because it represents a technique initiated during a period for which it seemed especially relevant, and has continued until the present time. During the past few decades, however, serious doubts have been raised concerning the worth of social service mission projects in solving twentieth-century church growth problems. Also, in contrast to the older historical Protestant denominations, a sharp increase in religious conversion has been seen in a third-phase movement, best characterized by Pentecostalism. These groups, usually financially and governmentally independent from foreign sponsorship, have brought renewal through emphasizing "spiritual salvation," not social service.[3] The phenomenal growth of the third-phase churches makes profitable an evaluation of the social service programs, and provides the

---

[2] Carter, Wm. E., *Protestantism in Four Societies,* mimeographed report, 1966, p. 3.

[3] For a detailed account of this phenomenon see Willems, Emilio. *Followers of the New Faith.* (Nashville: Vanderbilt University Press, 1967).

following question for this study: Do social service institutions, particularly educational institutions, contribute to or detract from numerical growth and the development of autonomous churches? "Autonomous" is here used to describe a church whose finances, internal government, and evangelistical outreach are sustained by the initiative and resources of its local membership.[4] The "development of autonomous churches" would involve either a totally self-supporting and self-propagating beginning or a gradual assumption of these responsibilities within a few (perhaps ten) years.

Answering the above question will involve the utilization of descriptive information obtained through personal interviews with Protestant missionaries and Mexican church leaders as well as the review of pertinent literature. Generalizations from these data will be presented at the end of this chapter.

Our method of approach will be to first examine some of the tenets and the consequences of the institutional and functional approaches. Then, using Latin America as an example, institutional theological education will be presented in the light of recent positive trends, some inherent weaknesses and possible alternatives. Finally, Mexico will provide the setting for an overview of comparative methods and results among prominent non-Catholic missions.

Institutional and Functional Approaches

The institutional approach is distinguished from the functional approach by the two-fold nature both of the guiding principles of an institution and its functional fulfillment in the lives of the religious participants. The institution usually has its written laws and proceedings, but these do not always match the "real" happenings. Likewise, the individual

---

[4]cf. Hodges, Melvin L., *On The Mission Field: The Indigenous Church.* (Chicago, Moody Press, 1953).

might seek acceptance in an institution, not because of its manifest purpose, but because of the *latent* function that is provided in which needs are met and/or frustrations released. The manifest, i.e., *stated,* purpose might be "preparing men to serve as full-time ministers of the church." But this is not necessarily the reason for which one enrolls. The latent or "hidden" function is often a phenomenon sensed and manipulated by the students of a school or members of a church, but which is out-of-touch with the administrators' official sphere of activity within the institution's stated goals and ideals. The institutional approach, then, involves observing the ground rules, as understood by the administration, with great emphasis on the manifest purposes of that institution.

The functional approach does not necessarily preclude the use of an institution; the principal consideration is found in *how* that institution is used. If it serves as an unbending model that must be emulated regardless of the social and cultural incongruities, then the approach is most definitely institutional. In this, the institution is duplicated, which becomes the purpose or end within itself. When the institution serves as a means to a more noble and culturally congruent end, not dependent on the institution itself, then there is sufficient flexibility for functionalism.

The functional approach allows a latitude within the structure of the institution (if any is used), permitting the adherents to demonstrate their "true selves." Fulfillment is found in certain latent functions of religion, e.g., social mobility, protest against the establishment, etc. A classic example of this is seen in Chilean Pentecostalism; the leaders of this movement have demonstrated extraordinary adaptability and flexibility in incorporating Chilean culture into their churches. Not only do they know how to meet the people's *felt* needs, they also have skillfully taken ritual and fit it into the culture, adopting existing institutionalized behavior, but modifying it to meet their own purposes and goals. This means simply that Pentecostalism has built for itself a set of symbols that serve to contribute toward group cohesiveness, while protesting against the established ecclesiastical order. Seemingly taking a purposeful opposite to just about every major tenet of Roman Catholic ritual, they have still designed and made possible for themselves a definite group identity. For example, they will *not* use images, will *not* burn candles, will *not* put crosses on their houses, and will pray almost at a shout. [5] Therefore, through allowing members to vent their frustrations against Romanism, the Pentecostals have made themselves distinctive, with an authoritarian doctrine, severe sanctions on rebellious members, and a wide-open ritual.

Basically, what has happened is that a new institution has emerged out of a functional approach that allows the adherents to mold themselves, in their own way, toward the goals that were desired all the time. The institutional approach, in turn, begins with a structured program and frequently frustrates the desired outcomes. It seems to the present writer that while such failures are often attributed to "disinterested and/or unspiritual people" or "disregard for the laws of God," a more palatable reason is to be found in the approach itself. People are often more interested in activities that bring real or imagined solutions to their problems than in joining an institution that seemingly remains aloof to those problems. This interest frequently leads them to search for answers outside the pale of the institutional religious establishment.

Religious Functions in Non-Religious Institutions

Religious functions, especially latent functions, are often carried out in the context of non-religious institutions. This concept demands a definition of religion not usually articulated among church-goers, but recognized by modern theologians. Paul Tillich, for example, presents religion as a system of beliefs and practices that constitute the "ultimate concern" of a society.[6]

---

[5] See Carter, *op. cit.*, p. 11.

[6] Tillich, Paul, *Theology of Culture*, (New York: Oxford Univ. Press, 1959), pp. 3-9.

In Latin America the ultimate concern, a designation which appears to be much more descriptive of the modern view of religion than the traditional institutional acceptance of Catholicism, obviously transcends hearing mass, visiting shrines, singing hymns, or reading the Bible. Paulo Freire's literacy work among peasants in Brazil[7] has demonstrated how that concern is sometimes expressed in a *concientizacion* that, based in politics and education, is designed to incorporate the disenfranchised into mainstream society. Nationalistic movements, even rebel guerila bands like the one with which the Roman Catholic priest Camilo Torres died, are convincing some church leaders that man is often more concerned with the "here-and-now" than he is with the "hereafter." Such has stimulated both concern and heated debate among the members of the World Council of Churches; this has been especially true since that organization absorbed the International Missionary Council, a body that traditionally has been more interested in evangelical thrusts than in social service. [8]

Forecast For Institutions

Today in Latin America there are conscious efforts being made to decide which institutions will figure in the ultimate concern of the people. Vallier draws heavily on Communism and Pentecostalism as being extremely important in the process of change and modernization in Latin America. The importance he sees is not one of direct contribution to the society, but one of pushing the Roman Church toward religious specialization, extricating it from secular involvements. The Roman Church's stance has been that of a political force, to the hurt of its needed religious influence. Vallier feels that since the church has not heeded the religious needs of the people, many have turned to other institutions in which to address themselves religiously. He further theorizes that this drift will force the church's hand.

---

[7] See *The Pedagogy of the Oppressed.* (New York: Herder and Herder, 1970).

[8] McGavran, Donald. "The Warren-McGavran Letters on World Evangelism," *Church Growth Bulletin,* XI, No. 6, July, 1975, pp. 466-469.

The point, then, seems to be that a significant percentage of Latin Americans is turning to more functional alternatives for the fulfillment of felt needs and/or release of frustrations, whether in a "culturally rebellious" Christian alternative such as the fast-growing Pentecostal movement or a theoretically non-religious idealism that promises social reform and satisfies "religious" needs. One of the interesting things about the transfer of religious functions to non-religious institutions is the fact that confidence placed in the religious institution is often ridiculed even as the same confidence is being placed in the new institution. A Messianic hope is supposedly brought closer to being obtained through transferring the object of that hope from the supernatural to the natural world. In the nationalistic movements that are so evident in Latin America today one readily recognizes the "religious" quest for freedom, liberty, dignity, and sovereignty. The fact that many Latin Americans have had to turn from the established church to express themselves provides a strong clue for mission approach. The more successful institutions are those which allow one to cope with life on his own terms and instill within him the pride, or hope, or confidence, or faith, or whatever is necessary to keep one in tune with his ultimate concern.

Theological Education

Probably the most frequently used institution in mission outreach is the Bible school or seminary for preparing a corps of native ministers. First established by the historical Protestant churches in the "second phase" of influence, and perpetuated by later missionary churches as well, several of these schools have been undergoing a metamorphosis that is seen as a positive move by leaders of major Protestant denominations. A trend within many of the established theological schools of Latin America appears to be that of amalgamation. One optimistic reporter from the Theological Education Fund of the World Council of Churches writes enthusiastically about the interdenominational fusing of seminaries and schools, citing as the "best example" the new Instituto Superior de Estudios Teologicos (ISEDET), the 1970 merger of the Union Faculty of Theology in Buenos

Aires with the Lutheran Seminary in Jose Paz.[9] The *Instituto Internacional de Estudios Superiores* in Mexico City has integrated five formerly scattered seminaries, including the interdenominational *Centro Evangelico Unido*. The *Seminario Biblico Latinoamericano* in Costa Rica has incorporated the help of several denominations "although retaining its links with the Latin American Mission."[10] Other examples can be found such as *Comunidad Teologica* in Santiago, Chile, in which Methodists, Presbyterians and Pentecostals have cooperated. Also, Protestants are increasingly establishing relationships with Roman Catholics through cooperative school programs. A few examples include Lutherans and Jesuits in Sao Leopoldo, Brazil; Episcopalians and Dominicans in Sao Paulo; and ISEDET and the Jesuit Faculty of Theology in San Miguel, Argentina. These happenings seem to have brought new life to an old system of institutional activity and are seen as very positive steps by ecumenically minded churches.

Associations

During the 1960's at least four associations emerged. Not yet powerful enough to decide school policy, they are attempting to bring together the thoughts of the member schools in order to standardize accreditation and textbook production. These are: *Asociacion Latinoamericana de Escuelas Teologicas* (ALET), covering northern South America, Central America and Mexico; *Asociacion Sudamericana de Institutiones Teologicas* (ASIT), covering southern South America; *Associacao de Seminarios Teologicos Evangelicos de Brasil* (ASTE), and *Asociacion Andina de Educacion Teologica* (AADET), a thus-far very weak organization intended for Bolivia, Peru and Ecuador. To the present, the expanded duties of these associations have not been carefully designed; it remains to be seen which problems will be included in their sphere of influence.

----

[9] Sapsezian, Sharon. "The Carribean, Central and South America," *Directory, Theological Schools,* Bromley, Kent, England: Theological Education Fund of the World Council of Churches, 1974, p. 221.

[10] Ibid.

Weaknesses

Savage[11] indicates several reasons why the contemporary Bible institute is generally falling short of its intended purposes: (1) Students use the school for social ambition and inexpensive education. (2) The composite of sub-cultures may be aggravated when the administrator is North American or European. (3) Some students from a rural setting have trouble readjusting to that humble life and, frustrated, seek employment in a city. (4) Dependence on the missionary and the United States support might rob the student of initiative and responsibility. (5) Conceptual barriers impede the communication of what might have been plainly said by the foreign missionary. (6) Often the real potential leaders are not in the seminary, but in professions and business.

Lores suggests that theological institutions are not advancing as they should because: (1) Latin Americans no longer respond readily to foreign-dominated institutional control; (2) the present-generation Christians are no longer content with a hope for the world beyond, but want something that functions here and now; (3) there is a cultural gap between those who would like to express their Christian faith in terms of their own setting and those who would perpetuate the cultural transplants which usually dominate in Protestantism; and (4) there are almost insurmountable financial problems in operating institutions in the traditional way.[12]

Alternatives

More and more, church leaders are recognizing the seemingly inescapable weaknesses in institutions not administered and financed by the local populace, and are turning to alternatives designed to eliminate some of the more predictable problems. Gaining popularity are "Evangelism-in-Depth," a crash course delivered in the

[11]Savage, Peter. "A Bold Move For More Realistic Theological Training," *Evangelical Missions Quarterly.* Vol. V., No. 2, Winter, 1969, pp. 65, 66.

[12]Lores, Ruben, "A New Day," *World Vision Magazine,* Vol. XV, No. 5, May, 1971. pp. 8-10.

churches, designed to make every member a church worker; and the prototype extension seminary begun by the Presbyterians of Guatemala in 1862.[13] Another departure from the resident seminary idea is found in the Chilean Pentecostal movement where ministers are trained on the job and in the street.[14] An imaginative program is found in Blay House Theological School in the Episcopal Diocese of Los Angeles,[15] in which mature folk, settled in their jobs, take a four-year theological program only on weekends. Chandapilla tells of moderate success in a teacher-disciple approach conducted on a person to person basis, in the student's home environment.[16]

The Mexican Case

Perhaps more than any other Latin American country, Mexico has been the scene of a fantastically complicated church-state relationship that, among other things, has given rise to a number of incongruities that make Mexican Catholicism a species of its own. Mexican history speaks of agents of both state and church terrorizing one another through various means (one of the most bizarre was that of the "Cristero Rebellion"[17]). The result is a paradoxical state of affairs; "Catholic" Mexico has vigorously curbed church economic and political power. But the same laws designed to limit Catholic activity also apply to the non-Catholic religious groups. The Revolutionary Constitution of 1917, drawing heavily on the anti-clerical thoughts of Benito Juarez and the

---

[13]Winter, Ralph D., *Theological Education By Extension.* (South Pasadena: Wm. Carey Library, 1969).

[14]Wagner, Peter C., "Theological Education in Latin America," *Christianity Today,* Vol. VII, No. 12, March 15, 1963, pp. 21, 22.

[15]Schonberger, Ernest. "The Episcopalian Weekend Seminary." *Church Growth Bulletin,* Vol. III, No. 6, July, 1967, p. 234.

[16]Chandapilla, P. T., "How Jesus Trained the Twelve–Training Leaders in India," *Evangelical Missions Quarterly,* Summer, 1969, pp. 210-218.

[17]A bloody conflict that came about after President Calles (1924-1928) began closing Catholic temples of worship.

Reformers of 1857, specifies that: (1) Associations called "churches" cannot own real estate of any kind, but must cede such properties to the Mexican nation (Art. 27). (2) The minister presiding at any type of religious service must be Mexican by birth (Art. 130). (3) In order to open new places of worship to the public, permission must be obtained from the Secretariat of Government (Art. 130). (4) Religious publications cannot comment on political themes (Art. 130). (5) Political meetings cannot be held in church buildings, nor can organizations be initiated that indicate a relationship between political and religious goals (Art. 130). (6) No religious corporation or minister may establish or direct schools of primary, secondary (Jr. High), normal or *campesino* adult education (Art. 3). (7) Religious ministers are denied the vote and cannot associate themselves with any örganization that is political in design (Art. 130).

These and other similar stipulations have necessitated different approaches from the somewhat standard entrance of foreign missionaries who usually rent a building, put up a sign, advertise openly, proclaim their message through the local media and then "open for business." Since all ministers for Mexicans must constitutionally be Mexicans by birth, theological training by established schools appears to be a logical approach for those mission boards that desire a reasonable reproduction of their own doctrinal convictions. This has been done on a moderate scale, both in and out of the Mexican republic.

The majority of the Protestant denominations in Mexico are products of European and North American churches of the same name and creed. However, several churches have been established by independent laymen who, having acquired their new faith, initiated a movement among their people; typical examples are The Apostolic Church of the Faith in Christ Jesus and The Independent Pentecostal Evangelical Church, both of which were begun by Mexicans who had converted from Catholicism while visiting the Uniteb States. Other denominations such as The Christian Interdenominational Church and The Spiritual Christian Church have been established by religious leaders who broke with another denomination.

Churches Established by Foreign Boards

Churches in Mexico which have been established by foreign boards have adopted an array of approaches:

1. The Plymouth Brethren mission has operated from the first under the assumption that Christian works initiated would be entirely financed by local funds. Therefore, with few exceptions, this mission has not provided funds for the support of churches, ministers, or ministerial candidates. Principally, they have purchased literature and prepared future pastors through correspondence and extension "home schools." The results have been impressive, both in numerical growth and active participation in administrative policy by the Mexican converts.

2. The Mennonite Church is presently engaged in an effort to become a "national movement." With occasional special-project help from the foreign church, they are investing primarily in literature, films, radio programs, and a few scholarships. Construction of church buildings is not common; they prefer to buy and recondition houses.

3. The larger denominations in Mexico (Presbyterians, Methodists, and Baptists) were established in a different way. The missionary societies, after having approved Mexico as a mission field, sent personnel with a set budget for the work. Missionaries usually began by seeking contacts through which good relations could be established with the government. Next, suitable properties to base the future operation were secured. Then, when converts were made, promising men with aptitude for the ministry were sent to an institute or seminary, often in the United States. Soon such schools were built in Mexico—with North American funds. Denominational organizations such as presbyteries, conferences and conventions were founded, staffed at first by Mexicans and North Americans, but later with fewer and fewer North Americans. As the Mexican churches matured they were expected to provide their own personnel and financing. This last expectation is being realized, although not as rapidly as originally hoped. It seems that American-made programs are often hard to fully finance with Mexican sources.

4. Other groups seek to make no distinction between the mission church and the "mother" church that is usually paying the bills. Mexican personnel are contracted and paid the same as their missionary counterpart. Examples of this group are the Episcopal and Confessional Lutheran churches, both of which have seen very slow growth.

A crucial point in the history of Protestant missions was the adoption of the "Cincinnati Plan" of 1916 in which the principal groups involved in Mexican mission efforts agreed to divide the nation into "zones of influence," instead of competing with each other in the same geographical territories. This ecumenical plan did not take into consideration the desires of the Mexican churches, nor were many Mexican Protestant leaders consulted. The result was a dissension that helped initiate a movement toward "independence" among the national churches. This movement gained prominence among the congregations of the National Presbyterian Church of Mexico. However, most churches are still in the process of becoming "independent," although Mexican leadership is often outspoken, even hostile, in favor of a national church, free from North American policy-making. As a consequence, there exist strong pressures in the United States to diminish financial contributions to the Mexican churches.

Mexican-United States Church Ties

At the present time there are three major kinds of relationships sustained between the Mexican churches and their North American counterparts. These are:

1. Churches that now govern and sustain themselves financially, but have a coordinating commission that involves the participation of a minority representation of the mission board that created them. Usually, the foreign representation is about one-third of the commission and has but one vote, no matter how many representatives. There exist cooperative relations through which there are interchanges of professors for theological seminaries, and personnel and money designated for special projects. Among these are the National Presbyterian Church, the Methodist Church of Mexico and the National Baptist Convention.

2. Churches that receive partial or total subsidy for various projects such as education, ministerial support, social work, and evangelism, but have a more or less autonomous administrative organization. They have representatives from the mission board, but these do not have the right to vote in matters concerning the national church. Examples are the Church of the Nazarene, the Associated Reformed Presbyterian Church, Bible Baptist Companionship, Association of Christian Churches and the Disciples of Christ. This group appears to be growing much more slowly than those mentioned in number one. One pastor complained that their ecumenical ideas had neutralized a formerly distinctive message and had reduced their effectiveness. A classic example of this was cited: The General Assembly of Congregational Churches of Mexico had 50 churches in 1913; this dwindled to 20 in 1930, and to 9 in 1975.

3. Churches that are a part of the foreign sponsoring church. These depend organically and economically on the foreign church. There is little or no evidence of a "distinct national identity." Money and basic administrative policies come from foreign sources. Mexican ministerial candidates receive full scholarships, and are later salaried by the foreign sponsors, usually the United States. Such are the Confessional Lutheran Church and the Churches of Christ.

Financial and Administrative Policies
When one talks with missionaries and local church leaders it becomes quite evident that both groups wish to encourage a trend toward administrative autonomy and financial self-sufficiency for the Mexican schools. But administrative autonomy can scarcely come without financial self-sufficiency, so the latter seems to be the key to the whole matter. In order to achieve the goal of financial independence for the Mexican theological schools, several plans are being tried:

1. Some have reduced funds over a specified period of time which, theoretically, will give the national churches time to arrange for the additional financial burden. This has had partial success, but often churches find themselves hard-pressed to sustain their programs. The Reformed

Christian Church in Mexico this year is reaching the end of a five-year financial withdrawal plan. They report that pastors and teachers will have to take a substantial cut in salary because the Mexican churches are just not able to bear the load.

2. Other mission boards have decided to channel their funds toward specific projects, such as social work or special kinds of schools. An example of the latter is the agricultural school in the state of Aguascalientes, sustained by the Disciples of Christ.

3. Still other groups will not establish or maintain works unless they are directly associated with preaching the Gospel. The Plymouth Brethren mission helps support evangelistical thrusts, but encourages the national churches to support their own institutions.

It should not be overlooked that there are several theological schools in Mexico that were established and have been sustained by national churches. Often these are less formal than those begun by the foreign mission board. In this category are the Christian Interdenominational Church and the Christian Spiritual Church. These are some of the more rapidly growing denominations in Mexico.

Conclusions

First of all, a generalization from the foregoing would be that the existence of institutions per se is not the primary problem, nor, perhaps, the solution. Several theological schools have had and continue to have impressive results. More important is the approach used in establishing and promulgating the institution's objectives. The more successful ones are seeking ways to assure self-government and relevance to today's problems through cooperative efforts and/or alternative approaches.

The literature shows that the primary purposes of some theological schools are frequently circumvented and relegated to ineffectiveness by the detractors of a foreign institutional approach. Therefore, unwittingly and unintentionally, the sponsors encourage deviation from the manifest purposes by offering alternatives too attractive to resist; viz., free secular education, upward social mobility, financial security, etc.

On the other hand, functional approaches have proved very effective in accomplishing political, social or religious goals that are always present in the doctrines expounded by the prime movers. These goals are not communicated through a set of rigid institutionalized behaviors, but rather are incorporated as a part of the local culture and ideals so that they appear to have been a part of that system all along. The local adherents are encouraged to lead, i.e., "function," as they see fit. They are never totally dependent on outside financial or personnel resources for carrying on their program. Therefore, although the main tenets of the doctrine might well have come from foreign sources, the organization functions independently, thus becoming a local effort, not an agency of a foreign effort.

Interviews demonstrate that those churches which have taken a more functional approach in communicating their message have enjoyed greater numerical growth. This growth, effected by an approach that allows ample latitude for participation by the converts, naturally lends itself to the tenets of autonomy. Therefore, for all practical purposes, numerical growth and autonomy are the inseparable results of the same phenomenon. In turn, those churches which have emphasized international and/or interdenominational organization have tended to lose their punch and even their identity in evangelistical thrust.

There appears to be a positive correlation, then, between self-perpetuating (autonomous) churches and the functional approach to missions. Pentecostalism heads the list as the most decentralized, independent movement and is also the fastest-growing in places where that type approach has been followed; e.g., Chile and Brazil. On the other end of the scale appear churches such as the Confessional Lutheran Church, which insists on international continuity, cooperation, finances, government and evangelistic program; this church is one of the slowest growing.

The question proposed in this chapter cannot be directly answered by the information gathered, because there is not adequate evidence as to whether or not an institution per se contributes or detracts from economic and governmental independence (autonomy). The question must be modified to read: "Does the *institutional approach* to missions contribute to or detract from numerical growth and the development of autonomous churches? To that question the evidences indicate a conclusive "detract" reply.

It seems to this writer that it is almost an impossible task in this age to transplant a prearranged institution onto foreign soil and then hope that the local adherents will make the institution their program. In places like Mexico, where special problems tend to invite institutional facilities, one should exercise great caution or the institution can easily become a symbol of foreign intervention and programming rather than a meaningful tool to promote the local church's goals. The institution might be used extensively by the local populace, but not necessarily for the purposes for which it was established. A better approach might be one that allows the locals to design, administer and perpetuate their own programs. If no formal institution emerges, that might indicate they are not needed or even desired by those who live in that particular culture. It seems safe to conclude that administrative and financial autonomy is desired by a great majority of the theological schools in Mexico, but that goal is much harder to achieve once outside influence and money have been accepted.

SUGGESTED READINGS

Carter, William E. *Protestantism in Four Societies.* mimeographed report, April, 1966.

Chandapilla, P. T. "How Jesus Trained the Twelve—Training Leaders in India," *Evangelical Missions Quarterly,* Summer, 1969, pp. 210-218.

Hodges, Melvin L. *On The Mission Field:* The Indigenous Church. Chicago: Moody Press, 1953.

Lores, Ruben. "A New Day," *World Vision Magazine,* Vol. XV, No. 5, May, 1971, pp. 8-10.

McGavran, Donald. "The Warren-McGavran Letters on World Evangelization," *Church Growth Bulletin,* XI, No. 6, July, 1975, pp. 466-469.

Sapsezian, Aharon. "The Carribean, Central and South America," *Directory, Theological Schools.* Bromley, Kent, England: Theological Education Fund of The World Council of Churches, 1974, pp. 220-227.

Savage, Peter. "A Bold Move For More Realistic Theological Training," *Evangelical Missions Quarterly,* Vol. V, No. 2, Winter, 1969, pp. 65-71.

Schonberger, Ernest. "The Episcopalian Weekend Seminary," *Church Growth Bulletin,* Vol. III, No. 6, July, 1967, p. 234.

Tillich, Paul. *Theology of Culture.* New York: Oxford University Press, 1959.

Vallier, Ivan. *Catholicism, Social Control, and Modernization in Latin America.* Englewood Cliffs, New Jersey: Prentice-Hall, Inc., 1970.

Wagner, Peter C. "Theological Education In Latin America," *Christianity Today,* Vol. VII, No. 12, March 15, 1963, pp. 21, 22.

Winter, Ralph D. *Theological Education By Extension.* South Pasadena, California: William Carey Library, 1969.

LEADERSHIP TRAINING IN MISSIONS

By ED MATHEWS

Mission work is a multi-faceted effort aimed at accomplishing the purposes of God. The methods employed in this global task have varied in each era since the Master issued His impelling order to "make disciples among all nations."

Perhaps one of the most important innovations[1] in mission during this century is Leadership Training by Extension.[2] The idea of training converts is not new. The Lord said "to teach them whatsoever He had commanded." But the *extension* concept is a dynamic breakthrough in world evangelism. Indeed, it is one of the fastest growing educational movements in history.

In order to grasp the significance of this phenomenon, it is necessary to compare some of the problems in traditional training programs with the basic philosophy behind extension work. This will not only reveal the factors which generated the idea but also give a rationale for its use around the world.

I. HISTORICAL BACKGROUND

Christian colleges and preacher training schools are relatively new. They do not have exclusive claim to being the "scriptural" method of training. Therefore, they must not be uncritically exported abroad. Instead, methods of training that truly meet the needs of the local churches should be developed in each country.

---

[1] Donald W. Kaller, "TEE: Brazil's Success Story," *Christianity Today*, February 13, 1976, p. 13.

[2] This movement is commonly referred to as Theological Education by Extension (TEE). However, the phrase Leadership Training by Extension (LTE) has been chosen for a special reason. The former concept usually emphasizes the training of preachers. And, although, there is considerable merit in this idea, the latter focuses on the training of leaders (who may or may not preach). In other words, LTE is a more comprehensive approach to the problem of stabilizing churches on the mission field.

The FORM of training must always be relevant to the culture of the people, while the FUNCTION of the leader must always be rooted in the will of God. Many missionaries have confused the two ideas. They have acted as if there was only one form and one function. This is unfortunate. There should be *many* forms of training in order to develop a biblically functional leadership in each of the various cultures of the world.

For example, there were no formal theological schools in New Testament times. The disciples of Jesus were trained "under the palm tree." Likewise, the apostle Paul used an apprenticeship method. His travel companions were trained "on the job." This is the form of training the early Church needed. For, as Kenneth Scott Latourette points out, sole dependence on formally trained leaders would not have enabled the ancient Church to expand so rapidly.[3]

In Alexandria, Egypt, about 230 A.D., a man named Origen formed an advanced theological school (from what had previously been an informal adult Bible study). The Church was being attacked by pagan philosophers. She needed a capable leadership to defend the faith. This new form of training grew out of the need of the local situation.

By the beginning of the sixth century, the invading Goths, Vandals, Franks, Visigoths, and Lombards had virtually destroyed the Roman Empire. If the Christian faith was now to survive among these pagans, training had to be done. The form adequate to serve this function was the monastery. A curriculum of reading, writing, and Bible memorizing preserved Christianity during the "Dark Ages."

Later, during the Protestant Reformation, the Bible was "rediscovered" by the common people. Suddenly individuals everywhere wanted to understand the word of God. Trained leaders were desperately needed. And, consequently, the

---

[3]Kenneth Scott Latourette, *A History of the Expansion of Christianity* (New York: Harper Brothers Publishers, 1970), I, p. 116.

academy established by John Calvin emphasized the exposition of scripture. Form was again closely related to function.

Seventeenth century England had hundreds of neighborhood grammar schools. These schools trained young men for the Church of England. Religion was the core of the curriculum. In 1644 all ministerial candidates were required to read Greek and Hebrew. Was this an arbitrary decision? No! The form of training was determined by the function for which the trainee was being prepared. The Anglicans were under attack by Roman Catholic scholars who were well-versed in the biblical languages.

The American colonies (during the first half of the eighteenth century) customarily sent young men back to England for training. However, several things made this an unacceptable arrangement. (1) It was expensive to go abroad. (2) There was no certainty that the students would return. (3) And, even if they did, it was difficult for them to readjust to frontier life.

All of this resulted in the development of a new, functional form of training. Circuit riding evangelists were produced by tutors who instructed a few apprentices in an "on the job" fashion. Class was held wherever the teacher and students were. This type of training was not inferior. It was merely different. For it fitted the circumstances in which it was used.

The first theological seminary in America was started by the Dutch Reformed Church at Long Island, New York in 1774. And, after the colonies gained their independence, the forming of special schools for training ministers became common. Seventeen such institutions were established during the early part of the nineteenth century.[4]

---

[4]Robert Kelly, *Theological Education in America* (New York: George H. Doran Company, 1924), p. 25.

Applicants to these schools were often little more than functionally literate. Few of them had any secondary schooling. [5] And, even after much academic upgrading, over 40 per cent of the ministers in 1926 (among the seventeen largest Protestant denominations in America) had attended neither a college nor a seminary.[6] Moreover, as late as 1960, about one-sixth of those listing the ministry as their principal occupation had had no college preparation.[7]

Special theological schools have been the most common form of ministerial training in America for *no more* than fifty years. However, the impression is often given that this is now the only option available (at home or abroad). And, where such an unexamined conviction is held, resistance has frequently developed against different forms of training that might indeed be more functional. Such an attitude is truly unfortunate (especially when the future of third-world churches, composed of poor, rural peasants are at stake).

No one can deny these third-world churches the right to have first-rate theologians who can formulate an indigenous expression of the Christian faith for their own people. But it must be remembered that the desperate need of younger churches is training that functions in *their* present situation and that satisfies *their* contemporary needs. Therefore, it is unwise to impose on them the recently acquired North American forms of training.

II. PRESENT DILEMMA

It is becoming increasingly clear just how unwise exporting Bible-school forms of training to foreign countries

---

[5]Christopher Jencks and David Riesman, *The Academic Revolution* (New York: Doubleday and Company, Inc., 1968), p. 28.

[6]Richard H. Niebuhr and Daniel D. Williams, *The Ministry in Historical Perspective* (New York: Harper and Row, 1956), pp. 274, 275.

[7]Jenks and Riesman, *op. cit.*, p. 211.

really is. Many problems are created. Frustrations result. And, in the end, the cause of Christ is often hindered instead of helped.

Failure To Train Enough Leaders. There are thousands of village churches on the mission field. Less than 5 per cent of them have elders. And the situation grows more desperate each year. For over 1500 new congregations are being started annually. Yet there are less than 200 graduates each year from the 35 training schools operated by the churches of Christ outside the United States. Obviously the Body of Christ can *never* be stabilized under these conditions.

The lack of trained leaders in these little churches is tragic. Schismatic and syncretistic movements are often formed. Christianity is seriously distorted. Christo-pagan groups result. This alone should cause serious consideration of an alternate (or of additional) means of leadership training.

Unbearable Cost In Training Enough Leaders. It is a well known fact that the average per student cost in a resident Bible school in the States is very high. Perhaps few may realize that the cost is about the same on the mission field. The budget for brotherhood training programs abroad is $3600 per student per year (which does not include the physical facilities that average $40,000 per school). At this rate, it would take over $20,000,000 to train *one* leader for *each* congregation on the mission field (if no new churches were started). There is simply no way to evangelize the world under such circumstances.

The problem of finances, however, is not just limited to the lack of funds. The effect of subsidizing the students' training is subtle, but very real. At the school they are introduced to a standard of living that is significantly higher than they had in their village. For the first time in their lives, they do not "work" in order to eat. And, after their training, they are often unable to readjust to village life. They become financially dependent upon North American money. The missionaries soon reach the saturation point in funding such a support program. They ask the village churches to begin helping these men. But the churches cannot offer the trainee a comparable wage. It becomes a vicious circle. Something has to give. And, unfortunately, the Bible school graduates often feel the most pressure. They become dissatisfied. And, within 5 years after they leave the school, over 50 per cent of them are no longer serving in churches.

Improper Selection Of Students For Training. Resident Bible schools generally train the wrong men. There are three basic aspects to the problem.

1. *Age.* Few if any older men with a family of six, eight, or ten children can attend a resident program. The school does not have facilities to care for them. Yet it is these very men who are the accepted leaders in the village churches. The younger men (who make up over 90 per cent of the student body in campus-based training programs) are not looked to for guidance. They are trying to fill a role for which they are not yet accepted by their own people. No wonder so many quit.

2. *Aptitude.* No training program can impart an aptitude for leadership. No one should expect this of a school. Yet many times the Bible institute receives students who have shown no prior evidence of leadership. It is merely hoped that the school can somehow do wonders with them. These men are enrolled because the school does not want to offend them and/or it desperately needs all the students it can get. Eventually a diploma may be given to them. And the churches take this to mean that these students are now leaders. But, in too many cases, disillusionment follows.

The criteria for choosing students should be carefully reexamined. Young men must not be selected because they are handsome, get good grades in school, are talented speakers, or possess similar qualities. *Maturity* is more important. The greatest tragedy of the traditional training program is that it excludes the mature men who most need the training.

3. Education. Most Bible schools abroad teach in English (which is generally a second language for those who attend). And entrance requirements demand that students have at least an eighth grade education. Yet over 70 per cent of the brethren in other countries have less than eight years of schooling. The real leaders are again left out.

Cultural Dislocation Of Students. The most common complaint leveled at resident schools is their lack of indigeneity. These institutions perpetuate a western pattern of leadership. And, in an age of increasing nationalism, this is like begging for trouble. A "solution" is often sought in replacing the missionaries with a national faculty. Nevertheless, the cultural dislocation continues because the latter are most often trained in institutions using western educational concepts.

A similar cultural problem may occur when students come from a rural setting to study on an urban campus. They have difficulty readjusting to their former way of living. And, even if they return to their people, they will probably not be able to minister effectively to them. Their training has separated them from their kinsmen. They think differently. Their values have changed. They are no longer the same. Their understanding of the Gospel was developed in isolation from their people. They attended a middle (or upper) class, urban school in order to work with poor, semi-literate, rural people. Consequently, their problems in planting and nurturing indigenous churches are legion.

III. EXTENSION CONCEPT

The extension philosophy requires a change in approach for those who are involved in traditional institutions. It demands a student-centered rather than a school-centered mentality. It first asks "whom?" before it asks "how?" Or it first determines *function* before it decides on the *form* of training.

Heretofore, entrance requirements were drawn up first. Those who could meet these stipulations were admitted (while the others were turned away). In other words, the person to be trained had to conform to the institution.

The extension concept reverses the process. It starts with the student. Every possible alteration in the structure of the school is made in order to train those who are ALREADY recognized by their own people as leaders. The school must not attempt to *make* leaders. It is to *train* the leaders that already exist. [8]

The term "extension" suggests *schools which operate where and when working people have free time,* namely, older men with families who must make a living.[9] It is a method that reaches the student in his own culture. "Extension" suggests *adapting the machinery of education to the life style of the trainee.* It is a new way for the living church to allow its real leadership to lead. The significance of extension training is its flexibility for doing a new thing in a challenging era of evangelistic opportunity.

The *extension* concept is not an attempted *extermination* of traditional institutions. It is not a case of "either-or." The two programs are complementary instead of contradictory. Many (though not all) resident schools are serving a worthwhile purpose. But few (or perhaps none) are doing all they can to extend their programs of training to those who need it most. A student-centered approach would lead these schools to extend themselves in five ways.

1. *Geographically.* The place (or places) where students are taught will be determined by the students. Many leaders are unable to leave their homes and move to an urban campus. And, for reasons already reiterated, probably none of them should. If they are to be trained, then, the school must go to the students.

---

[8]James H. Emery, "The Preparation of Leaders in a Ladino-Indian Church," *Practical Anthropology,* vol. 10, no. 3, 1963, pp. 127-134.

[9]James F. Hopewell, "Training a Tent-Making Ministry in Latin America," *Theological Education by Extension,* edited by Ralph D. Winter (South Pasadena, California: William Carey Library, 1969), p. 75.

2. *Temporally.* Classes will meet when the students can attend. This takes into consideration not only the time of day but also the season of the year. Farmers can study during the heat of the day. Factory workers must meet early in the morning or late at night. Farmers may not be in class at all during planting and harvesting. Factory workers will attend any season except holidays and vacation. A student-centered training program will adjust itself to the schedule of the trainee.

3. *Culturally.* Leadership training will be adapted to each culture or sub-culture. Students from one culture will not be required to take their training in another culture. This reduces the danger of frustration for both the students and the teacher. It helps the student avoid cultural dislocation during training (since he is never extracted from his own society in the process).[10]

4. *Economically.* Extension training will not require the construction of a campus. It will take less faculty to operate. The students-per-teacher ratio will be much higher. The trainees will keep their jobs. They will not be subsidized either during or after their training. And, since the students will pay for their study materials, an extension program can be financially self-perpetuating in a short time. This makes leadership training by extension a truly indigenous program.

5. *Academically.* A student-centered approach to training will develop ways of instructing both the literate and the illiterate. It will gear the processes of education to the level of the trainee. This will require a great amount of creativity. But can a school exclude a man from Christian nurture simply because circumstances have excluded him from academic accomplishments?

---

[10]This is one of the most difficult aspects of the extension concept to achieve. See William J. Kornfield, "The Challenge to Make Extension Education Culturally Relevant," *Evangelical Missions Quarterly*, vol. 12, no. 1, January 1976, pp. 13-22.

The missionary faces an enormous task, especially in a time when many see education as a traditional and inflexible institution that does not respond to the needs of the hour, a force that merely preserves the past. He must shake off whatever traditions that prevent him from training leaders in such a way that they will be able to effectively and responsibly guide their own people. The extension approach poses both a challenge to traditional practices and a viable option in the present dilemma of training Christian leaders.

IV. EARLY EXPERIMENTS

The first extension work was done by the Presbyterians in Guatemala. In 1962, after 25 years of operation, their seminary in the capital had prepared only 10 pastors for the 200 churches in their denomination. This is typical of other groups throughout the world.

Many solutions were considered. They studied the possibilities of offering more scholarships, giving correspondence courses, of conducting night school classes, etc. But, finally, they realized that one of their major obstacles was the location of their seminary in Guatemala City. Most of their churches were among the Indians 100 miles away. These rural people could not come to the capital. So they moved the school closer to the people. This was a radical step. But it was not radical enough. The school was still culturally and academically isolated from the Indians.[11]

Therefore the resident school was decentralized. Those who could not come to the seminary were able to receive the same training where they lived. But this bold, new step required new educational material. Traditional textbooks were inadequate. And thus began the most difficult phase of the transition—the writing of programmed lessons. But it was soon learned that the semi-literate, rural Indians were getting

---

[11] Ralph D. Winter, "New Winds Blowing," *Church Growth Bulletin,* edited by Donald A. McGavran (South Pasadena, California: William Carey Library, 1969, vols. I-V, p. 242.

better grades (in the same subjects) than the resident seminary students![12]

The future was beginning to take shape. Extension training was coming of age.

This pioneering experiment had many shortcomings. But weaknesses were constantly corrected. And, eventually, it was realized that the good outweighed the bad. For the door of training had been opened to leaders who could not otherwise be trained. They could receive their training within the context of their sub-culture. Furthermore, extension methods proved economical.[13] For example, in 1963, when the resident and extension systems operated simultaneously, 70 per cent of the faculty and 80 per cent of the budget was assigned to the training of 5 resident students while the rest of the resources of the seminary served the 65 extension students.

Much work is ahead. More experiments are needed. But the possibilities are almost unlimited in solving the countless training problems on the mission field. Extension training is no longer a theory.

V. WORKABLE SYSTEM

The purpose of extension training is "to equip the saints . . . to build up the Body of Christ," *Ephesians 4:12.* And, of course, the measurement of success in such a program is the souls saved and the churches planted. In other words, those who are *already* leaders are equipped to teach their own people to make disciples. It is an evangelistic tool that spreads the Kingdom and glorifies God.

---

[12] Ralph D. Winter, "This Seminary Goes to the Students," *World Vision Magazine,* July-August, 1966, pp. 10-12.

[13] Ralph Covell and C. Peter Wagner, *An Extension Seminary Primer* (South Pasadena, California: William Carey Library, 1971), p. 75.

Extension programs will take different forms in various places. For example, they may be added to resident schools.

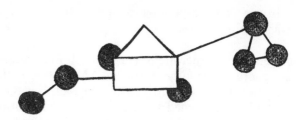

Night classes may be held once or twice a week on campus for those who cannot attend during the day. And additional classes may meet in neighboring villages on Saturday.

But, where a resident school does not exist, extension training may appear as a chain of classes visited by an itinerant teacher.

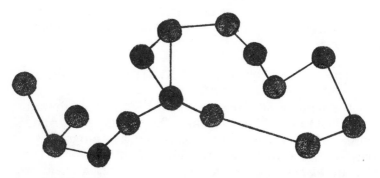

One of the first steps in the development of an extension program is announcing the idea to various churches. The need and purpose for such classes must be carefully explained in order to capture the interest of the people. Each congregation should be allowed to select those *they* consider to be their leaders.[14] These leaders, then, will choose the

---

[14]This helps to eliminate the frustration of training the wrong people, namely, those who are not yet respected as leaders.

best time and place for the extension classes to meet. When deciding such matters, the sociological factors, economic circumstances, and local customs of the trainee must be taken into account.[15]

It is easy to find students. Those who are depended on for leadership are always eager to get whatever training is available to them. Consequently, some missionaries are training from 50 to 300 leaders at a cost of less than $50 per student per year. And, when the local brethren teach the classes, the cost per student drops to virtually nothing.[16]

The students will study specially prepared (self-instructional) lessons during the week. The teacher will come once-a-week (or once every-other-week) for a couple of hours to help the trainees apply to their lives the truths they have learned. However, there are two requirements: (1) the students must faithfully prepare their lessons for each class and (2) they must teach what that have learned to their congregations during the following week. In other words, leadership training by extension is an in-service program which matures the *whole* church.[17]

The instructor must not dominate his classes. He must not lecture (or preach a sermon). The "palm tree meetings" must focus on leading the students to *experience* (that is,

---

[15]Therefore, as much as possible, the teacher should allow his students to settle on the time and place (only making suggestions that are necessary in order to develop a workable itineration schedule). Whether under a tree, beside the path, in a home, whether early in the morning, in the heat of the day, or late at night, appointments properly staggered allow teachers to meet several times in one day, numerous classes on the same circuit and, hence, reach more students in fewer days at less cost than any other method known. This is simply good stewardship.

[16]The trainee should be learning to teach the courses *from the beginning*. That is, a missionary (or national instructor) should not teach the same subject in a particular area more than twice.

[17]This is why it is suggested that *only* the leaders be trained in the extension classes. Their congregations become their laboratories for applying what they have learned.

relate to their daily lives) what they have studied. The teacher is there to clarify and amplify the information. He should lead the trainees to live what they have learned. The emphasis is on both *knowing* and *doing.* This is achieved in three ways.

Participation. It would be a great loss if—in the intimate fellowship of small extension classes—the students (and teacher) did not develop an openness in discussing freely and sincerely the specific, personal applications of the lesson.

Purpose. The reason for the class must be evident at all times. No lesson should become an end in itself. Every prayer, discussion, and activity must point toward service in Christ and in His Church.

Progress. Important to the vitality of the program is a sense of achievement. Extension students have many hardships and handicaps to surmount. It is not easy for them. But when they share the news of souls saved and churches started it will all seem worthwhile. Very few will want to drop out. In fact, experience shows that less than 5 per cent do.

The students will NOT be working for a diploma. Instead, a graduate is a trainee who teaches others to convert the lost, plant a church, and nurture that congregation to the point where it will establish other churches. Then (and only then) will a student be considered a trained leader. This is measurable. And it is biblical.

Nevertheless, people have questions about the quality of teaching (and learning) that occurs in an extension program. These questions are to be expected and should be answered.

Does the extension student have as much time to study? No. He has considerably less time than a resident student for study *each week.* Yet he will have as much in the long run since he stretches his program over several years. The external pressures that surround the student in either system are what rob him of his study time. The learning depends chiefly on self-discipline (not on whether one is a resident or extension student).

Is the home an inferior atmosphere for learning? The extension student must study at home where he is interrupted by his family and friends. After completing the extension program, he will probably continue studying in the same surroundings. It seems better to learn to do so early. A resident institution usually provides a superior study atmosphere (as well as external discipline). However, the real test comes when the student leaves the campus. Will he remain mentally alive?

Can the extension student expect to be adequately trained? The person who gets all of his training before beginning his work with a church will not know what parts of the information that he learned is worthwhile. He may have concentrated on matters of little significance. On the other hand, an extension program provides constant *in-service* training whereby the student comes to know the relevant issues that beg for solutions. Therefore, he has an opportunity to learn more of what is useful than a resident student.

What are some problems in leadership training by extension? There are many. One of the major challenges to the extension philosophy is the "bandwagon" mentality. Any new idea can become the "in" thing. Every program—as long as it is given the name "extension"—could be hailed as the cure for the present leadership shortage in the church. Systems with poorly written materials and uninformed teachers should not be dignified by simply superimposing the word "extension" on them.

There are no shortcuts! Everyone should be well prepared before attempting to begin an extension program. The tools are available. The information is accessible to all. An ill-conceived training program is the fault of those who begin it. Any criticism must come to rest at their doorstep. The extension movement cannot be blamed for what it does not endorse.

Leadership training by extension is a promising aid to world evangelism. Although it alone is not the final solution, it suggests the proper direction. Jesus said to "make

disciples" *and* "teach them," *Matthew 28:19,20.* Extension
training relentlessly presses toward that goal. It will not be
satisfied until a biblical leadership is found in every church
throughout the world. It spares nothing (in the way of self
examination and revision) in order to obey the Master.
Secondary goals do not replace the primary objectives. For
the means of measuring the difference is precise: "the things
you have learned . . . commit unto faithful men who will . . .
teach others also," *II Timothy 2:2.* Hence a particular form
of training is justified only if it produces a functional leadership for each specific cultural context in which the church
exists.

SUGGESTED READINGS

Covell, Ralph, and Wagner, C. Peter. *An Extension Seminary Primer.*
South Pasadena, California: William Carey Library, 1971.

Emery, James H. "The Preparation of Leaders in a Ladino-Indian
Church." *Practical Anthropology.* vol. 10, no. 3, 1963, pp.
127-134.

Hopewell, James F. "Training a Tent-Making Ministry in Latin
America." *Theological Education By Extension.* Edited by Ralph
D. Winter. South Pasadena, California: William Carey Library,
1969.

Jenks, Christopher, and Riesman, David. *The Academic Revolution.*
New York: Doubleday and Company, Inc., 1968.

Kaller, Donald W. "TEE: Brazil's Success Story." *Christianity Today*
(February 13, 1976) pp. 13,14.

Kelly, Robert. *Theological Education In America.* New York: George
H. Doran Company, 1924.

Kornfield, William J. "The Challenge to Make Extension Education
Culturally Relevant." *Evangelical Missions Quarterly.* vol. 12, no.
1, January 1976, pp. 13-22.

Latourette, Kenneth Scott. *A History of the Expansion of Christianity.*
New York: Harper Brothers Publishers, 1970.

Niebuhr, Richard H., and Williams, Daniel D. *The Ministry in Historical Perspective.* New York: Harper and Row, 1956.

Winter, Ralph D. "This Seminary Goes to the Students." *World Vision Magazine* (July-August 1966) pp. 10-12.

Winter, Ralph D. "New Winds Blowing." *Church Growth Bulletin.* Edited by Donald A. McGarvan. South Pasadena, California: William Carey Library, 1969. Volumes I-V.

MASS MEDIA IN MISSIONS

B. E. DAVIS

Perhaps no other phenomenon of the twentieth century has provoked more discussion, inquiry, and argument than the rapid proliferation and exploding technology of the modern mass communications media throughout the world. Elaborate and expensive research studies are conducted by the hundreds each year, heated disputes are conducted, glowing reports are heard about the media's potential, and sobering protests are made about the many calamities and damage being wrought by the media upon society.

Religious mass media users also seem fascinated by the marvels of the new technology. Some acclaim the media as a modern-day miracle wrought by God, while others seem adamantly unconvinced that they can be used effectively in religious work.

At least three distinct viewpoints toward the power and potential of the mass media seem to exist within religious circles:

A. *"The mass media are virtually unlimited in their ability to carry the gospel throughout the world."* Committed to allowing every individual in the world to hear the gospel at least once, many dedicated Christians firmly believe in the unlimited power of the gospel to produce results, if only people can be exposed to it. Their philosophy seems to be: "Preach the word, as often and as widely as possible, and God will produce results." The media are seen as an almost magical means of proclaiming Jesus, and thereby converting the entire world.

B. *"The mass media are powerful, but only under certain conditions; these conditions must be delineated so that wise choices may be made in order to achieve maximum results."* While believing strongly in the power of the gospel, this second group of media users feels that maximum effectiveness in proclaiming the gospel can be achieved only through a thorough understanding and wise use of the mass media. They believe not only that some media activities may be worthless, but that unwise or uninformed usage of the media may even produce harm to the evangelistic effort. Thus, true stewardship would demand considerable research and planning, before media efforts are initiated.

C. *"The mass media do not produce enough conversions or prospects to justify their expense."* This third group of Christians also believe fervently in the power of the Gospel and are devout in their convictions that the Gospel must be proclaimed widely, but remain unconvinced that the mass media are effective enough in evangelistic work to warrant the thousands—even millions—of dollars required to use them. They make such assertions as "Only *personal work* can convert the sinner," or "Nothing can ever be as powerful as a *one-to-one* relationship." Thus, they prefer personal conversations, private teaching sessions, and one-to-one contacts, rather than mass media efforts.

Which of these three views toward the mass media is correct? Without presenting a full discussion of the complexities involved in the question at this point, we can say that both the first and third viewpoints are based on an overly simplistic and naive attitude toward communication in general, and toward mass communication in particular. The remainder of this chapter will set forth in fuller detail the many problems and opportunities presented to those who would use the mass media in missions, and suggest a model for their most effective utilization.

The Nature of the Communication Process

The word "communicate" comes from the Latin word *communicare,* which means "to make common."[1] Communication therefore involves a striving for mutuality, commonality, or sharing.

---

[1] *The American Heritage Dictionary of the English Language.* (1970), s.v. "communicate."

As reasonable as this now seems, such a view of communication has not always existed. Many of the early writings and analyses of the communication process have been faulted by an unfortunate emphasis on a *single communicative act,* seen basically as a *unilateral* activity, something the communicator *does to* the receiver of his message. Although terms such as "source" or "receiver" are still retained in discussions of communication, more recent analyses of communication have emphasized the activity as an *ongoing process, a simultaneous interaction* occurring between the individuals involved. Such a view elevates the activity to the larger context of a continuing relationship between two or more individuals who alternately switch roles as "Source" and "Receiver" and who constantly and simultaneously *act upon* and *react to* each other, so long as the communicative relationship exists. The cybernetic term "feedback" has been seized by communication theorists and used to epitomize this continuing interaction, especially the flow of reaction from the "receiver" back to the "source."

The communication process may be illustrated by the following diagram emphasizing the continuing interaction.

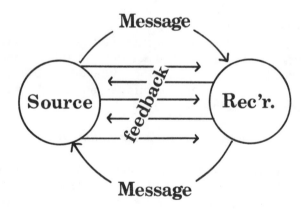

A given individual involved in an interpersonal communication activity is not only acting as an encoder of a message which he sends forth to another, but he is simultaneously decoding and interpreting "feedback" messages from the other person. Similarly, the "receiver" in the situation is not only decoding messages from the "source" and interpreting them for his own use, but is also simultaneously (perhaps subconsciously) encoding "feedback" messages and sending them back to the other person.

Now, let us look specifically at *mass* communication. Is mass communication basically the same process as just described, with no significant differences? First, let us consider the unique characteristics of mass communication.

The Uniqueness of Mass Communication

A moment's reflection reveals that communication through the mass media (newspapers, magazines, books, movies, radio, television) is significantly different from communicating to another individual in a private conversation, or even communicating to a large group of people in a public assembly. Certain characteristics of mass communication make it unique, and demanding of special attention.

A. Mass communications generally require *large formal organizations* for their production and distribution (broadcast stations, printing plants, publishing firms).

B. Mass communications are aimed at *large audiences,* numbering often in the millions of people in many parts of the world.

C. The audiences for mass communications are *highly heterogeneous* in composition.

D. Mass communication messages are aimed at the *largest "common denominator"* within the audience. That is, messages are constructed so as to appeal to the largest possible portion of the audience. Aim is taken, not at the elite, the affluent, the educated, nor at the impoverished, the unlearned, the socially impotent, but at the "typical" individuals, the people who are present in largest numbers within the reading, listening, or viewing audience.

E. *Feedback*, described above as vital to effective inter-personal communication, is generally slow or non-existent; being supplied either by formal research, correspondence, or other similar means.

F. The source of a mass communication message is generally seen as *impersonal* by the audience, since he is unknown to the audience in his private life.

G. The audience is *located at a distance* from the source, and individual members are separated from other members of the audience, yet all can be reached simultaneously by the mass communicator. Thus the mass communication audience differs from all other communication audiences. As McQuail points out,

> It is an aggregate of individuals united by a common focus of interest, engaging in an identical form of behaviour, and open to activation toward common ends; yet the individuals involved are unknown to each other, have only a restricted amount of interaction, do not orient their actions to each other and are only loosely organized or lacking in organization. The composition of the audience is continually shifting, it has no leadership or feelings of identity.[2]

Such psychological factors as "social facilitation," often mentioned in public address studies, or acceleration of effect due to interaction among audience members, are generally missing with mass media audiences.

To the religious communicator, perhaps most familiar with large assemblies such as exist in public worship services, or with small groups such as exist in private Bible studies, such mass communication characteristics are highly significant. One who approaches mass communication with the assumption that the same tactics used elsewhere will prove effective in this situation also is due for sad disillusion-ment.

---

[2] Denis McQuail, *Towards a Sociology of Mass Communication,* Themes and Issues in Modern Sociology (London: Collier-Macmillan Ltd., 1969), p. 10.

Advantages Shared by All the Mass Media

Because of their inherent characteristics, the mass media do have several general advantages that make them especially useful for religious communicators:

A. *The mass media can place a given message within reach of more people in a short period of time than any other form of communication.* The sheer magnitude of the numbers involved prohibits the use of interpersonal contact, or even mass meetings, when one wishes to reach a large group of people (such as an entire nation or a continent) within a short time. There are now more than two billion non-Christians in the world. Mass media present the logical alternative in such situations.

B. *The mass media can penetrate locations where personal presence may not be possible.* Although economic and/or political factors may present problems in some cases, the mass media generally are able, as no other medium, to reach areas and places where it would be impossible for a missionary to be in person. The mass media can leap physical, geographic, social, and even political barriers, and convey the message of Christianity.

C. *The mass media can disseminate the Christian message with great financial efficiency.* One unfamiliar with the huge numbers of people reached through the mass media may be staggered by the seemingly prohibitive cost of producing such a communication. But, one must weigh the many dollars involved against the many hundreds of thousands of people who can be reached. Professional mass communicators speak of "CPM" (cost per thousand) in mass media work. For example, a given radio program may cost $10,000 per year to produce and broadcast, but if 100,000 people hear the message and respond in a desired manner, then the CPM would be only $100, a most efficient usage of funds.

D. *The mass media permit the presentation of the message in a highly attractive format.* The use of specially prepared audiovisual aids to the message (recordings, photographs, art work etc.) can be of inestimable value in proclaiming the Gospel. Mass media make possible—even demand—the production and use of such highly attractive materials for maximum effectiveness.

E. *The mass media make it possible to use highly credible and effective spokesmen as an aid to proclaiming the message.* Research indicates that a spokesman who is perceived as highly trustworthy and expert will have greater effectiveness in communicating a message than an individual without these characteristics. The mass media permit such an individual to be brought before large numbers of people over an extensive area, to help overcome the apathy or resistance of some people to the message.

Not all missionaries or evangelists are equally capable communicators in all situations. Some are more effective with small groups or interpersonal contacts, while others are more effective in public speaking situations. Very capable, effective mass media spokesmen can be used to augment the work of local missionaries, by programs or publications carefully chosen for their value in that specific situation.

Specific Advantages of the Print Media:

Beyond the general advantages outlined above, the print media of mass communication possess certain specific qualities that make them useful in religious communication:

A. *Permanence.* Many an oral communicator, or religious broadcaster, has wished he could somehow preserve his message so his listeners could ponder the meaning more deliberately, or review the message after its initial presentation. The print media make such preservation possible. Studies indicate that many print publications may be read not only several times by a given individual, but may even be passed on to others, so that the message may have its impact multiplied.

B. *Multiple exposure.* A listener to an oral proclamation, or a broadcast message, may have only one, fleeting exposure to a certain thought or point. The print media permit a re-examination of the point, or even continuing discussion of the point with others, since the printed message remains accessible. This is especially valuable with new or difficult teachings, which may require some time to be fully understood and absorbed.

C. *Flexible rate of exposure to the message.* With a broadcast message or any oral presentation, the listener is at the mercy of the speaker, insofar as rate of exposure to the message is concerned. A rapid speaker, presenting new or difficult material, may easily outdistance his listeners' thought processes. The print media, however, permit the reader to pace himself. He may read as slowly and deliberately as needed or desired. The advantages are obvious.

D. *Circumstances of exposure to the message controlled by the reader.* When a public assembly is convened, or an oral presentation is made through the broadcast media, the listener must be physically present when the message is given, if he is to hear it. An uninformed or apathetic listener may not find it convenient or desirable to make his schedule conform to the speaker's schedule, and thus may miss the message. With the print media, however, an individual may take the printed message with him, and examine it later, when he has adequate time, and is in an unhurried frame of mind. He is not forced to react to a deeply significant message in the midst of other activities, when he may not be prepared to give it favorable or even courteous attention. Every missionary or evangelist should try to insure that the message of Christ will be given adequate consideration by his audience.

E. *Purposive selection of portions of the message.* Not all portions of a given message will be equally relevant or interesting to an evangelist's listeners. However, during an oral proclamation, either in a public assembly or a radio-television program, the listener has no choice but to sit patiently (or not so patiently) through those portions of a message which are already highly familiar or are less relevant to his needs, until more significant portions of the message come to his ears. With a printed publication, however, the reader may skim through certain portions until he comes to a paragraph or a section that speaks directly to his needs at that specific time. While such skimming of a message obviously is subject to abuse by uninformed or untaught readers, the practice has certain obvious inherent advantages.

F. *Use of illustrations, photographs, artwork, or typographic devices.* "Redundancy with variation" is a well-known technique of effective communication. That is, permit the receiver of your message to have more than one exposure to your message, in more than one form. Illustrative material such as photographs, drawings or other graphics may clarify and enhance an otherwise difficult or uninteresting message. Printed publications seem especially appropriate for this type of mass communication.

Weaknesses of Print Media:

Printed publications have a number of disadvantages and weaknesses which should be considered by the religious communicator when he is planning his strategy.

A. *Motion and animation are not provided through the print media.* Even with illustrations and graphics, printed messages are relatively static, in comparison with film or television. Even with photographic illustration, a given event or activity is presented in "stop-action" form. Choosing the right stop-action photograph to typify a complex or extended activity may be difficult. Cultural or semantic differences among readers may produce misunderstanding or misperception of the intended meaning. For example, a fairly standardized picture of Jesus—quite familiar to Western eyes—depicting Him with his hand raised in benediction, was interpreted by a large number of African viewers as "a white man telling a black man to stay down."[4] The inability to illustrate an entire event, in sequence, is a liability of print media that should be recognized.

B. *The print media demand that readers be at least functionally literate.* In many emerging nations of the "third world," large numbers of people cannot read or write. In

---

[4]B. F. Jackson, Jr., Ed., *Communication Learning for Churchmen,* Vol. 1, Comm. for Churchmen Series, (Nashville: Abingdon Press, 1968), p. 47.

some specific locations, a tribe or sub-culture may not have a written language at all, thus posing a serious obstacle to the religious communicator. Even the use of drawings, photographs, or other non-verbal messages presents problems with receivers who are not accustomed to the use of printed matter.

C. *The print media demand considerable time and space to adequately describe or explain a complex principle.* Verbalization of certain Christian concepts such as love or righteousness or spirituality is difficult any time, perhaps being better explained by a living example or object lesson. Trying to communicate such abstract principles becomes doubly difficult when you must work only with printed words on the page. Apathetic listeners may not be willing to dedicate enough time or energy to reading a long dissertation on some difficult theme, in order to understand the Gospel message.

D. *Once a message is formulated, printed, and distributed to the readers, modifications or explanations of misunderstandings are difficult.* Although the writer of a religious tract, book or pamphlet may spend considerable time making sure his message says just what he would desire, a misunderstanding of that message in some remote corner of the world, where the print medium is the only contact, may never be corrected. The religious writer may have only one opportunity to correctly communicate his message. If he were personally present, he might easily answer a question, or correct an error, but when he must rely totally on the printed message, such interaction is not possible.

E. *The print media do not permit the use of the warmth, tonal inflection, and varying emphases of the human voice.* Familiar as we are with the Gospel, we may sometimes forget how important the proper use of emphasis, inflection, and vocal expression are to the correct presentation of the message, especially to one who has never heard the message before. In comparison with the vibrancy and warmth of the spoken word, the printed word may seem somewhat lifeless or uninteresting to a pagan. In trying to overcome this problem, missionaries or evangelists should avoid dull, technical discussions of theological concepts when using print media for proclamation of the word to non-Christians, but should attempt to "write as you talk," as personally and cordially as possible.

Specific Advantages of the Broadcast Media:

The electronic media (radio, television, and sometimes film) also have a number of inherent strengths which make them useful to the missionary or other religious communicator.

A. *The broadcast media can reach people who might not be accessible through other media.* Many people might be uninterested or even antagonistic to a "religious tract," or book or Bible study lesson, but may still have their attention caught involuntarily by a message from the Christian communicator on radio or television, in the midst of a line-up of other programs. Although many might never purposely seek a religious program on radio or television, many will listen (perhaps only tolerantly, at first) to a striking or interesting message from a religious speaker, even while using these media primarily for entertainment or other purposes. Such fleeting opportunities have produced dramatic results at times, and ought not to be neglected by the Christian speaker.

Furthermore, the broadcast media can reach people who cannot read or write. The transistor radio, capable of being produced in great numbers, at relatively low cost, has been distributed in virtually every part of the world. Radio can speak to people in remote, uncivilized areas, where schools and literacy pose serious problems for the print media user.

Donald McGavran has pinpointed the significance of radio in remote regions of the globe:

> The cheapness and portability of the transistor set has given the medium a new portability and a new dimension and a vast measure of influence . . . In Guatemala, six times as many people listen to radio as read newspapers . . . And

once it is turned on, it is left on from morning to night, pouring out fuel for hopes and dreams. The possibilities that exist in this force are enormous. [5]

B. *The broadcast media can locate and surface interested prospects for conversion.* Radio and television programs typically create their own audiences, by offering content or formats that are specially appealing to certain people. Those individuals with an existing interest in Christianity (regardless of their source of knowledge) can be reached and encouraged to respond through religious messages broadcast into a given target area.

C. *The broadcast media can provide a warm, personal touch in the presentation of the message.* The sound of the human voice, and, in television and film, the sight of the speaker himself, can bring a valuable added dimension to the message of the gospel. Compassion, concern, kindness, and genuine interest in the listener can often be expressed most effectively when both the audio and visual channels of communication are used together.

D. *Radio, especially, is an intimate medium, producing a unique relationship between the speaker and the listener.* The novice may mistakenly visualize the radio audience as a faceless, impersonal mass of indefinable people. But the experienced radio broadcaster knows that he is talking to very small groups of people, perhaps only one person. In the mind of this listener, the imagination is creating an image of the personality, appearance, and characteristics of the speaker, all based upon the quality of his voice. The listener, if the speaker is effective, has the feeling that the performer is speaking to him alone. Often, especially with long-running programs, a sense of intimacy and deep loyalty to the program can be established, more distinct and pronounced than that produced by any print medium of communication.

---

[5] Donald McGavran, "Radio and Church Growth," *Church Growth Bulletin*, VI (November 1969), pp. 17-18.

Weaknesses of Broadcast Media:

As with each of the other mass media, broadcast media also have their specific weaknesses, disadvantages and limitations, including the following:

A. *In some cases, especially in some parts of the world, the broadcast media may have a negative image.* In a number of despotic monarchies, for instance, radio and television may be totally censored or controlled by the national government, or may be used by the national government for propaganda purposes. Thus, these media may be perceived in a very unfavorable light by the inhabitants of these nations, making their use for evangelistic purposes questionable if not impossible. Certainly the missionary or radio-TV evangelist should avoid any impression of affiliation with the authorities, or any identification as being officially sanctioned or commissioned by those in power. Of course, the converse is also true; i.e., the religious communicator should avoid any affiliation or identification with illicit broadcasting operations such as "pirate" stations, or "black-market" operations. In some cases, radio-TV programs by anyone other than nationals of the country may be forbidden by the authorities.

B. *In many areas, the religious broadcaster may have great difficulty in obtaining an acceptable broadcast time.* One may discover that access to prime time is either forbidden or prohibitively expensive, or that religious programs are permitted only on the weekends or very late at night. In such cases, one must carefully weigh the advantages and disadvantages of the alternatives and make a solemn evaluation of the feasibility of the program. In some instances, broadcasting funds might be more wisely allocated to other purposes.

C. *The attention span for broadcast messages is very short.* Although the frenetic pace of radio and television programs in the United States is not characteristic of media systems throughout the world, it is still true that people generally will listen to a given program for only a limited time. Not only will listeners tune in to the program after it has already started, but many will become impatient or lose interest, and turn to other stations or turn the set completely off. Changing the station of a radio or TV set is one of the easiest things in the world to do, and a listener may quite casually tune away from the message of salvation, or give it only partial attention. This one factor alone should motivate a radio or television speaker to attempt to captivate his listeners immediately and maintain a high level of interest and attractiveness throughout the program. This is difficult, but is vital to the effective use of the broadcast media.

D. *The broadcast media provide only a brief exposure to specific facts or points the listeners may need to remember.* Although some might jot down an address, a name, or a scripture reference while listening to a radio or TV program, many will not or cannot. The broadcast message does not have the inherent permanence of the printed message. Thus, the broadcast evangelist must provide repetitive exposures to those parts of the message that he wishes his listeners to remember; e.g., address, name, facts, etc. Even then, many will miss the information or soon forget it.

Unique Limitations of Mass Communication

The mass communicator, especially the religious mass communicator, faces certain obstacles and limitations which are either peculiar to the mass communication situation, or are found to a greater degree in the mass communication situation.

For instance, the audience's tendency to perceive the source in mass communication as an institutionalized, impersonal messenger impedes any effort by the source to deal warmly and sensitively with personal needs and problems. The communicator is seen as a "representative" of some organization or institution, not a feeling, concerned individual who can empathize with the reader or viewer of the message.

This leads to a second problem for the religious communicator; viz., how to avoid institutionalizing the gospel. That is, the gospel proclaimed via the mass media may be perceived as the official pronouncement of some church or religious organization, rather than the deeply intimate, personal word of salvation from a loving, sympathetic Savior.

Thirdly, the very size and heterogeneity of the audience in mass communication inhibits any attempt to deal with individual needs, or problems experienced by only a small portion of the total receiving group. For example, the mass communicator should strive to speak or write to each group within his listening or reading audience in its own language, if possible. Yet many language groups and dialects are spoken only by a relatively small number of people in a small geographic area. Since mass media are especially adapted to large numbers and large geographic areas, their utility for a specially-focused usage may be questionable, from an economic and efficiency viewpoint.

The absence or slowness of the feedback in mass communication means that the source must send messages to his intended hearers with no other guidelines than previous experience, hunch, or personal opinion. To some extent, he is "flying blind" in trying to communicate; no responses or reactions from his audience reach him until it is too late to modify his message for greater effectiveness. Of course, the experienced mass communicator can use his acquired wisdom and experience with considerable success, and research and study can tell him much about the general characteristics of his hearers, but misunderstandings and communication break-downs are easier to avoid or rectify when the communicator is able to read instantly the feedback coming back to him.

Another problem frequently encountered in mass communication is the divided attention the average person gives to any mass media message. Even when a mass media message captures our attention, it is often only for a fleeting moment, or must compete with other activities for the concentration of the reader or listener. Far from being assembled in a secluded church building with other religiously-oriented people who have the same purpose in mind, the average mass media listener in many nations of the world is caught up in the hurly-burly of everyday activities.

He therefore listens to a television program with only half an ear, he generally is busy doing something else while listening to a radio program, or he is willing to give only a few moments to a given printed message, especially one from an unknown or distrusted source. To say the least, to speak meaningfully to such a person in this frame of mind is difficult.

Closely related to the problem of inattention is the mass communicator's difficult task of finding the proper message content, and the proper rate of presentation of that content, for his audience. Although seen most vividly in the electronic media, all mass media are beset with the problem of pacing. Too much information at one time, or given without adequate time for the audience to digest the information, will inhibit understanding. Time considerations in the broadcast media, and space considerations in the print media make this problem especially relevant for the mass communicator. "Information overload" is often committed by religious communicators because of the pressure of the urgency of the message, or the source's deepseated compulsion to "declare the whole counsel of God." However, a good rule to follow might be: Don't give too much information at one time, or the whole communication will tend to block.

The final problem associated with mass communication that we shall mention is somewhat abstract and difficult to grasp quickly. It also overlaps to some degree the other problems we have discussed. It is this: the medium chosen for the presentation of a message has a profound effect upon the content and effect of the message.

To see the importance of this concept, consider how, in the world of secular mass media, the coming of televised news reports affected the communication of the news. Not only does the news get to us more quickly now than it did in the days of newspaper reporting, but we feel the impact of the news stories more deeply. Marshall McLuhan has gone so far as to say that "the *medium is* the *message,*" and then subtly modified this expression to say "the medium is the massage," to point up how the media mold, form, and influence our lives while we are blissfully unaware of it.[6]

Furthermore, research indicates that each of the mass media has a given *image* or *reputation* for the average viewer or reader, so that a magazine article has quite a different reception than a radio message, or a television program, or newspaper story.

Transferring this idea to the field of religious communication, can you see how a Christian evangelist should use wisdom and discretion in choosing the medium for his message? At the very least, surely one should consider the general image of the magazine or paper he is using, the reputation of the radio or television station on which he is broadcasting, the context in which the message will be presented to the reader or listener. What goes before, or follows after, the message? What kinds of material surrounds the message? For what kinds of message content is this publication or broadcast station generally known?

A problem of even deeper significance is tapped by the question: Does a mass media presentation, so tightly confined by time and space limitations, have to offer such an over-simple, superficial version of the gospel that its real vigor and beauty are lost? Such queries must continuously linger in the periphery of the religious mass communicator's awareness, and keep pulling him back toward the center, the heart and core, of the gospel story, and away from the empty showmanship and crass commercialism that characterizes much mass media work today.

Ways Mass Media Are Used in Missions

Mass media are being used widely, in a broad assortment of ways, by those engaged in mission work today. The following list, although not exhaustive, will illustrate the major approaches:

---

[6]McLuhan, Marshall, *The Medium Is the Message; An Inventory of Effects.* (Bantam Books, N. Y., 1967).

A. *Many mass media programs may be designed to instill awareness and impart introductory information about the church and the mission effort.* Quite logically, many who hear a newly-arrived missionary in their country, or who are exposed to literature or broadcasts being distributed by an unknown missionary, will want to identify and evaluate this new message they hear. Although the gospel itself is the hope of salvation, one cannot really separate the message from the messenger. Thus, effort can legitimately be expended in providing historical and descriptive information about a group of missionaries, especially those moving into new fields.

Of course, many foreign governments demand proper identification before allowing entry into their country. But, simply establishing legitimacy with the governmental authorities is not enough. The recipients of your message need to know who are you, and what group you represent. "Is this new group different from the other 'Christian' missionaries we have heard?" "Is this some little splinter group that will not amount to anything, or does it represent a substantial, enduring effort that will continue?" "Who are your sponsors?" "Who provides your financial support?" "Why are you here in our country?" Such questions are entirely legitimate, and the missionary should not be offended by them. He should welcome the opportunity to fully identify himself, and legitimize his presence in the place.

B. *Many mass media programs are designed to prepare the way for a major missionary effort.* This has been described as the "softening-up process", or "seed-sowing". Just as John the Baptist was sent before the Lord to prepare the way for his coming, mass media programs may be very effective in providing initial exposure to the Gospel, to lay the foundation for an intensive evangelistic effort later. The objective with this technique is to accomplish preliminary acquaintance with the missionary and the message, so that the mission team will not be confronted with people who are unfamiliar—perhaps even hostile—to the mission effort.

C. An extension or adaptation of this technique is to continue to use the mass media for this "seed-sowing" operation, even after becoming established on the field, *to open doors and stimulate inquiries from the people, which may be followed up with personal contacts.*

Donald McGavran has cautioned against being content with mere "seed-sowing", and mistakenly assuming that proclamation alone fulfills our responsibility:

> . . . many Christians are firmly committed to a theology of seed sowing, which might also be called a theology of search. It arose in the era of missions just ending. It maintains that in Christian mission the essential thing is not the finding, but going everywhere and preaching the Gospel . . .
>
> . . . the trouble is that mere search, detached witness— without the deep wish to convert, without wholehearted persuasion, and with what amounts to a fear of the numerical increase of Christians—is not biblically justified. Mere search is not what God wants. God wants His lost children found . . . [7]

D. *Mass media are sometimes used to provide both basic and advanced study of the Bible, and aggressively seek conversions.* Missionaries in certain areas have achieved some success in offering a complete array of gospel messages, including discussions of the "deeper things of God", leading the listener all the way to acceptance of Christ. Such a technique is generally used only in areas where mission efforts have been in existence for some time, where one might expect to find people who are ready for more advanced study of the Bible along with the spiritually illiterate. For instance, a verse-by-verse study of the Gospel of Mark was conducted through a daily radio program in Mexico, with reported success. Such an approach in another area, however, might produce few results.

The assortment of the media used in mission work is broad and varied, including:

---

[7] Donald McGavran, *Understanding Church Growth*. (Grand Rapids: Eerdmans, 1970), pp. 34-40.

International stations, broadcasting fulltime Christian programs.

International stations, broadcasting Christian programs along with secular programs.

Local and regional broadcasts designed for one city or one region of an area.

Gospel tracts, books, pamphlets centered around one theme.

Free distribution of Bibles and portions of Bibles, translated into various languages and dialects.

Bible correspondence courses.

Gospel magazines, carrying both exposition of scriptural teachings and news about the work of the church.

News letters and personal correspondence, directed both to fellow missionaries and to prospective converts.

Bible study guides, outlines, and workbooks.

With such a wide variety of communication media being used by evangelists and missionaries, one might expect great results to be produced. However, close evaluation of the techniques being used frequently reveals a number of significant errors and misconceptions existing among religious mass communicators.

Errors Frequently Committed By Religious Communicators:

A number of religious leaders and knowledgeable scholars have deplored the mistakes and weaknesses found in religious communication. A former speaker on the well-known "Mennonite Hour," Dr. David Augsburger, has declared:

> If we do not change our methods, we change our message, because we only reach those who understand old words and techniques ... A good share of Christian communication techniques are still in the 1930's. [8]

---

[8] Huffman, James, "Christian Broadcasters Tune Toward Future." *Christianity Today,* XIV (May 22, 1970) p. 35.

Donald McGavran, well-known church growth authority, has pointed out that one reason churches do not grow and proliferate is that many churchmen use too simplistic communication methods.

As the Gospel is broadcast in North America the message falls on the ears of a potential audience of at least 150,000,000 persons, to whom ... it is more or less familiar.
Christian broadcasting in Africasia, however, falls on the ears of Marxists, Hindus, Buddhists, animists, and Moslems. At least half of these are illiterate. The Christian message is not familiar. On the contrary, it is totally strange. Under these conditions, it is simplistic to suppose that even the unchanging Gospel, beamed over the radio waves to this audience in substantially the same way it is in North America, will bring non-Christians of many different cultures to Christ ... radio should convey the message of salvation to each community *in ways which make it possible for obedience to the Gospel to become a real option to its members.*[9]

The following list, while not exhaustive, includes some of the more glaring errors committed by religious mass communicators:

A. Use of the English language only, in cross-national and cross-cultural communication.

B. Few, or extremely limited, ethnographic studies or audience analyses of the audience to whom the message is being directed.

C. Failure to separate elements of American politics, economics, social customs, and cultural trappings from the pure and simple Gospel of Christ.

D. Little or no research regarding success or failure of the communication effort.

---

[9]McGavran, Donald. *Understanding Church Growth*, (Grand Rapids: William B. Eerdmans Pub. Co., 1970), p. 104.

E. Choosing topics for presentation which are of concern to the speaker or writer, but having little relevance or significance to the audience.

F. Failure to commit enough work and/or money into mass media work to permit a significant impact.

G. Expectation of results before enough time has elapsed to permit the effort to bear fruit.

H. Placing too much faith in the mass media alone, without complementing them with personal follow-up or additional materials.

I. Acceptance of undesirable air-time for radio programs, without protest or efforts to obtain other times.

J. Failure to devote enough preparation time and effort into mass media messages. Mass media work is often perceived as highly secondary to more popular mission work, and is allocated only incidental attention.

K. Failure to deliberately set specific purposes and goals for a mass media program to accomplish. Much mass media work is done simply because it is traditional or expected, and no real objective is established.

L. Failure to recognize the unique characteristics of the mass media audience, with the result that many broadcasts are presented as if the listeners were identical to the speaker's personal acquaintances.

Of course, no one mission effort commits all of these errors, but many of these mistakes are widespread. Many who are dubious about the ability of the mass media to produce results either have no clear idea of what the mass media should be used for, or commit one or more of the above mistakes. In the following section of this chapter, we shall delineate where the strengths of the mass media really are, and offer suggestions for their effective use.

Lessons from Diffusion Theory

Diffusion (the study of the spread and adoption of new ideas, devices and technologies by a particular group or social system) has a body of theoretical concepts and principles that are related significantly to the use of mass media. With its origins deep in the writings of early sociologists and anthropologists, diffusion theory is now recognized by communication experts as contributing much to our knowledge of the process of change, and the problems of gaining acceptance of innovations. Several research findings and principles from this area apply to the field of religious mass communication.

For instance, diffusion theorists tell us that the innovation decision-making process consists of four steps:

1. *Awareness*—the gaining of first knowledge or preliminary information about an innovation.

2. *Persuasion*—the consideration of arguments, both pro and con, leading to attitude formation or change.

3. *Decision*—the arrival at a decision to adopt or not adopt the innovation.

4. *Confirmation*—the strengthening and reinforcing of the decision to adopt or not adopt the innovation.[10]

Numerous research investigations have revealed that mass media have great power during two of these steps; the *awareness* step, and the *confirmation* step. On the other hand, the interpersonal communication media (personal contact with friends, family, trusted associates, etc.) are most influential at the *persuasion* step, where the potential adopter discusses the feasibility of the new idea with his friends, acquaintances, or opinion leaders.

This has considerable significance for religious mass communication. Consider the parallel between the innovation decision-making process, and the process by which one becomes a Christian:

---

[10]Rogers, Everett and Floyd Shoemaker, *The Diffusion of Innovations: A Cross-Cultural Approach* (New York: Free Press. 1971).

Innovation Decision-Making	*Becoming A Christian*
Awareness	Hearing the word, Rom. 10:17
Persuasion	Believing the word, Mk. 16:16
Decision	Repentance from sin
	Baptism into Christ
	Luke 10:3, Acts 2:38
Confirmation	Growth in grace and
	knowledge, 2 Pet. 3:18

Although the parallel is not perfect, one may see that the innovation decision-making process is very similar to the process in which one is first exposed to the gospel of Christ, and then moves through various stages of decision-making to the point of actually committing his life to Christ.

Applying the research findings regarding the power of the mass media (and assuming that the parallel is valid), we can see that mass media should be used primarily (a) in the proclamation of the basic fundamentals of the gospel, to make people aware of the message, and provoke interest in it, and (b) to strengthen, confirm or encourage people who have already become Christians. Although conversions may occur through the influence of the mass media alone, these conversions will be comparatively few in number. Most individuals who become Christians will do so after *personal contact* with ministers, Christian friends, or trusted associates. Insistent admonitions and pleadings to become a Christian are most effective when done in a personal, face-to-face relationship with the prospective convert, either as an individual alone, or part of an assembly.

This should not be taken to mean that the mass media are to be used only to "publicize the church," or to conduct a "public relations campaign" for the missionary; far from it. But it does mean that the most frequent results seen from mass media work among non-Christians, especially pagans, will be inquiries, requests for more information, or perhaps clarification and discussion. These are *entirely legitimate and worthy contacts,* and represent *opportunities for follow-up* and initiation of personal teaching and persuasion to become a Christian.

Further, the mass media may be used to strengthen and encourage those who are already converted. One of the continuing problems in virtually every mission program today is the large number of "drop-outs," people who respond to the gospel, but then grow weak and discouraged, ultimately going back to their former life. The mass media can be powerful instruments to help teach, encourage, and strengthen new converts, confirming them in the faith. This is not done by presenting messages designed solely for them, but their continued exposure to the messages proclaiming Christ to the world may produce reinforcement and recommitment in their hearts.

In the third place, both research and personal experience have shown that *mass media are most effective when used as part of a multi-faceted, many-pronged program of outreach and communication.* In view of the fact that mass media are most effective in imparting awareness of a message, and in reinforcing those who accept it, and the interpersonal media are most effective at the persuasion and decision steps of the conversion process, it seems logical and reasonable to combine both mass media and interpersonal media, thus capitalizing on the strengths of both.

Numerous examples might be cited to show how such a multi-media approach might be implemented. Since 1958 the Southern Baptist mass media ministry has utilized a concept known as "televangelism," in which evangelistic films have been broadcast on various network programs, and viewed in numerous viewing and discussion groups, in churches, private homes, or other small assemblies. Both "churched" and "unchurched" people view and then discuss the films, which are televised according to a previously announced schedule. The producers of these programs consider them very effective.[11]

Roger Shinn of the United Church of Christ produced a series of 30-minute films for television in 1965, for much the

---

[11] T. Harold Ellens. *Models of Religious Broadcasting* (Grand Rapids; Wm. B. Eerdmans Pub. Co., 1974), p. 104.

same type of viewing and discussion by small groups. In Pittsburgh alone, 800 viewing and discussion groups met regularly to watch and discuss the program.[12]

The Herald of Truth, produced by the Highland Church of Christ in Abilene, Texas, has produced a number of 30-minute films for prime-time television showing in selected markets. Pre-broadcast efforts were directed towards publicizing the programs, arranging for private or small-group viewing and discussion groups, and even including an additional half-hour segment on the broadcast where a panel of ministers and teachers could respond live to telephone messages and questions from the audience. Impressive figures on total audience, and follow-up personal contacts have been reported.[13]

Even in the secular field, similar multi-media programs have proven remarkably effective. In the early 1950's, in India, Dr. Paul Neurath found his "Radio Farm Forums", combining radio broadcasts and small group discussion, to be *more than twice* as effective as either radio or personal contact alone.[14] Similar results were reported for the Canadian Farm Radio Forums[15] in the 1930's, and for the "Telescuola"[16] government educational programs in Italy.

The secret behind these results is simple: The communicator takes the best of two worlds—utilizing mass media for what they do best, and personal contact for what it does best. Such a strategy would seem directly applicable, with few problems, to religious mass communication in the mission field.

---

[12]Ibid, p. 100.

[13]Clois Fowler, "Herald of Truth", personal conversations with author, 1973-74.

[14]J. C. Mathur and Paul Neurath, *An Indian Experiment in Farm Radio Clubs* (Paris: UNESCO, 1959.)

[15]Daniel Lerner and Wiebur Schramm, eds., *Comm. and Change in the Developing Countries* (Honolulu: East-West Center Press, 1967) p. 13.

[16]Ibid, p. 14.

Even when small viewing and discussing groups are not possible to arrange, *an aggressive, vigorous, personal follow-up ministry should accompany any mass media effort.* The "climate" can be set, first awareness can be accomplished, good impressions and stimulation of inquiries can all be accomplished through the mass media (either print or broadcast), and then personal contacts can be made through the inquiries and questions that come. Such a flexible and effective combination is far more productive than placing all trust and confidence in any mass media, pulpit preaching, private Bible class, or small group work *alone.*

The following additional generalizations about the use of the mass media should be considered by the missionary or other religious communicator:

1. The short-range effectiveness of mass media may be small, but the long-range, cumulative effectiveness may be great.

2. The mass media are able to establish a "climate of acceptance" for the message of Christ, by saturation of the receiving population with the message.

3. Mass media may legitimize and authenticate a work of mission, thereby encouraging mass conversions and people movements.

A Suggested Strategy for Missionary Mass Media:
In summing up the discussion in this chapter the following points seem to be especially significant. We have accepted the notion that mass media are powerful, but *only when used knowledgeably.* The mass media *do* accomplish much in religious communication, but *not what many dedicated evangelists and missionaries think they accomplish.* The religious communicator who wishes to avoid wasting money and prevent eventual frustration and disenchantment had best spend considerable time investigating the theory and concepts that guide the utilization of mass media, and in planning in great depth just how the media will be used. The success of the national radio ministry called "Heartbeat," heard several times daily on the NBC radio network, can probably be largely attributed to the fact that the speaker,

Landon Saunders, spent more than one full year in intensive research and planning before a single program was broadcast.[17]

Now, what specific strategy can be suggested for the use of mass media in missions? The following points can at least serve as a stimulant for thinking in the proper direction:

1. *Identify clearly and precisely just what you wish to accomplish by your mass media work.* Don't begin a radio program or a Bible correspondence course simply because "everybody else does it," or because it seems like a "cheap way to reach a lot of people." Know just what you hope to accomplish, and let that objective be your guiding star for all that follows.

2. *Invest enough time, money, and effort into your mass media program to permit success.* This minimum investment is often much higher than some think. One could question, for instance, whether one 5-minute radio program per week will accomplish enough to justify its cost. A small two-inch ad in a local newspaper may not be noticed by enough people to pay for itself in results. Bible lessons, religious tracts and other publications printed on cheap, unattractive paper with sloppy copy and artwork may well do more harm than good. Don't fail because you are unwilling to spend a few more dollars, or invest a little more effort, which may be vital!

3. *Don't place all your trust and energy into mass media alone (or any other medium of communication alone, for that matter.)* As suggested earlier in the chapter, use a broadscope, multi-media approach. Determine just what percentage of your time and money should be allocated to each individual area of concentration, and maintain a diversified, well-balanced program of evangelism.

4. *Promote group study, group commitment, and group conversions, through your mass media and personal contact combination.*

[17]Landon Saunders, "Heartbeat", personal interview, 1973.

5. *Use the mass media to strengthen, inform, legitimize, and publicize your ministry.*

6. *Use a localized focus by including local references as much as possible.* Although broadly-aimed programs can be effective, their success can be increased when the listeners can know that you are talking specifically to them and their locality.

7. *Conduct research (both qualitative and quantitative) into the characteristics of your audience.* No mass media communicator can reach his readers or listeners effectively unless he knows what kind of people he is attempting to reach! Don't assume that, since everybody needs the gospel, every individual can be approached in the same way! Study your audience. Know their special needs. And then, show how the Word of Life can help solve their problems!

8. *Be as warm, friendly and personable as you can be!* No suggestion is being made here that you should assume an artificial personality, or adopt an obsequious, fawning manner in your communication. This would not only be dishonest, it also wouldn't work! But, mass media have the problem of being an impersonal medium. The radio, or printing press, or microphone interjects itself between you and your audience, so they see you as somewhat removed from their lives. Fill your heart with love and concern, and then let it show in your voice, your writing, and your whole demeanor.

9. *Use repetition. Remember that not every person is going to hear or read every word you say.* Give opportunities for adequate exposure, even multiple exposure, for maximum effect.

10. *Don't demand that God give you instant success, and don't usurp credit from the Lord for the success you do achieve.* Even though we know a Christian mustn't "cast his pearls before swine," or waste his time and energy in an unproductive region, we also must remember that success requires time. Sow the seed! Then, water it! Then, trust the Lord to give the increase!

SUGGESTED READINGS

DeFleur, Melvin L. and Ball-Rokeach, Sandra. *Theories of Mass Communication. Third Edition.* New York: David McKay Co. 1975.

Ellens, J. Harold. *Models of Religious Broadcasting.* Grand Rapids: William B. Eerdmans Pub. Co. 1974.

Jackson, B. F. (Editor) *Communication–Learning for Churchmen, Volume One.* Nashville: Abingdon Press. 1968.

Television–Radio–Film for Churchmen, Volume Two. Nashville: Abingdon Press, 1969.

Lerner, Daniel and Schramm, Wilbur. *Communication and Change in the Developing Countries.* Honolulu: East-West Center Press. 1967.

Nida, Eugene. *Message and Mission.* New York: Harper and Row. 1960.

Rogers, Everett and Shoemaker, Floyd. *The Diffusion of Innovations: A Cross-Cultural Approach.* New York: Free Press. 1971.

Schramm, Wilbur. *Mass Media and National Development: The Role of Information in the Developing Countries.* Stanford: Stanford Univ. Press. 1964.

Sellers, James E. *The Outsider and the Word of God.* Nashville: Abingdon Press. 1961.

GROUP EVANGELISM IN MISSIONS

GLOVER SHIPP

Two are better than one, because they have a good reward for their toil. (Ecclesiastes 4:9, RSV)

Team or group evangelism is defined as "two or more individuals organized for a sustained effort to spread the Gospel."[1] Group effort can accomplish a task otherwise hopeless for an individual alone or for many individuals functioning in an uncoordinated way. Especially in times of crisis there is strength in unity of purpose. Benjamin Franklin once said: "Gentlemen, if we do not all hang together, we shall all hang separately."

The Principle In The Bible

Moses was given his brother Aaron as a spokesman, to compensate for Moses' lack of fluency, thus making a "complete" liberation team for the Israelite slaves. Later, the need arose for a company of judges to share with Moses in the burdensome task of civil jurisprudence. Barak needed a Deborah; Naomi a Ruth; David a Jonathan; Jeremiah a Baruch. Nehemiah succeeded in the enormous task of reconstructing the walls of Jerusalem, because of his capacity to organize a dedicated task force (Nehemiah 3-6).

Jesus sent out His disciples in teams of two, to evangelize, and he developed a compact force of twelve thoroughly prepared apostles to fulfill the great commission. Paul journeyed almost always with a company of colleagues—first, Barnabas and Mark, and then Silas, Timothy, Luke, Titus and many others.

---

[1] Morris, Don H., "The Power of an Idea," *Horizons.* May-June, 1961, p. 1.

Need for Companionship in Service

Why is there this consistent thread throughout the Bible of the need for companionship in service? Because man functions better and is discouraged less frequently, if he has at his side others with like purpose. When Moses became tired, the Lord raised up help for him. When Elijah was hiding out, afraid for his life, he was given an assistant, Elisha. When Paul was alone in Athens, and later in Corinth, he reached a low ebb in spirit; but he took on new life, however, with arrival of Silas and Timothy (Acts 17:15-16, 18:1-5).

Man is a social creature. He has the need to be with his own "birds of a feather". Very few people are successful loners; most function best in company with others who can complement their strengths and compensate for their weaknesses. In the spiritual realm, this need is recognized by Paul in his use of the spiritual figure of the body (I Corinthians 12:12-28). Each member functions according to his abilities and gifts, supporting and strengthening, in his own essential way, the functioning of the body as a whole, as well as being guided and strengthened by the entire body.

An Integrated Whole

This principle, of various elements making up an integrated whole in the Lord's service, has been largely forgotten in recent centuries by many missionary planners. With dismaying frequency, one man has launched alone into the "outer darkness" of world evangelism. Some succeeded, sticking out the intense loneliness and discouragement, but many others failed, returning home with shattered health and/or faith. In Brazil, we have witnessed such mismanagement of human power. The same note has been sounded time and time again throughout the world, as otherwise potentially successful workers leave the field disenchanted, primarily for lack of companionship on the battle line.

Although infrequently used in the past, mission teams as such are not a new concept. Francis of Assisi and his companions, for example, served in voluntary poverty in the attempt to bring order out of chaos concerning the religion and morality of Middle Ages Italy; and so did the Jesuits, who tamed savage Brazil for Catholicism. In the last century England launched many mission teams to other countries in its farflung empire. Only in recent years, however, has this basic principle of evangelism been adopted on anything like a consistent basis. While many religious bodies still practice the "one man to one nation" or "one man to one city" approach, the notion of sending entire groups of families to unreached areas came to be held by several men of vision following World War II.

Beginning of Exodus Movements

Out of this same stirring came concrete action, in the form of "Exodus Movements" to major cities in the northeastern United States. While successful in themselves to a greater or lesser degree, these movements gave birth to the idea of well-organized mission teams, especially prepared and qualified to work in major foreign cities.

We next saw the development of small teams which entered Italy, Germany, Japan, Guatemala and other areas, and then came the formation in the late 1950's of the Brazil team, which brought to Sao Paulo an initial total of 13 couples. Most of the persons in this group had prepared together at Abilene Christian University before their arrival in Brazil.

Foreign Teams Formed

This "new" approach to overseas missions was observed by many and copied by some. Other teams were formed, going to Australia, Austria, Jamaica and later on, to Argentina and other countries.

Meanwhile, our Belo Horizonte mission team was formed in 1962, under the name of "Operation '68." At first, it was to be something of an Exodus Movement of largely self-employed Christians to the carefully selected foreign metropolis. To this end, extensive planning was put into the movement. As it turned out, most of the 15 families involved during its first years on the field were fully supported by churches in the States, with but three being classified as purely "vocational" missionaries. Some of the more recent workers have maintained themselves by teaching in the local American school, but most have had support from churches in the States.

Since the arrival of the Belo Horizonte team in Brazil, other mission groups have been formed. The Buenos Aires, Argentina team, the Quiche-Indian team in Guatemala, and the Zambia team in Africa, have arrived on their respective fields and are functioning with moderate to excellent success. Other groups are still in the process of formation and preparation. It appears to be a coming pattern now at some Christian colleges and preacher training schools to select a city or country, and then to concentrate on preparing a qualified team to enter it.

What are some of the considerations involved in the decision to organize and/or participate in a group thrust into a foreign target area? What are some of the positive and negative factors involved in team evangelism?

Positive Factors

On the positive side of team evangelism, we have pointed out man's need for companionship, especially in the strange surroundings. This may be illustrated by the present writer's experience on more than one occasion, as he found himself stranded in some remote city of Brazil. Even with a briefcase full of names to contact, it was extremely difficult when alone to get at the task and to keep at it. But when he had even one other colleague with him, the searching out and teaching of these same persons became interesting and challenging. A man needs companions in arms.

Secondly, team evangelism provides more than just companionship "in battle." It also provides companionship in solace and in mutual encouragement. One man's low point may be offset by another's high. One man's discouragement may be relieved by a colleague's understanding "hand on the shoulder." Team evangelism, then, is a pooling of individual emotional strengths, just as a tired battery may be brought back to life by an energized one. It develops strong common personal bonds—David and Jonathan relationships—between the colleagues. Deep, loyal friendship develops and becomes a real blessing.

Pooling of Human Resources

Team evangelism is also a pooling of other areas of mutual support. It is a case of all complementing the abilities and strengths of each other, as well as compensating for the others' weaknesses. No one man can be all things to all people, nor can he do all of the things that may be required of him on a mission field. At best, a missionary is a man who must wear several hats—preacher, teacher, counselor, printer, parent, public relations man, fund-raiser, financier, church planter, proxy elder, writer, linguist, practical nurse. . . . Often, he becomes confused and frustrated by his many roles, not really succeeding at any of them. In the group effort, he isn't required to become all things. He can gravitate naturally toward those areas of work where he is best prepared and most successful. In a missionary team, there is room for writers, printers, and those with other specialized skills, whereas in the lone-family thrust, men with certain professional skills may either find little time to utilize them on the field, or more likely, never be given an opportunity to even enter mission work. After all, our usual image of a missionary does not normally allow for the presence on the field of highly skilled technicians.

The team that went to Belo Horizonte, Brazil in 1967-68 was purposely organized to include people of varied professional backgrounds. There were: a business administrator, an airplane pilot-photographer, school teachers, a house builder, an artist-journalist, a professional music writer-arranger and a doctor, as well as several who had years of preaching, Bible teaching, and youth camp experience. Some criticized us for taking "non-preachers" to the mission field. But were we to organize a new team today for some other city, we would not change this principle, but rather, would encourage various specialists to join us. We thus have in our team what might be described as "unity in diversity." Not all are called to preach publicly. Some are skilled at preaching on paper, or at freeing the evangelists from record-keeping and financial details. Our pilot, for example, is not a polished public speaker. But he is an "old pro" at carrying men and printed matter to every area of vast Brazil. But in the process, he is able to teach men all over the country on a quiet, one-to-one basis.

Maximum Use of Specialized Skills

Only in a team effort can such specialized abilities be put to their most effective use. Only in a team effort can the collective skills of all of its members be blended together, to create an end result that is even greater than the sum of its parts. Perhaps this is one of the most valuable, yet mysterious, aspects of a mission team. It can become a unique, living personality in itself, functioning as all of the body of Christ should function.

Most mission fields are far from home and far from the sponsors' supervision. A mission team can provide some of the gentle (and, if necessary, more stringent) pressures needed by some missionaries to produce and to conform to expected norms of behavior. Alone, a man may let down his standards over a period of time, but in a group, he thinks twice before ignoring pressure from his on-the-field peer group.

Group evangelism is a give-and-take process, with emphasis on the giving. A firm understanding of the group dynamics process is essential to team missionary effort. No one person is the permanent "chief of operations." No one man will be able to run roughshod over the opinions and will of the group.

Financial Muscle

Since team evangelism is definitely a case of giving, herein lies one of its strengths. By pooling its collective resources of money, time, and talents, it will accomplish much that otherwise would not be possible. In the area of finances, the Belo Horizonte team receives as a group a certain amount each month from each of its members, according to his ability to participate. This money is then utilized for various programs which could not be sustained by one or two men working alone. These programs include publications, correspondence courses, a Bible camp and many other areas of outreach. Interestingly, the pooled funds (separate and apart from each team member's church contributions) amount to more than many smaller congregations' monthly budgets.

Don Vinzant, former Sao Paulo missionary, notes that a whole group can share in the cost of expensive facilities and equipment, language instruction, the hiring of lawyers or brokers, and the shipping of goods as the need may arise. He also suggests that it is easier to raise support for individual team members, because of publicity generated by the team thrust and the confidence brethren have in the stability of the group involved.[2]

"On-the-field" blessings also include the combined resources, both spiritual and material, of all of the congregations involved directly in the team effort. For example, in times of special opportunity, need, or crisis on the field, sponsoring and supporting churches can all analyze the situation and provide such advice or resources that only one or two churches would be unable to realize.

Pooled Personal Resources

Pooled resources also include a team's ability to assist members who are ill, injured, traveling, or on leave. One of our colleagues was stricken recently with a critical heart attack. His teammates immediately went into action, providing around-the-clock hospital vigil, financial aid, help

---

[2]Vinzant, Don. "Steps Into The Mission Field," Chapter 1. Unpublished mission textbook, written by members of the Sao Paulo, Brazil mission team.

on documentation, arrangements for his return to the States and a host of other details. If a team member goes on leave, his work doesn't come to a sudden halt. Rather, it is carried on, at least nominally, in his absence. His home is cared for and his other interests are served while he is away. He is given a loving send-off and a warm welcome on return.

Mental and Spiritual Resources

Perhaps the most useful areas of pooled resources are those in the mental and spiritual realms. One man, working alone, may arrive at what he believes to be an excellent new idea or approach to a problem. In team evangelism such "brainstorms" can be examined, tested, left to simmer down and then re-examined. In Proverbs 11:14 the King James version states the matter well:

> Where no counsel is, the people fall: but in the multitude of counsellors, there is safety.

Certainly, this point is true. An entire mission group can be wrong in one of its collective decisions, but the chances of this happening are much less likely than in the case of individually made decisions. The New English Bible puts a different but also a practical slant on this verse:

> For want of skillful strategy an army is lost; victory is the fruit of long planning.

It is our experience, after more than a decade of group decision-making in regard to our work in Belo Horizonte and elsewhere in Brazil, that real success generally comes only after much soul-searching and careful planning of the whole team. The problem-solving process as practiced by a group is tedious, but the end-results are worth the effort.

Spiritual growth for a man, and a group, can be stimulated by pooling spiritual resources—experience, past study, areas of specialization, research, books, prayer life and worship. No one person can be a master of every aspect of Bible knowledge, spiritual life and church work, but several Christians together, functioning as integral members of the same body (I Corinthians 12:14-31), can cooperate for the good of the whole, with one supplying strength where another is weak, and vice-versa. Vinzant comments:

> In a group some may be down emotionally because of culture shock, poor physical health, neglected spiritual life, etc., others will be in better spirits. Thus the group is protected because one can encourage the other.[3]

Yoke-Fellows in Christ

A mission team should learn this lesson well. Team members must work together as yoke-fellows, never as competitors. One perpetual critic or laggard in a group can hold back the entire team's progress. They also must learn to communicate their needs, their weaknesses, their sins and their complaints. Of course, this is what James teaches all Christians to do in their interpersonal relationships (James 5:13-16), but serving together on a team absolutely requires mutual understanding. There is no place in which to hide from a problem that may arise. There is no transferring to another congregation in order to escape an interpersonal problem. Misunderstanding must be faced honestly and if at all possible, through prayer and brotherly love, resolved.

Team evangelism as in any team effort, requires considering the other person as more worthy than oneself. This requires a generous portion of humility and of Christian maturity, as taught in Philippians 2: 1-4:

> So if there is any encouragement in Christ, any incentive of love, any participation in the Spirit, any affection and sympathy, complete my joy by being of the same mind, having the same love, being in full accord and of one mind. Do nothing from selfishness or conceit, but in humility count others better than yourselves. Let each of you look not only to his own interests, but also to the interest of others.

---

[3]*Ibid.*

Longevity on the Field

Because of the many advantages of team evangelism, especially in the areas of mutual companionship and encouragement, the chances of longevity in mission service on a particular field are enhanced. Even the chances of entering the field initially are improved, because of the presence of a team on which to rely and with which to serve as an integral part of a whole operation. Of the thirteen men who went to Sao Paulo, Brazil in 1961, five are still active on the field after more than fourteen years. Of nine American men who went to Belo Horizonte in 1967, six are still in Brazil, after more than eight years.

Impact on the Field

With a strong continuity of personnel and activity, mission teams can have an impact on their host society that might never be achieved by an individual working alone. A team's presence is more strongly felt over the years. In researching mission methods before coming to Brazil, John Curtis made this observation:

> The group method may possibly serve to impress the nationals of a country that the group means business and is there to stay.[4]

Nationals have often watched a new religious movement brought in by some zealous missionary, but then as he moves on, or his work for some other reason declines, it is abandoned—a stark testimony to its temporary nature. For this reason many are hesitant to become connected with another potential failure. The long-term presence of a mission team can help reassure the nationals that this venture is planned, determined and permanent, and thus facilitating their acceptance of the church and their incorporation into it. Among team members contact is made with a number of

---

[4]Curtis, John and Curtis, Joy. "A Study of Sao Paulo, Brazil and Church Growth Within That Growth Metropolis." Thesis presented to Sunset School of Missions, Lubbock, Texas, 1974. p. 67.

top government and business officials. This is another type of rich resource whose benefits can be pooled. For example, materials or technical knowhow are needed for construction of a meeting place. Among the teammates someone generally has the necessary contacts for its design, engineering and construction.

This same continuity of personnel and program can also have a cumulative impact on the church as back home. Over a period of time brethren come to know of and to respect the work and trustworthiness of a seasoned team. Thus, if handled correctly, new projects and personnel for the team can be provided more easily than might otherwise be the case.

The Other Side of the Coin

Are there any weaknesses in team evangelism? Certainly! For example, any team effort involves human personalities, some of which run counter to each other. Add to this the fact that most missionaries are strongwilled and at least fairly well dedicated to their task. If they were not determined people, they never would have gone to the field in the first place. Strong willed, determined individuals hold intense points of view. Put several such people together and the results can be anything but calm. Not every man can work as a partner, or let us say, as a servant, considering the welfare of others ahead of himself (Philippians 2:3-4). Interpersonal problems and clashes can be the greatest difficulty to overcome in any team effort. This is true, not only for the men, but also for wives and children. Many a time an otherwise smooth-working team grinds to a halt because of complaints and/or gossip among wives or eruptions among children.

Veteran missionary and writer T. Stanley Soltau makes this pertinent statement about missionaries serving together on the field:

It is true that a few individualistically minded missionaries have a difficult time getting along with their fellows, and they do their best work if they are left alone in a station. On the other hand, when two or more families, working individually or as families, are compatible, the combined impact of their work and influence is cumulative. The moral and spiritual discipline which they undergo as they work together, checking and counterchecking on each other's efforts, precludes the tendency toward becoming dictatorial and "difficult." In the long run they will accomplish much more, both quantitatively and qualitatively, than had they been placed singly and along in different places. [5]

It is often traumatic to accept this, but there are times when it proves impossible for two or more to serve together in the same group. The only solution is for them to work separately in the same city or preferably, in separate localities. This is not a new phenomenon, as we see by reading about Paul and Barnabas' rupture in Acts 15:36-39. In such case, however, for the good of the team and of its individual members, the separation must be made as peacefully as possible, hopefully with a demonstration of forgiveness.

Problems of Communication

A related handicap, which perhaps precipitates many other more serious difficulties and misunderstandings among team members, is that of a failure to take the time and effort required to maintain good communications in the group. Many tensions arise because someone unintentionally overlooked, snubbed or otherwise hurt a fellow team-member.

Mission teams require considerable time for planning and communication. The problem-solving process can be frustratingly slow and tedious. For this reason, some become reluctant about participating in brainstorming sessions and business meetings. If they do attend, through group pressure, they may arrive late and leave early, seldom entering into the discussion. Their attitude frequently is, "Let's quit talking about it and get with it!" Of course, there is a tendency for

---

[5] Soltau, T. Stanley. *Facing the Field,* (Grand Rapids, Michigan: Baker Book House, 1965), p. 88.

any group to unnecessarily prolong discussion. There is also a tendency to waste time in idle chatter, or even harmful gossip, in the name of problem-solving. But the problems must be faced and solved.

"Mission Compound" Syndrome

Another disadvantage of team effort is the tendency to rely only on each other as social outlets, thus narrowing the individual member's contact with nationals. It is easy to thus develop a "mission compound" attitude and huddle together to the point of seeming to deliberately exclude nationals from intimate friendships.

This tendency can also include the work itself. A mission team may come to make all decisions and rely only on team members for leadership and supportive roles on the field, rather than drawing nationals into the program, including its decision-making processes and its leadership. This is a serious mistake!

Too Much Reliance on Others

Sometimes an individual team member comes to rely too heavily on others in every aspect—failing to master the language, shirking his own responsibilities and producing less than his own share of results. He can bask in the glory of team accomplishment, while hiding from the brethren back home his own lack of productivity. Riding on the shoulders of others is beneficial and essential for a newcomer, who must learn the language and adapt to the culture and the work, but for the experienced missionary, this is dishonest and unfair to his colleagues and to the work. He must carry his own load, as well as sharing in the burdens of others (Galatians 6:1-6). This obligation includes financial, moral, emotional and spiritual concerns, as well as that difficult area of plain hard work.

There are times when a team may expect more from a colleague than he is qualified or prepared to deliver. Group pressure can be awesome, if consistently applied. At the very least, it can force a member into tasks that he finds disagreeable and discouraging. He must sacrifice individual freedom to serve with a team, but he must not be forced into "a right-handed task," when he is really a "southpaw" by nature. His individual abilities, rights, and freedom of thought and action must be protected, despite his participation in the team.

There are other times when the team must investigate honestly the behavior and/or lack of productivity of one of its members. One possibly negative aspect of team outreach is that such a task is distasteful and awkward, because the person involved is also answerable to his sponsoring elders and to the Lord, and not just to his teammates. So the team will sometimes patiently, or critically, wait out a situation that should have been dealt with much sooner.

Another area of possible difficulty of a large "foreign" nucleus of team members, is that they may easily earn a reputation of "foreign domination" of the work. This can be destructive, if there are strong nationalistic tendencies in the host nation.

Constituency of A Mission Team

Having considered plus and minus factors involved in team evangelism, let us move on to other aspects. For example, what type of individuals and families should make up a mission team? Should the team be an homogenous, closely knit group, before arrival on the field? What is the optimum age range for team members? Should the group be made up of single workers, young marrieds, parents of small children, or older people, who have largely or totally reared their children? What about the level of maturity, the goals, the ability to work with others?

A mission team must plan and work closely together. Obviously its members must be compatible, with the ability to complement the others in the team, rather than compete with them. The rugged individualist, the overly strong-willed and the self-centered have no place in a team effort. Those who seek to be *the* "chief of missionary operations" cannot function well in a team. Those who must have their own way at all costs are destructive to group success. A successful team member is one who seeks the greatest good for all, rather than for himself. He fights for his own ideas, but for the sake of group unity, knows when to yield gracefully and to cooperate in the work to be done, even if the decision as to how to accomplish it goes against his own opinion.

A Practical Dreamer

A good group man is a dreamer, but who is also practical. He is goal-oriented. That is, he is able to set high goals for himself, for the team, and for the work, and then he sets about to determine how best to meet these goals. However, a man who *only* dreams may become carried away with his own fantasies, without ever considering their practicality.

David Mickey suggests another characteristic of an effective team member:

> The good group member accepts responsibility readily, and leaves no room for criticism that he is not carrying his part of the load. In group work each member must fulfill his goals, if the others are to achieve theirs.[6]

A group man can and should be a specialist in one or more areas, but must also be adaptable. He may have to learn new areas of ability on the field, or change his skills to meet new and different situations. The present writer came to the field as a professional artist, designer and journalist. But he soon found that to function here in Brazil in the area of Christian publications, which was his major goal, it was going to be necessary to retrain, to learn new methods and technical vocabulary, to adapt to new tools and materials, to understand new attitudes and to have a great deal of patience. All of this he has learned to some degree and so is

---

[6]Mickey, David. "Steps Into The Mission Field," Chap. 14 (See footnote No. 2).

able to be producing materials in the Portuguese language, but still at a slower, more frustrating pace than he could have done in his own language and cultural and professional setting at home.

Adaptability is a real key to successful group evangelism. There is no such thing as *one* super mission method. Situations, needs and opportunities constantly change. A mission team must adapt to these changing situations or perish. The missionary himself must be adaptable to a new language, culture, environment, methods and workmates. A rigid type of person who sees everything as a dichotomy, who believes that the way it was done back home is the only way to do it on the field, or who belives he can only eat, drink or wear items to which he has always been accustomed, is in for serious trouble on the field and so is his mission team.

A Flexible, Mature Person

Each missionary must be flexible in methods and life style. He must be adaptable to the other personality types on the team, in the church on the field and among the nationals in general. Perhaps a good way in which to describe him is that he should be humble, a pillar of strength when necessary, but also tactful and gentle, not abrasive in personality. He should be a person of mature thinking, which need not necessarily correlate to his physical age. Some will show considerable maturity even in their early twenties, others may never. And along with maturity of judgment, it would be helpful for him to have had experience.

Other Vital Characteristics

Howard Norton, veteran missionary in Sao Paulo, describes the successful mission team member:

> A group member must be willing to try new ideas and not become despondent when some cherished plan does not materialize . . . Flexibility, which means the ability to adapt to changing conditions without undue upset, is an important character trait of group members.[7]

---

[7] Norton, Howard W. "Steps Into The Mission Field," Chap. 2.

He goes on to list other qualities:

1. A group member must be spiritually strong.
2. A group member must be doctrinally sound and well versed in the Scriptures.
3. A group member must be in good health, physically and mentally.
4. A group member needs to have training and experience for the job he intends to do.
5. He should have a history of successful work with other people.
6. He must have the ability to bear tedium. (Note: There is much detail to bear, both in general mission service, and especially in group work.)
7. He must practice perseverance.
8. He should be known by the rest of the group, or at least by many in it, before coming to the field.
9. He must be willing to listen to others preach and teach ... On a football team, not everyone in the backfield gets to carry the ball on each play ... It is important that the group member be a man who is willing to watch others perform and rejoice in their success. [8]

Need for Patience

To the above list, the result of more than a decade and a half of team partnership, I would add one other key characteristic: *Patience.* Perhaps no other desire, except for increased faith, trust in the Lord, vision and understanding has been expressed more often in our prayers in Belo Horizonte, than the word "patience." It is a characteristic in great demand, but often short supply, among missionaries. We tend to want instant results and instant understanding among our colleagues. We want mature, indigenous churches almost overnight. We want all of our plans to be realized now. But this is not the way in which it normally happens.

This is a good place in which to mention the need to make and fulfill a long-term commitment, as a characteristic

---

[8]*Ibid.*

of the good group man. He must make a firm decision to cast his lot with the Lord and with a specific team of His servants, and then to stick with his decision. Building the church, especially in another cultural and religious heritage, is the process of a generation at best. There is a vital place for short-termers in a team effort, but the basic core of the team must be committed to continuing in its task in the field, perhaps for decades.

In summarizing the traits of the good team member, the following points also come to mind: He should be friendly, open-hearted and open-minded (no one can successfully serve at the side of a sour or domineering type). He should be willing to hear the other man and to fairly weigh his ideas. But he should also have an independent mind, capable of analysis and original thinking. Above all, he should be sincerely involved. Utterback says that any group "should be composed of persons genuinely interested in the problem to be discussed."[9] This sounds axiomatic, but it is strange how often a group finds itself in supposed partnership with one or more persons whose interests run counter to those of the group itself.

The Family Age and Attitude

A prospective team member's age, marital and family situation all enter decisively into the picture. Arguments fly pro and con over the optimum age range for beginning missionaries and their families. This does not appear to us in Belo Horizonte to be as important as the attitudes of the family in question. Our own team has had members whose ages ran from the early twenties to the sixties. While it is more difficult on the whole for older persons to adapt and learn the language, it is not necessarily impossible, and they can function in areas closed to the young. Middle-aged, older people and retirees, often overlooked in the demand for youth in missionary outreach, can be quite effective,

---

[9]Utterback, William E. *Group Thinking and Conference Leadership,* Revised Edition, (New York: Holt, Rhinehart and Winston, 1964), p. 15.

especially in those parts of the world where age and experience are held in high esteem. Several of our families had teenage children when they arrived in Brazil. Despite prophecies of doom it was discovered that the teenagers benefited greatly by their stay in Brazil, and they also performed a valuable service while there. Their middle-aged parents have shown a higher-than-average longevity on the field, due perhaps to their having already been through the mill—of education, work and human experience in general, and thus being more content to stick out the added frustrations and crises of the missionary endeavor.

It is essential, however, that both the wife and children favor the idea of foreign evangelism, especially in a team thrust, and that they be compatible with the other families involved. When the idea of their going to Brazil became a serious possibility, the writer's entire family met around the dinner table for a conference on the matter. Problems of moving, adjustment, language, education, returning for college in the States and the long separation from parents were all considered. When it came time to make the awesome decision, the teenage sons opted for Brazil ahead of their father.

Preparation is Vital

Once a team is carefully and prayerfully put together, it should spend time in joint and individual preparation for the venture. Teammates should come to know each other as well as possible and should all participate in the advance planning. To throw a group of strangers together and expect them to automatically become a smoothly operating missionary machine is to invite disaster. Our own team was five years in forming and preparing before the first unit left for the field. During this time, especially the last two years, there were frequent retreats and planning sessions. A lengthy handbook called *Operation '68 Master Growth Guide,*[10] was drawn up, after much research and prayer, as a guide for all the team

---

[10]This manual, although in some respects out of date now, is available for study. A copy may be researched at The Mission Center, Abilene Christian University or at other sources available through the Belo Horizonte team.

members. Every effort was made to acquaint all teammates and supporting churches with each other and with the project. This included a monthly group newsletter called *Brazil, Oba!,* regular bulletins shared by the committed and prospective workers, personal correspondence, frequent telephone conferences, visits in the homes and other means of communication, as well as the retreats and planning sessions.

But even with all of this effort to communicate and build team understanding and spirit, some were not well acquainted with each other when we arrived in Brazil, and some were hazy about proposed methods. Some proved to be incapable of working closely with others, and some returned home early, frustrated by their stay. The entire prospective team must feel a real *esprit de corps,* a real sense of "familyhood" among its members and should have a real sense of having participated fully in planning before departure. Otherwise, there is a great likelihood that a spirit of comradeship will never develop under the pressures faced in the work. Such a spirit will "grow" on the field, but it must be there, at least in essence, beforehand.

Individual Preparation

A mission team is no stronger than the potential strength of all of its members. If one of its partners is well prepared and another ill prepared, the result will be for the two of them only mediocre preparation. If one has studied the language and culture of his new host country, the mission methods and other areas of preparation before coming, while the other made little or no specialized preparation, the second man will inevitably retard the progress of the first. Of course, no two will have the same capacity nor the same opportunities to learn. But every effort should be made, collectively and individually, to see that all members, including wives, have the best preparation possible before going. (How very often wives are overlooked in the process of both preparation and decision making. This is a dangerous oversight and will haunt the group later on.)

In many cases, some knowledge of the language can be obtained before departure. This will facilitate learning it on the field and will also reduce some of the initial frustration as the workers attempt to find houses and furniture. The history and culture of the target area should be researched by every team member. If the preparation period is long enough, courses can be taken in cultural anthropology, mission history and methods, principles of church growth, group dynamics and other studies beneficial to success on the field.

Individual and Group Goals

Most worthwhile things in life are realized by setting goals and then aiming one's energies at accomplishing them. Individual members of a mission team should set personal goals of preparation, language mastery and personal growth and service on the field.

Then the group itself should collectively set goals—for preparation, departure and development of the work. These goals must be the product of group consideration and consensus, not just based on someone's individual decision. A longtime Brazil colleague, John Pennisi, says this about group goal-setting:

> ... interest and cooperation are created within the group through participation in the establishment of goals. When the individual has the opportunity to express himself and to participate in the decisions that affect him, he feels that the group is of benefit to him and not merely to the leader along.[11]

During its preparatory period, the group should determine certain *basic* goals and understandings, both immediate and long-range. The Sao Paulo team set the following goals in its early planning:

1. Number of workers in the group.

---

[11]Pennisi, John L. "A Study of the Problem of Church Leadership in the Light of the Dynamics of Group Management." Masters Thesis, Abilene Christian College, Abilene, Texas, October, 1959, p. 50.

2. General goals compatible with the group's manpower.
3. Length of time the group plans to work together.
4. Philosophy of mission work to be adopted.
5. Financial strength of the group.
6. General consideration of the size, political outlook, and cultural makeup of the target nation.

Once goals are set by the group, they should be kept in mind and pursued diligently. Pennisi additionally lists several essential steps in areas of goal-reaching and problem-solving:

> First, a clear perspective of the problem must be obtained and boundaries placed around the scope to be discussed. Second, all must settle on a definition of terms and concepts, in order that semantics may present the least difficulty.
>
> Third, an understanding of the long range objectives must be developed, in order that the more immediate goal may be determined in consideration of them.
>
> Fourth, identify the problem concretely by bringing in all facts in the matter, studying them carefully.
>
> Fifth, reconsider the long-range goals and the effect that they have upon the problem.
>
> Sixth, determine the possible solutions and fully understand what each means, without ridiculing any proffered course of action.
>
> Seventh, evaluate each solution in the light of the long-range objectives.[12]

Unity in establishing goals, and then in reaching them, is dependent upon "how well the members personally like each other, how well they like the shared goals and how much they realize that they need one another to reach their goals."[13]

---

[12]Ibid., p. 60.

[13]Laird, Dr. Donald A., and Eleanor C. *The New Psychology for Leadership,* (New York: McGraw-Hill Book Co., 1956), p. 135.

Maintaining Goals and Spirit

Utilization of the above principle in group work will help guarantee the fulfillment of group goals and the continuity of its spirit, both in preparation and functioning on the field. Individuals will flag in zeal, especially as the preparation period drags month after month and perhaps year after year. Group spirit must be maintained, by every means possible, during this critical time.

One mistake that deeply hurt our group spirit (one that future teams might avoid) is that of entering the field in separate waves. When our first group (one family independently and seven families together) left the States, the departure caused a letdown in spirit for those who were to follow, as well as a serious breakdown in communications, and unity among the members of the total group. When the second wave of five families arrived a year later, friction developed between what had become, in essence, two separate teams. How much better it would have been to hold the team together, both in preparation and arrival on the field.

Choice of Locale

Now that we have roughed out some guidelines for *forming* a mission team, where should it go? Among the requirements for selection of a country and city, the following were included in our list during the process of selection: It must be receptive: to the gospel, to the entry of a team of Americans, and to vocational opportunities. It should be a growing nation, with a reasonably stable government. Finally, it should have large, unreached metropolitan centers, from which to choose a target city. Brazil was one of the nations that met all these requirements for us, with Belo Horizonte selected as the next promising city, after Sao Paulo, in which to open a new work. The selection process should have much research, and direct, on-the-field investigation. It also requires time, patience, and a heaping portion of prayer.

Not Every Area Suitable

Obviously, not every area is conducive to team evangelism. Rural or small town settings, where missionary colleagues are scattered over a wide area, would complicate greatly a group operation. The area selected should be homogenous; that is, a large city that is conducive to the presence of a team of families, or a closely knit tribal area that can be worked from a central point.

How central? A "missionary compound" approach is probably unwise, especially in these days of strong nationalism. Team members must live close enough together to maintain effective communication and joint effort, but they should not live "in each other's pockets." To some extent, availability of housing and its price will dictate where team families should live, at least early in the stay.

Organization of the Work

Once on the field, a team must devote time to organization of the work. During our first few months in Belo Horizonte, we met almost daily to hammer out procedures and solve unforeseen difficulties.

One area of very vital concern in the functioning of a mission team, as well as its morale, is that of continuing internal communication. We attempt to assure good communication by means of: notes distributed to each member, telephone calls and a regular group bulletin (distributed to the team, as well as to a select group of friends, supporters and former colleagues). We also meet once a week in what we call "Chat-N-Chew" luncheon sessions, where ideas are shared and filed mentally for future reference. Despite the best intentions, however, someone on the team will inevitably complain, "Nobody ever told me about that!"

Communication is more than announcing facts. It is also gaining the other person's attention and sharing with him heart-to-heart. No two of the workers in a team will have identical experiences, goals, vocabulary, educational level or communicative skills. As pointed out by Beal, Bohlen and Raudabaugh:

> In heterogenous groups ... it is particularly important that each group member makes sure he is communicating with all other group members.[14]

They further state that group members feel unsure of themselves, and therefore defensive and suspicious, when they do not have two-way communication. Evidently, even open words and acts of hostility are received with more certainty, if there is a practice of open communication among group members.[15]

To Everything A Season

It is essential that a missionary team discipline itself to regular times for business, fellowship and recreation. It should also maintain adequate records of its work and its finances. It must know who is responsible for what, simply because "what is everybody's business is nobody's." It must discipline itself to requiring completion of assignments, participation by all members in the work, in the finances, and in the times of group discussion and fellowship. It is our considered opinion that a man who voluntarily joins a mission team, and then refuses to participate wholeheartedly, has forfeited his right to team membership. To avoid such a reversal of attitude after reaching the field, our team requires all prospective team members to sign an agreement of participation, in the work and in financial and moral commitment to it. A copy of our agreement form is found in an appendix at the end of this chapter.

Organization includes the necessary machinery of: chairmanship of meetings, minutes-taking, keeping of and

---

[14] Beal, George M.; Bohlen, Joe M.; Raudabaugh, J. Neil. *Leadership and Dynamic Group Action,* (Ames, Iowa: Iowa State University Press, 1962), p. 86.

[15] *Ibid.*

reporting on finances, responsibility for official group correspondence, and other group-assigned tasks.

Ted Stewart, another veteran group worker, lists the following reasons for sound structuring of group work:

1. Organization is needed to give unity and order to the group effort. Group goals can never be accomplished going in ten different directions.
2. Group organization is also needed to distribute fairly the load of responsibility to all group workers.
3. Good organization avoids the opposite extreme of duplication of effort and time.
4. Another advantage of organization is concentrated efficiency in every area of work.
5. Good organization also enables individuals to feel more satisfied. When responsibilities are not clearly defined, group members lose their initiative and joy of personal achievement. Bad organization is often the cause of much individual frustration . . .[16]

Necessary Meetings

Team effort requires regular meetings, despite the time they take up. And meetings require rules and records, as noted by Howard Norton:

> Even as a brief meeting at midfield to discuss ground rules is necessary prior to a football game, it is necessary for a group to decide jointly the norms which will regulate its discussion periods (and business methods).

> Written records are worth the effort because the minutes record all formal decisions of the group and thus cut down on misunderstandings that might arise.[17]

Rules are necessary to the orderly processing of decisions. Faulty memories and changes in the group, as well as legal

---

[16] Stewart, Ted. "Steps Into The Mission Field," Chapter 2 (See Footnote No. 2).

[17] Norton, Howard W. *op. cit.,* Chapter 3.

considerations, require accurate record keeping. There are also historical considerations, because someone later on might want to research the development of that particular work. Record keeping includes sound business procedures for handling of funds, payment of group bills, processing of documents and other such matters.

A distinct characteristic of both the Sao Paulo and Belo Horizonte teams is the absence of a single group leader. However, all discussion periods, business meetings, and group functioning need coordinating by a chairman. For this reason, a chairman is selected by the group to serve only for a specific period of time. Thus, leadership is spread around in the group.

Depending upon the size of the group and the complexity of its work, a certain number of committees is necessary. Both of these Brazil groups have a Steering Committee, composed usually of the chairman, the secretary and the treasurer for the year, or other men selected by the team. This committee coordinates group activity, handles internal conflicts and difficulties and represents the team in various official and legal realms. Committees may also be formed to care for recruitment, publications, evangelism, public relations, facilities, Bible camps and other such matters. Because our team in Belo Horizonte is now fairly small, we have simplified the committee structure. Except for the Steering Committee, specialized areas are assigned generally to one man, who reports to and counsels with the entire group about his area of responsibility.

Individual Assignments

A mission team's individual assignments must be based partially on need but partially on individual abilities and desires. Considering only one aspect of assignment making, to the neglect of others, can create problems. For example, the present writer is no carpenter or handyman. But for a time he was made responsible for maintenance of the Bible Camp near Belo Horizonte, a clearcut case of a square peg in a round hole. On the other hand, his group assignments from the beginning have included responsibility for creating printed materials, a happy choice for all concerned.

Job Description Chart

In our team approach, we have tried to consider the human resources available, as well as the task to be accomplished, and then to match these up as well as possible. It is most important that each member understand and accept his part in the functioning of the whole structure. Here is our present group "job description" chart:

SCHOOL OF THE BIBLE
Individual Assignments

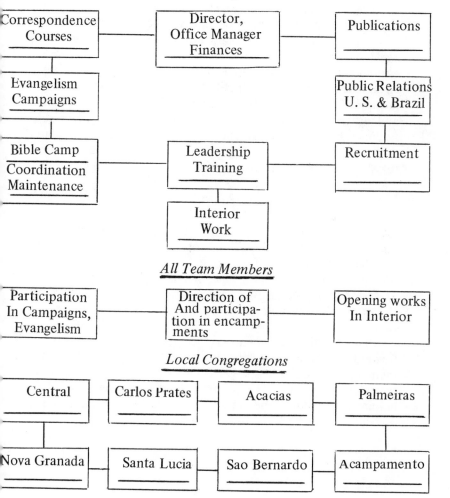

Correspondence Courses	Director, Office Manager Finances	Publications
Evangelism Campaigns		Public Relations U. S. & Brazil
Bible Camp Coordination Maintenance	Leadership Training	Recruitment
	Interior Work	

All Team Members

Participation In Campaigns, Evangelism	Direction of And participation in encampments	Opening works In Interior

Local Congregations

Central	Carlos Prates	Acacias	Palmeiras
Nova Granada	Santa Lucia	Sao Bernardo	Acampamento

As indicated on this chart, each man has at least one assignment in his area of specialization. He also serves in other areas, including working with one or more congregations. All team members also share in responsibilities connected with our Bible camp and with major evangelistic campaigns.

Each member also shares in group expenses. Our mission team is registered officially and functions in Brazil as a School of the Bible. This gives us legal recognition as a team, with the right to transact business, apply for visas for new workers and such like. We operate a group office, which also doubles as a center for correspondence courses, publications, courses for church leaders and other projects, such as large-scale campaigns that are beyond the capacity of the young churches here. In order to function in this way, we expect each team member to contribute his share each month for group office rent, printing, postage, Bible camp maintenance and other expenses. Thus, we can have a reasonably stable financial base for our growing commitments. Careful records of all transactions are kept, approved by the group and registered according to Brazilian law.

One For All, All For One

Each team member accepts a responsibility to the entire team—a "one-for-all and all-for-one" spirit. When one member suffers, all suffer. When one rejoices, all rejoice. It is not at all uncommon for one member to spend part of his Stateside leave attempting to reinforce the work or shore up the support of another member.

The good team member "can often help to create a favorable climate by expressing good will toward the other members, by complimenting others on their contributions, by encouraging others to speak (and participate) and by helping to pacify the short-tempered and to harmonize divergent views."[18]

---

[18]Utterback, *op. cit.,* p. 53.

But let us suppose that divergent views still exist, or that friction arises. How does a team handle these? Conflicts will occur, even in the most understanding of groups. Missionaries too are human. Misunderstandings arise, due primarily to strongly held views about the work and about how others in the group should or should not be performing. Each other's faults are seen in the bright light of day-to-day reality. On this point David Mickey observes:

> In a close group relationship, where each member of the group knows the others so well, individuals are let to see their own weaknesses and inabilities.[19]

Some cannot tolerate this mirroring of their own faults, as pointed out by Miller:

> A person who has never learned to crucify this pride system of his life, to cleanse his inner life until it can stand the transparency of genuine interpersonal relationships, will retreat further behind shame, false fronts and intrigue ...[20]

And just as the individual discovers his own weaknesses, as reflected by the group, he also comes to see the weaknesses in the lives of other members of the group. It is the obligation of all involved to gently encourage and correct each other. They must be willing to help and be helped. They must be ready to forgive and ask forgiveness, to criticize constructively and to receive loving criticism.

Financial Support

One area of potential misunderstanding between team members on the field, or between the team and sponsoring churches, is that of financial support for workers. To diminish this possibility, we in Belo Horizonte have tried to maintain a somewhat uniform set of guidelines for level of

---

[19]Mickey, David. *op. cit.,* Chapter 14.

[20]Miller, Paul M. *Group Dynamics In Evangelism,* (Scottsdale, Pennsylvania: Herald Press, 1958), pp. 48-49.

support of present and future team families, depending largely on number and age of children in the family involved, since their schooling can be a real financial and logistics problem on the field. Other major expenses, apart from housing, are transportation, telephone (which is usually quite expensive in other countries, but indispensable to communication within the group) and the purchase of major household appliances. In addition, the family's budget must include resources for settling in, for language study and for sharing in group expenses. The former two expenses are almost always higher than anticipated.

One Sponsor or Many?

Some have questioned whether it is better for each worker to be sponsored separately or whether all in the group should be under the sponsorship of the same Stateside congregation. It is imperative that all team members be answerable to an eldership, somewhere. The first system, that of a different sponsor for each family, has been followed by the Sao Paulo and Belo Horizonte teams, whereas the entire Buenos Aires, Argentina group is largely sponsored by one church. If there are various sponsors, support and accompanying interest in the work are spread out over a larger area and have a generally wider financial base. Also, if one congregation decides to withdraw its participation, the entire effort is only hampered, but not killed outright. The method does have the disadvantage of having to keep a number of elderships informed and approving of the work being done.

This is no easy task, since decisions are generally reached by the consensus of the men at work on the field (that is, by those who should generally be most qualified to make such decisions). At times elderships at home, not understanding the real situation and the process by which a particular decision was reached, disagree with it, thus placing their man in the untenable position of being pulled in two different directions by two opposing loyalties. If this two-way stretch continues, he must either part company with the team over the matter, or part company with his sponsor. Fortunately for our team, such a problem has seldom arisen, but it can.

Mutual Confidence Among Sponsors

In such an arrangement (various sponsoring churches), it is wise to develop early in the program a sense of mutual confidence between the team and the sponsoring churches. This can be done by careful communication and better yet, by occasional joint meetings of the elderships of the churches involved, to discuss the work in general, as well as visits by team members on leave to the various sponsoring churches of his fellow workers.

With such a spirit of mutual confidence, sponsors will more readily accept team decisions, even in the extreme case of disciplinary action recommended by the team against one of its members.

The other system, that of one sponsoring church for all team members, has certain advantages, perhaps chief of which are simplified communication and better coordination of team effort and its relationship to the sponsor. However, there are certain handicaps, one of which is the risk of a team's rising or falling together, depending on the mood of the moment in its sponsoring church. Another is that the entire team may be held back unnecessarily by limitations imposed by the lack of vision or resources of its single sponsor.

Evaluation of Work

Any efficient team must have periodic means of evaluating both its progress and the processes by which it reaches its decisions and realizes its progress. In this way, it will direct its energies toward the task at hand, rather than heading off at tangents, as enticing as they may seem at the moment. In the book, *Leadership and Dynamic Group Action,* the importance of group self-evaluation is stressed in these words:

. . . systematic, rational evaluation has great potential in leading group members and the group to greater productivity. Members participate the most in group activities when they understand the goals and objectives of the group and evaluate the group as making satisfactory progress toward these goals.[21]

Continuing Recruitment

Most who enlist in a mission team are determined to stick with their commitment. They want to be a part of a successful group venture and for this reason, pledge a definite period of years to the work. To become really useful to the work, a period of several years of on-the-field experience is essential. They often have the rosey-eyed notion that their fellow team members will be nearly perfect and that no one will create problems, become discouraged or return home. But this is not the case. Even with the best of intentions, relations and planning, there are misunderstandings and disappointments, with some leaving the team from time to time. Illness, lost support, changing interests and circumstances, disillusionment and just the very changing nature of life itself contribute to changes in a team's personnel. To maintain its program of work, a team must recruit new families.

This is a difficult experience for all. It has been our observation that the times of greatest stress in group work are the final two or three weeks before departure, the first few months after arrival (the settling-in period), those moments of frustration in language learning, periods of division in the ranks of the team, serous calamities, such as loss of support, sudden illness, major accident or death, strife among national congregations, departure of a key member of the team and the arrival of a new member. The right kind of recruit must be sought out, prepared, documented and visaed (a tedious task) and then incorporated into an already operating program. He doesn't have the benefit of previous experience and may not be absorbed readily into its nature and spirit. He

---

[21]Beal, Bohlen, Raudabaugh. *op. cit.,* p. 120.

may not agree with its methods, and, of course, nothing irritates a group much more than a newcomer's challenging its time-honored practices, which have been hammered out, over the years, on the anvil of hard experience. It is possible, however, for a newcomer to see things from a fresh point of view and for this reason his ideas should be given fair consideration.

The newly arrived worker goes through all of the agonies of adjustment and language-learning, which can be aggravated by his seeing the "old pros" operating and communicating so easily. They, too, may be irritated by his "slowness," forgetting how it was for them a few years earlier. It is often better to assign a more recent arrivee to lead in the orientation of the newcomer, because he can identify better with the problems of the novice. Once on the field, continued care must be given to the newcomer's absorption into the group, the work and the culture. His permanent attitude about his new co-workers and the environment in general becomes pretty much set during his first weeks and months on the field.

It is essential, then, that replacements be given careful consideration. We here in Belo Horizonte put them through a screening process that is designed to point out potential strengths and weaknesses before the person leaves home. Questions we ask in recruiting are: What is the optimum size for our team? What talents are needing to be replaced or incorporated into the work? What kind of temperament does this person have? Can he make the necessary adjustments to life and service here? Will he be a real asset to the work, or a liability? To help us answer these questions, we ask him to submit to us a statement about his personal background and references, as well as the already-mentioned agreement form. We also try to arrange for various ones of our number to visit in his home prior to his departure for the field.

Long-Term Implications

Team evangelism, then, involves many considerations. Any such team should be carefully and prayerfully formed. Its task, especially if in an area newly opened to evangelism, is monumental and should be begun with all of the advance preparation possible. Its task has long-term implications, which call for long-term commitments. Some in our Belo Horizonte team felt earlier that, surely, five years would be sufficient for mounting a strong, self-perpetuating work in our city. Now we see it as the task of a generation, considering the almost total lack of prior Bible knowledge on the part of its citizens, as well as their background, steeped as it is in tradition and superstition. To change a nation of people is an extremely slow process, one that must look ahead to the rise of a new Bible-oriented generation.

Despite the great cost, energy and time involved, it is well worth all the extra efforts to launch the right kind of mission team. Its total impact for good can and probably will continue for many generations.

An Age of Teamwork

This is an age of teamwork—in sports, "brain" pools, research, industry and even teaching. It is time for the "sons of light" to be as wise as, if not wiser than, the sons of this world. Major population centers all over the world require concentrated assaults by crack teams, well prepared and dedicated to long term service. In Brazil alone, several cities of a million or more inhabitants each are still strategic targets for team evangelism. To this end we launched several years ago a strategy for conquest, called *Breakthrough/Brazil.* According to this concept, several teams are to be formed and placed in these centers, to establish strong nuclei of Christians and to eventually reach outward to secondary cities in each area.

Teams for All Major Cities

Such a strategy ought to be devised for all major centers where the church is either non-existent or still weak. For too long we have largely ignored the major cities—the Calcuttas, Shanghais, Tokyos, Londons, Parises, Montreals, Mexico Cities, Rio de Janeiros, Recifes, and Buenos Aires'. Or, if we have ventured into them, it has often been with but one or two families and little real strategy for conquest. In fact, it is almost guaranteed in advance that one or two men will come to feel intimidated by the masses of humankind about them and frustrated by their lack of physical strength and time to penetrate successfully.

For too long in our mission planning we have followed the mentality of Israel in the period of the Judges: "Every man did that which was right in his own eyes," (Judges 21:25). We should rather have followed the example of cooperative team effort demonstrated by Nehemiah and company: "And so we built the wall, for every man had a will to work."

If other nations and their great cities are worth evangelizing, and we know that they are, the task is worth doing in an all-out, permanent way. One means of achieving this is through the formation, placement and long-term service of "tough", dedicated teams of God's men in every strategic metropolis on earth. Let us raise up a generation of team evangelists, in order to assure the eventual firm securing of the Eternal Kingdom everywhere in the world. Properly taught nationals will then form their own teams to carry the Good News to every surrounding area and to other metrpolitan centers.

In this way, we can more likely say at the end of our generation, "And so all Asia (or Africa or South America . . .) heard the Word."

APPENDIX

FORMAL AGREEMENT FOR PROSPECTIVE WORKERS
Belo Horizonte, Brazil, Mission Team

October, 1970

Understanding that a missionary team effort is precisely that—a team effort—that it is a privilege rather than a right to serve with a team dedicated to evangelism, regardless of the place, and that in a team approach to evangelism, the individual is willing, when necessary, to relinquish his own "rights" for the good of the whole team and of the work, I agree to accept the following conditions to my serving with the team in Belo Horizonte, Brazil:

1. Strive at all times to hold Jesus and His church in the highest esteem, and to support their welfare at all times.
2. Strive to grow in spiritual things, and in prayer, especially for the work.
3. Do my best to become proficient in the language, knowing that it will normally require several years of formal study.
4. Participate in a program of orientation into the culture and the work here.
5. Participate regularly in business meetings and planning.
6. Accept the will of the team, as expressed in formal business meetings, even if such will is contrary to my own will. (The only exception being a situation in which that will is in direct violation to my conscience as a sincere Christian.)
7. Accept my full share of responsibility in fulfilling the over-all program.
8. Accept my full share in the financial obligations of the team and of the work, barring an unforeseen personal financial crisis.
9. Be the best possible example of Christian love, patience, and forgiveness, knowing that there will be differences of opinion, and personality conflicts, as well as other irritations and frustrations in our work together.

10. Be a loyal, constructive representative of the team and of the church, both on the field and on trips home.
11. Attend services and functions of the group and of the church, even if at first there is a language barrier.
12. Accept, if the need requires it, total group action in case of emergency, illness, support crises, and/or problem of a doctrinal, moral or emotional nature in my life or that of my family. And I will do my share to act in like crises among others on the team and in the church.
13. Be alert to the spiritual, mental, and physical welfare of ourselves and our families as much as possible. This will include days of rest, vacations, physical exercise, devotional periods, and opportunities for mental growth.

_____

(Signature)

_____

(Date)

SUGGESTED READINGS

BOOKS

Beal, George M.; Bohlen, Joe M.; and Raudabaugh, J. Neal. *Leadership and Dynamic Group Action.* Ames, Iowa: Iowa State University Press, 1962.

Budd, Richard W. and Ruben, Brent D. *Approaches to Human Communication.* Rochelle Park, N. J.: Hayden Book Company, 1972.

Cartwright, Dorwin and Zander, Alvin. *Group Dynamics Research.* Evanston, Ill.: Row, Peterson and Co., 1960.

Gordon, Thomas. *Group Centered Leadership.* Boston: Houghton Mifflin, 1955.

Gulley, Halbert E. *Discussion, Conference and the Group Process.* New York: Henry Holt, 1960.

Homans, George C. *The Human Group.* New York: Harcourt, Brace, 1950.

Laird, Dr. Donald A. and Eleanor C. *The New Psychology for Leadership.* New York: McGraw-Hill Book Co., 1956.

Maier, Norman. *Principles of Human Relations.* New York: John Wiley and Sons, Inc., 1952.

Miller, Paul M. *Group Dynamics In Evangelism.* Scottsdale, Penn.: Herald Press, 1958.

Soltau, T. Stanley. *Facing the Field.* Grand Rapids, Mich.: Baker Book House, 1965.

Stogdill, Ralph M. *Individual Behavior and Group Achievement.* New York and London: Oxford University Press, 1959.

Titus, Charles H. *The Processes of Leadership.* Dubuque, Iowa: William C. Brown Co., 1951.

Trecker, Audrey R. and Harleigh B. *How to Work With Groups.* New York: Morrow, 1952.

Uris, Auren and Shapin, Betty. *Working With People.* New York: The MacMillan Co., 1952.

Utterback, William E. *Group Thinking and Conference Leadership* (Revised Edition). New York: Holt, Rinehart and Winston, 1964.

Wagner, Russel H. and Arnold, Carroll C. *Handbook of Group Discussion.* Boston: Houghton Mifflin, 1950.

PERIODICALS AND BULLETINS

Brown, Ida Stewart. "Working Toward Goals." *Adult Leadership,* Vol. 1, No. 4, Spring, 1948.

Lippitt, Gordon L., and Schmidt, Warren H. "My Group and I." Washington, D. C.: *Educator's Washington Dispatch,* 1952.

Morris, Don H. "The Power of An Idea." *Horizons,* May-June, 1961. Abilene, Texas: Abilene Christian College.

"Evaluating Programs and Performance." *Adult Leadership,* Vol. 1, No. 11, 1953.

Understanding How Groups Work, Leadership Pamphlet No. 4. Chicago: Adult Education Association, 1955.

UNPUBLISHED MATERIALS

Sao Paulo, Brazil Mission Team. "Steps Into The Mission Field." Soon-to-be published book on group missionary preparation and operation. Address: Caixa Postal 30.217 01000, Sao Paulo, SP, Brazil.

Shipp, Glover H. "Missions And The Local Church." Scheduled for publication in 1976. Address: Caixa Postal 1514, 30000 Belo Horizonte, MG, Brazil.

THESES AND MANUALS

Belo Horizonte, Brazil Mission Team. "Master Growth Guide," Operation '68/Brazil. Los Angeles: Operation '68 Team, 1966.

Curtis, John and Joy. "A Study of Sao Paulo, Brazil and Church Growth In That Growth Metropolis." Thesis submitted to Sunset School of Missions, Lubbock, Texas, 1974.

Pennisi, John L. "A Study of the Problem of Church Leadership in the Light of the Dynamics of Group Management." Masters thesis submitted to Abilene Christian College, Abilene, Texas, 1957.

WOMEN IN MISSIONS

BY JOYCE HARDIN

The dictionary defines a missionary very simply, as one with a mission or one who undertakes or accepts a mission. A missionary woman, therefore, would be defined as a female who has a mission or who undertakes a mission.

The word missionary may be used in a very broad sense but in religious circles, it has come to indicate those who have accepted the challenge of preaching in a different culture and is used synonymously with dedication, religious sacrifice, adjustment and "purpose in life."

Outside religious circles, the word missionary may still mean one who preaches in a foreign culture but the synonyms are often quite different. Writers have tended to deal rather harshly with the missionary, ridiculing him, maligning him and poking fun at his way of life. He is often pictured either as a spineless misfit or an arrogant religious bigot. Always in the background is the missionary woman—long suffering, unattractive, meek, and obviously unhappy. Cartoonists have drawn the missionary as a milk-toast character, out of touch with reality, perhaps looking pious or self-righteous as he stands in the cannibal's cooking pot. Again in the background is the missionary woman, wearing out-of-date clothing, her hair in an unattractive bun, wringing her hands helplessly or singing a hymn as her husband prepares to meet his Maker. The single missionary woman has fared no better and has often been pictured by the novelist as becoming a real woman only after she has forsaken her religious mission and rejoined the "real" world. (The missionary woman in the movie *African Queen,* for example.)

In reality, missionaries are very much like other Christians. They have the same weaknesses and strengths and in a group would probably not be distinguishable from anyone else. However, the missionary does face a different set of challenges and problems and must learn to cope with life in a foreign culture. This does serve to make him unique.

The woman who becomes a missionary whether as the wife in a missionary team or as a single woman who has accepted her own particular mission is still a woman. She will face the same problems, frustrations, and blessings as women everywhere but these will be compounded by the fact that she must meet these problems in a new and alien setting which will cause additional problems and add new challenges.

The fact that this present volume includes a single chapter on the missionary woman does not mean that the missionary woman is still a background figure. Rather, it indicates a realization that the missionary woman has a unique and important role to play in the success or failure of missionary endeavor.

The missionary man may face the difficulties of learning a new language and dealing with a different set of customs in a new culture. Although he may find it necessary to modify his techniques of preaching or teaching, basically his work remains the same. He is still doing that which he has been prepared to do. For the woman, however, her entire way of life may be completely reversed. She must make a home in a new style dwelling, cook strange foods, watch her children adapt to customs that are alien to her and, at the same time, adjust to the new role of "missionary," which she may discover demands much more than she had ever considered. The single missionary woman's adjustment may be less severe in that she does not have to care for a family but she may find her mission severely hampered by the fact that she is single and is a woman.

The success or failure of the missionary woman to adjust to her new life has important implications for mission work as a whole. If the single woman is not able to cope with her problems, she may return to the States and the work will lose a valuable worker. If the missionary wife is unable to adjust, the entire family may return to the States and two valuable workers will be lost. If the adjustment is only partial, the family or individual may remain on the field but the influence for good may be severely hampered and the welfare of a Christian family jeopardized.

This chapter cannot begin to answer all the questions and solve all the problems related to the missionary woman. It will however, attempt to point out certain problem areas and suggest some solutions in the hope that prospective missionaries may be forewarned and thus better able to prepare themselves to become more effective servants of the Lord.

Missionary Motives

"You're going to be a MISSIONARY? You're actually going to spend the rest of your life in a foreign country, teaching heathens? WHY?"

Probably the above questions have been asked, more than once, to every prospective missionary. The answers given will vary according to the individual, but basically they will follow a general trend. The missionary will answer that he has chosen his vocation "because of a desire to preach the gospel to a lost world."

However, if the missionary will look more closely into his or her inner self, he may discover other motives than just a desire to evangelize. These are not necessarily wrong, when combined with a true love for souls but it might be well for the missionary to fully know himself or herself. Basic motives will have a definite influence on the missionary's success or failure. If the true motive is love for souls, the missionary will be willing to do whatever is necessary to satisfy that need, but if the true motive is something else, the end result may be frustration and failure.

The list of motives for missionary women could be as varied as the women themselves. However, the following are perhaps the most pertinent, as related to the missionary woman:

1. *Pioneer Spirit.* Many a missionary woman has been moved to become a missionary because of the promise of adventure. There are no new lands to conquer but there are new cultures to learn. It sounds exciting to meet new peoples and venture into areas where few Christians have gone.

Perhaps every missionary should have some of this motive, for entering a new culture will certainly be an adventure. However, adventure soon becomes old. The pioneer may tire of carrying water, living in a mud hut, or shopping in a local market. If the pioneer spirit is the only motive then it soon may not be enough.

2. *Travel.* Related to pioneer spirit is the desire to travel. Again it is exciting to travel to new and distant places. However, the tourist, who exclaims over the primitive life in Africa can take her pictures and return home. The missionary must stay and the primitive life becomes hers. Unless the desire to travel is combined with a desire to serve it will not be strong enough to overcome the obvious obstacles.

3. *Obeying as a Form of Duty.* The Christian who realizes that God has commanded that the world be reached may decide that she must accept this challenge in a foreign setting in order to have salvation herself. But there is obedience without a true love for souls, the mission may become mere form without real substance.

4. *Can't Make It in the States.* There is also the Christian who cannot seem to fit into any real niche in the home church. She is unable to find any real area of service, and so decides that being a missionary is her calling. The fallacy is, of course, that she will probably not find an area of service in the mission field, either. A misfit in one society is probably a misfit in another.

5. *Resists Authority—Needs to Work on Her Own.* This motive may apply to the woman who would like to do more than the home church allows and perhaps take more of a leadership role than the elders will permit. The mission fields offers to her an opportunity to make her own decisions and avoid the restraints of traditional authority.

6. *Guilt.* Another motive for becoming a missionary is guilt. Unable to accept God's forgiveness for past sins or to forgive herself, the Christian woman hopes that by sacrificing as a missionary and giving up home and friends, the guilt will be absolved. Unfortunately, instead, the guilt may be

compounded by the problems met and unsolved on the field itself.

7. *Group Hysterics.* Often an individual or couple will decide to become missionaries because their friends are making the decision or because it is the "in" thing to do. Wives are sometimes reluctant to express their own feelings or misgivings because to do so would alienate them from the group. If the mission is accepted because others are accepting a similar mission, the new missionary may later be confronted with more difficulties than she is able to overcome.

8. *I Married a Man.* This may not be an actual motive but it is often the only reason that many missionary wives have for finding themselves in the mission field. They have given very little thought themselves to their own responsibilities and duties, and are merely following their husband's decision. When a woman does not share her husband's desire to serve, she may find it difficult to adjust to the life she must lead. This may lead to resentment, unhappiness, and an unwillingness to continue the mission.

9. *My Parents Were Missionaries.* Some missionary children feel an obligation to continue the work begun by their parents. Certainly this is commendable. It is also expedient, since cultural adjustments will be minor and language no difficulty. However, the mission must become theirs, not their parents. The desire must be to serve the Lord and not just to please parents.

The missionary woman needs to examine the real motives behind her decision to become a missionary. If there is no true love for souls, no real desire to evangelize a lost world, then the life of a missionary may be very difficult.

Missionary Qualifications

If a school principal interviews a prospective teacher, he begins by asking for teaching credentials. An executive wants to know how fast the secretary can type. The medical board carefully reviews the records of a new doctor. Even a high school student takes aptitude tests to determine whether he is more suited to be a mechanic or a lawyer. Likewise, there are certain qualifications or characteristics that should be present in the prospective missionary. The following list is by no means all inclusive, but is suggested merely as a beginning point for self-evaluation.

1. The missionary woman should be a strong Christian. This includes a knowledge of God's word as well as a deep spirituality which includes a dedication to service and a positive reliance on prayer. There is often a mistaken idea that becoming a missionary will increase spirituality and offer more time for prayer and study. Unfortunately, this is usually not the case. If anything, problems and frustrations may make it more difficult to later grow spiritually.

2. The missionary woman should be one who is more than usually resourceful and bouyant.[1] Creativity and imagination are needed to make a home in a strange culture and to adjust to a new cultural frame of reference. Likewise, there will be disappointments and discouragements and the missionary will need to be able to resist depression and to turn failure into success.

3. The woman who has been exposed to many kinds of people at different levels of society tends to relate better to a new culture than one whose background and contacts have been limited to people of her own socio-economic background. Also, the individual who has had environmental mobility tends to adjust more rapidly to the environment of the new country.

4. The missionary woman must be educated, not necessarily academically, but rather she should have an intellectual curiousity that goes beyond that required for

---

[1] Some of these qualifications have been paraphrased from: Cleveland, Harland, Mangone, Gerald J., and Adams, John C., *The Overseas Americans.* (New York: McGraw Hill Book Company, Inc., 1960), page 171.

mere academic study. This would include an interest in people, places and ideas. Because the missionary woman usually demands of herself a particular service, it would also be wise to train for a particular mission. Education (teaching), home economics, nursing, nutrition, secretarial skills, language expertise, and anthropology are just a few areas that are of great value on the mission field.

5. The missionary woman should have a very minimum of racial prejudice. Feelings of prejudice toward any group of people will carry over in dealing with all other groups of people. Prejudice cannot be concealed and a missionary with feelings of superiority will have limited influence at best.

6. The missionary woman must have a talent for building. This includes not only building a home but being able to start classes, build congregations, and develop intimate relationships with people who speak a new language and live in a different culture.

7. The missionary woman must be healthy, both physically and mentally. In a new culture, the physical body will be beset by new germs and diseases, and mental health will be endangered by the frustrations and complications of culture shock. Even the very healthy will suffer, but poor mental or physical health will be a serious liability from the outset.

8. The missionary woman needs to be emotionally mature. She must be able to finally depend on God and herself. She cannot be emotionally tied to her mother, or her stateside life. She must be able to adapt to new social situations and to accept defeat as well as success. In addition, the single woman must be able to cope with the inevitable loneliness, and also be able to handle such matters as visas, bank transfers, household problems, etc., that she will encounter as she lives on her own.

10. As to age, the missionary woman must be young enough to learn a new language and adapt physically and mentally to a new culture, and old enough to be mature in thinking and acting.

Preparation

The importance of missionary training and preparation is just beginning to come into its own. A mere "calling" is no longer considered the only prerequisite to becoming a successful missionary. Preparation is as vital for the missionary woman as for the man, and the reader is referred to the chapter on preparation in this volume. Suffice it to say that unless the woman also receives training, the mission team will be severely handicapped.

Cultural Adjustment

It has already been suggested that the woman may have a more difficult adjustment to make to life in a new culture. This is due to the fact that her sphere of service more often involves the home and the physical living situation. It is in these areas that cultural differences are most noticeable and most frustrating.

In order to overcome the inevitable culture shock, the missionary woman needs to have an understanding of customs and culture and a command of the native tongue. She must also develop an honest appreciation of the society in which she lives, and which will include a respect for the people of the nation and a desire to incorporate into her own life as much of the culture as possible.

Cultural adjustment or empathy can be fostered by a systematic study of the culture, beginning with an understanding of one's own cultural milieu and then moving into an anthropological study of the new culture itself. The acceptance and use of new customs, as well as becoming adept in the native tongue, will aid cultural adjustment. Finally, seeking and developing new relationships with people will provide avenues through which respect and genuine love can grow.

As the missionary woman conscientiously reaches out to the new culture and to the people of that culture she will find that adjustment will follow naturally and easily.

The Missionary Wife

It might seem that a special section on the missionary wife would be unnecessary since the responsibilities of being a wife and mother should remain the same, whether abroad or at home. However, there are two additional factors which have a strong effect on the Christian missionary family and particularly the missionary wife.

First, of course, is culture itself. The woman's responsibility to create a home becomes more difficult. Not only must she make adjustments in every phase of her life from child rearing to dishwashing, but she must also find the time to study language and learn about the new culture.[2]

Second, the missionary wife will find that she must meet new role expectations. Although her responsibilities should not be any different than the Christian wife at home, she will find that there are pressures to assume new roles, many outside the home. Her husband may want her to join him in his evangelistic activities. And, if the desire to preach to a lost world is hers as well as her husband's, she may feel that she must take an active part in the teaching program. The home church may even expect more of her than they do of other Christian women.

If the new duties are those with which the missionary wife is comfortable and there are no small children to suffer from a lack of maternal guidance, then there will be no difficulty. However, if the wife is pressured to fit into positions for which she is not prepared, the results can be disastrous. Not everyone is suited to be a teacher or a social worker or a secretary.

---

[2]The reader is referred to the following volume which deals specifically with culture adjustment:

Hardin, Joyce. *Sojourners: Women With a Mission.* (Korea: Korea Consolidated Corp., 1973).

A clear definition of roles will help the new missionary wife clarify her new life and help ease the initial adjustment. A constant reviewing of roles may be necessary for they may change as children grow older or as new talents are developed. Regardless of what other responsibilities she assumes, the missionary wife must not forget that her primary duty is to build a home.

Marriage Relationship

The marriage relationship of the missionary couple is of utmost importance to the success of the mission endeavor. If the marriage relationship is weak, the problems and difficulties of mission life will create even greater divisions. Not only will the family itself be emotionally unbalanced but the struggling new church will lose the living example of what a Christian family can and should be.

Prospective missionary couples are urged to strengthen their marriage relationship by whatever means available: reading the excellent books on marriage that are now available, visiting with marriage counselors, attending marriage seminars or encounter groups, and, certainly, praying and planning together.

There are many factors involved in a successful marriage relationship but the following are suggested as being particularly pertinent to cultural adjustment:

First, the missionary couple should be able to *communicate*. In some cases, there may be no others with whom to share ideas and thoughts. Communication involves not only a discussion of problems but also a sharing of joys and hopes.

Second, the missionary couple must be able to *accept* one another, to recognize problems that may be too deep to explain and to realize and accept without threat the irritations and emotions that may develop in the new culture.

Third, the missionary couple must provide *mutual support*. Culture shock often gives a feeling of being alone, but marriage should provide at least one other person to whom an individual can turn to for support and confidence.

Fourth, the marriage relationship must be characterized by *intimacy*. This is not merely sexual contact but a relationship characterized by transparency and authenticity, which permits each partner to be open, honest, and real.

Finally, the missionary couple must pray, study, and play together. The wife must never cease to be a wife and the husband must accept his role as the head of the family, spiritually as well as physically.

Missionary Children

Wherever American missionaries are found, one also finds missionary children and the myriad of child rearing problems multiplied by life in a different environment. Since children themselves adapt easily to new situations and new languages, such problems are more parent-problems than children-problems.

If children are allowed to develop in ways that encourage communication and intercourse among peoples of different cultures, not only will they mature naturally and easily in the new culture but they will also open the doors and hearts of the local people.

However, if parents communicate their own fears and prejudices to the children or if they attempt to isolate them from the local culture, the children can become a barrier to cultural adjustment and creatures of a quasi-environment, living in the midst of a culture but not a part of it.

Parental responsibilities for child rearing are the same regardless of geographic location. The family is still the chief agent of the child's socialization process. Problems arise when parents are too busy with other activities (preaching included!) to give children the love and attention they need. When servants are available, parents may be tempted to delegate too much of their responsibility to others and forget that children also suffer from culture shock but are without the abilities to communicate their uncertainties or to understand their emotions.

Child rearing in a new culture is often complicated by cultural differences. A Korean mother does things differently than her American counterpart. The missionary mother may wonder whether she should do things the "American way or conform to local standards. The answer lies in deciding what is important and what is not. She must not endanger the health of her children but she should keep an open mind and be willing to learn from the new culture.

The dilemma of educating missionary children is a very real one and one that each family must solve for itself. Basically there are three solutions and each should be carefully reviewed before a decision is made:

First, *the children may be taught at home* by use of a correspondence course. Teachers do not need to be professional educators and the schooling is quite adequate. Obvious problems lie in keeping a definite schedule and the lack of give and take with other children.

Second, *the children may be sent to an English language school,* which is generally available in almost every country and major city of the world. Advantages of this solution include the absence of language difficulties and the similarity to a Stateside education. On the other hand, boarding children may be necessary and such schools may tend to isolate children from the real culture in which they are living.

Third, *the children may be sent to a local school.* Such a decision can help children and the entire family identify more closely with the local people. They learn to cope with many new situations and feel a part of their new country. However, local schools may be inferior in quality and the language may be a great disadvantage.

Every missionary family must evaluate its own situation and make a decision based upon its own needs. Children are definitely a part of the missionary team.

The Single Missionary Woman

The annals of missionary history chronicle the deeds, sacrifices and commitment of early single missionary women. These women were pioneers in every sense of the word.

Today, more than ever, single women are looking toward the mission field as an area of service. The amount of good they can do cannot be measured. They are needed as teachers, personal workers, secretaries, doctors, and in every field of Christian endeavor. Although they cannot preach publicly or assume church leadership, single missionary women can be a powerful influence for evangelism.

The fact that a missionary is single does not immunize her from the inevitable culture shock. She feels it just as forcibly as her married sister. It may actually be more difficult for her to overcome because she does not have a mate in whom she can confide and find support.[3]

An additional cultural problem comes as a result of the very fact of her single-ness. In many of the world's cultures there are no single women of marriageable age. Marriage is accepted as a matter of course for every woman. In the case of some Latin countries, there are only three kinds of adult women: wives, nuns and prostitutes.

The absense of a spouse may place the single woman in a sort of status limbo. The new culture may not quite know what to make of her and she may be frustrated by their attitudes and the barriers they present. She will need a very careful study of the local culture in order to determine where and how she might fit in.

The problem area that seems to affect most single missionary women the greatest is that of loneliness. This may be compounded by the cultural problems just mentioned.

---

[3]It is often suggested that single women go in pairs to offset this problem.

However, if she is willing to share her life with others, and, in turn, share theirs, she will find that she has little time to be lonely.

A special problem for the young single missionary may be in her relationship with the opposite sex. This would certainly be true if she is seeking to develop cultural empathy and be accepted by the local people. If she assumes the same freedom as she had in the States, she may find herself in embarrassing situations if local customs dictate a different behavior. Here again, a close study of the culture will help her clarify and modify her behavior in regards to dating and other relationships with the men with whom she has contact.

Another problem area faced by single missionaries involves their relationships with the missionary families. Being single places her somewhat outside the inner circle. She may be asked to assume duties such as typing, baby sitting or grading correspondence courses when she feels her ministry is personal evangelism or teaching. She may not be consulted in group decisions that involve her welfare as well as those of the families. If the single missionary woman is working with a group, it is recommended that she reach an agreement, beforehand, as to how she will fit into the group's plans and mission.

The single missionary woman must not forget that she is still a woman and her place in the work of the church is outlined in the Scriptures. Crossing oceans or borders does not give her a permit to usurp the authority given to men.

Since the single missionary woman does not have a family to care for, she has more time than her married counterpart for language and cultural study. Likewise, she has more time for evangelistic activities. Thus she has great potential for both cultural adjustment and Christian service.

Personal Adjustment and Identification

The success or failure of a missionary woman will depend largely on her ability to adjust to the local culture and become accepted by the local people. Language and cultural study will facilitate this end but in the final analysis, acceptance and adjustment is made on an individual basis and is directly related to the extent to which the individual is able to identify with the people with whom she is working.

Identification involves the totality of interhuman relationships. It is not cheap imitation or a loss of personal identity but rather the missionary becomes more of herself as she grows toward others.

Identification is possible only if one recognizes its limitations: first, that identification is made with individuals and not nations and, second, that it will be partial at best. An American can never lose her Americanism but only subdue and modify it.

The process of identification begins with a genuine regard and respect for the people with whom the missionary is working. Feelings of superiority will not produce identification. The process grows through involvement in the lives of individuals, as the missionary makes an emotional commitment to others. It includes a willingness to give as well as to receive and to learn as well as to teach.

Identification does not come automatically. The missionary must make an effort to adjust and to find her niche in the new society. This process is a very personal one and with possibilities as limitless as the missionaries themselves. Each woman is unique and will take with her into the field her own aptitudes, attitudes, talents and hobbies that will make her process of adjustment and identification equally unique. Each must develop her own strategy and plan for promoting and facilitating her own personal identification.

There are many ways in which the missionary may find and develop the interpersonal relationships from which identification evolves. The following list is suggested only as a small beginning:

1. *Community Participation.* The missionary must recognize that the new country is now her home. She must become involved whether at the village well or the large city civic center. She must be an interested participant in local affairs.

2. *Local Politics.* The missionary should be aware of local politics. This means knowledge, but not intervention. She is not in the field to create political change but certainly she should not be ignorant of what is happening, politically, in her adopted country.

2. *Local Events.* An awareness of local events will help the missionary become more a part of the new society. She should read the local newspaper, know about holidays and special events and be cognizant of important milestones in the lives of the people around her.

3. *Hobbies.* A hobby need not be left at home as the missionary packs her bags for overseas living. Not only does a hobby relieve pressures and tensions but it can also serve as a catalyst for many personal encounters with people of like interests. For best results, the hobby should be considered worthwhile by the local people. (Chess in primitive South America would probably not be as effective as a study of flower arrangement in Japan.) A hobby may develop on the field as the missionary becomes expert in local folk lore, antique pottery, music or the native religion.

4. *Use of National Products.* The use of products made on the local economy will not only foster identification but will help the missionary develop a pride in local achievements. As much as possible, food, clothing, and household furnishings should come from the host nation.

5. *Local Club Work.* Women's clubs and interest groups flourish in most cities of any size. Even primitve tribes have some sort of women's alliance. The missionary would do well to become a part of such groups. They will help her find friends with common interests, provide an outlet for service and give her countless opportunities for making contacts that could lead to new Christians.

6. *Acceptance of Local Customs.* The missionary's acceptance of local customs will help her become less foreign in her own eyes and in the eyes of the local people. Adopting local customs should be a natural outgrowth of respect and appreciation. That which may begin as a conscious imitation of something appreciated will evolve into a closer relationship with people of shared customs and ideas.

7. *Special Talents and Interests.* As each missionary looks at herself she will find new ways in which to increase relationships with local people which will develop into closer identification.

Planning and carrying out a strategy for personal identification will help result in a more enjoyable and profitable sojourn for the missionary woman. She becomes not only the bearer of "Good News" but the receiver and participant of a true learning experience which will create relationships through which Christ can be communicated.

The missionary woman has a multiple responsibility in world evangelism. As a wife and mother, she must help her family live successfully in a new culture. As a woman, she must develop her own talents and grow spiritually and mentally. And, as a Christian, she must find her own avenues of specific service and be fully committed to bringing others to Christ.

SUGGESTED READINGS

Bawcom, Louanna M. *Journey with Joy,* Winona, Miss.: J. C. Choate Publications, 1968.

Butlar, Joyce Marie. "A Study of the Role of a Single Missionary Woman Functioning as Part of a Team Working in Buenos Aires, Argentina," unpublished Master's thesis, Abilene Christian University, 1976.

Hardin, Joyce. *Sojourners: Women with a Mission.* Inchon, Korea: Korean Consolidated Co., 1973.

Tuggy, Joy Turner. *The Missionary Wife and Her Work.* Chicago: Moody Press, 1966.

Williamson, Mabel. *Have We No Rights?* Chicago: Moody Press, 1957.

PREPARATION FOR MISSIONS

by

DANIEL C. HARDIN

A question frequently asked by students who have completed their first survey of the Old Testament is: Why did God wait so long before fulfilling the promise He made to Abraham?[1] If all mankind has need of the cleansing blood of Jesus Christ, why did God not send Him to the earth 2000 years earlier? The most reasonable answer seems to be that God was waiting until the time was right[2] . . . until everything was ready. Though God is not willing that any should perish[3], He evidently recognizes that there are essential perimeters of time and preparation that cannot be casually violated.

God's dealings with man are fundamentally and thoroughly permeated with evidence of planning and preparation. Christ was destined before the foundation of the world[4] but was made manifest only when God's intricate plan was carefully unfolded during the course of history.

It is, therefore, with this understanding of God's attitude about adherence to systematic and conscious planning that the following suggestions are made. It is not the writer's intention to place a stumbling block before the anxious beginner, to suggest that all prospective missionaries need the same preparation, nor to insinuate that the reader is not already partially or fully prepared. Rather, the twofold pur-

---

[1] Gen. 12:1-3, Gal. 3:8.

[2] Gal. 4:4,5.

[3] II Peter 3:9.

[4] I Pet. 1:20.

pose of this chapter is to help the conscientious candidate by supplying guidelines to aid him in the identification of his strong and weak points and also to offer suggestions for capitalizing on the former and shoring up the latter.

SPIRITUAL DEVELOPMENT

One may be keenly aware that the fruit of the spirit is love, joy, peace, patience, kindness, goodness, faithfulness, gentleness, and self-control [5] without having any accurate knowledge of his own productivity in these areas. For example, if one has never been face to face with a hate producing situation, he may not fully comprehend his own capacity for loving. Likewise, if he has never become aware of the extremes of sorrow and strife he may not know his own potential for radiating joy and peace.

T. Stanley Soltau asserts that although the spiritual power needed on the mission field is not unlike the spiritual power needed at home, the mission field may be much more demanding due to "the absence of any of the helpful influences and spiritual 'props' which are so common and so accessible at home."[6] At first, the missionary may not be conscious of the fact that he misses the fellowship of the home town church, misses the stimulating sermons of a favorite preacher, misses the encouragement of family and friends, or even the familiarity of traditional surroundings; but, as time passes the absence of these "props" can become catastrophic.

The missionary's spiritual strength is the most significant armament he will carry with him into the mission field. It will serve as a shock absorber against the impact of frustration, mistakes, weaknesses, and, in general, the manifold darts of Satan. This spiritual strength is a reservoir that can-

---

[5] Gal. 5:22, 23.

[6] T. Stanley Soltau, *Facing the Field* (Grand Rapids, Michigan: Baker Book House, 1965), p. 124.

not only see him through times of stress but supply him with the power necessary for effective evangelism and service.

Superficial, erratic, or casual attachment to God, Christ and the Holy Spirit, will not satisfy the demands of an exacting mission field. Of course, it will not prove satisfactory at home either, but the failure will be more obvious and perhaps damaging in the context of a strange environment. Therefore the prospective missionary should pay close attention to the development of his own spirituality. There are at least three important areas that bear directly on one's spirituality and a brief look at each of these might help in evaluating and improving spiritual growth.

1. Devotion.

First, attention should be given to devotion. Cook suggests that the development of good devotional habits is essential for training in spirituality.[7]

Devotional habits would include Bible reading for communion with God (as opposed to sermon or class preparation where the aim is the development of pre-determined concepts rather than openness to the communication of God), meditation, prayer, and combinations of these kinds of activities. The harried missionary, unless he has already built up a strong devotional habit, will not likely find the time and opportunity for the development of such habits while on the field.

Perhaps the most unrealistic concept harbored by many people is the idea that once a person goes into a mission field, he. will automatically increase his spiritual activities and development. On the contrary, the absence of brethren who might encourage, the time consuming problems of living in a strange culture, and the overall pressures of foreign work can easily have a negative effect on one's spiritual development.

---

[7] Harold R. Cook, *An Introduction to the Study of Christian Missions* (Chicago: Moody Press, 1967), p. 123.

So, do not wait for the field experience, to begin developing spiritually! Start now and build up devotional habits that will help overcome the negative influences of the field.

2. Bible Training.

Second, the missionary must realize that he is likely going to a tribe or nation that already has a long history of religious activity. Their own traditional religion may contain a wealth of merit. They may have high moral values, deep faith, sacrificial giving, and a host of elements worthy of admiration and praise. They may even be worshippers of Jehovah, and who have been calling on his name for many years. Why then is a missionary needed? Obviously, he is needed only if he has something to offer which they do not yet have and, under the best of the above circumstances, the only thing they may lack is accurate truth.

Jack P. Lewis, of the Harding Graduate School of Religion, insists that the missionary needs a great deal more than, "a few scriptures and the gift of gab." He points out the need for *missionary scholars* who know Greek and Hebrew and who can, therefore, be masters of scripture as well as fund raisers and public relations experts. Certainly, the missionary should be adept in wielding the sword of the spirit. [8]

The amount of formal Bible training a prospective missionary should have will vary from individual to individual. Those engaged in Bible translation, in depth Bible instruction, or confrontation with false teaching may need a great deal more formal training than the evangelist to a receptive preliterate society where, temporarily at least, the simple gospel message is sufficient.

However, even the vocational missionary who plans to specialize in the area of his vocational training must not

---

[8]Jack P. Lewis, from a lecture delivered to the Summer Seminar in Missions at Abilene Christian University.

short-change himself in the matter of Bible study. Harold Cook points out that every doctor, nurse, teacher, typist, etc., should also be a capable evangelist.[9] There may be many great services to perform along the way but the ultimate goal of mission work is reconciling men to God through Jesus Christ[10] and every missionary should be prepared to persuade men to be reconciled.

There are many institutions which have been designed to provide students with adequate Bible training. There are non-degree programs, Bible chairs, liberal arts colleges, graduate degree programs, and special short term seminars and conferences. The prospective missionary should evaluate any program critically and try to enroll in one which provides a combination of pure doctrine and sound scholarship.

The number of months or years of study needed for a particular individual will depend on his past training and experience as well as his future plans. However, there are few, if any, experienced missionaries who complain that they are over qualified in the area of Bible knowledge. Therefore, the prospective missionary should not rush his training and preparation in this critical area. The fields may be white unto harvest and the laborers may be few, but a worker with a dull sickle is not the answer.

3. Interpersonal Relationships.

Spiritual growth, as suggested earlier, involves the production of certain types of fruit. By its nature this fruit cannot be produced except within the context of one's relationship with his fellow beings. Love for God cannot be genuine unless it is manifested in love for a brother.[11] Joy

---

[9] Harold R. Cook, *op. cit.,* p. 125.

[10] II Cor. 5:18.

[11] I John 4:20.

cannot be complete unless our fellowship with others is perfected,[12] peace must prevail between brethren,[13] and patience must be shown to all.[14] The "fruit of the Spirit" scripture is concluded with these words, "If we live by the Spirit, let us also walk by the Spirit. Let us have no self-conceit, no provoking of one another, no envy of one another."[15]

Harold Cook writes that dissensions between missionaries cause most of the breakdowns in missionary ranks.[16] Add to this the breakdowns in communication and fellowship between missionaries and local persons and these will likely account for the remainder of whatever problems may exist. The argument between two siblings, a divorce between a husband and wife, or the wars between tribes or nations all reflect the difficulty man has in getting along with his fellow men.

Selflessness and consideration for others is central to Christianity and these virtues are especially important to successful mission work. Missionaries are not only human beings but they are humans who have voluntarily placed themselves under tremendous pressures. Culture shock, language shock, fatigue, and disappointment are but a few of the weights that plague the typical missionary. Far from home and the familiar cultural cues that generally offer him some support, the foreign missionary must rely almost entirely on his own spiritual reservoir. And though that reservoir is unlimited through participation in the Holy Spirit the missionary who has not exercised himself in drawing upon this source may stumble and fall when the real tests come.

---

[12] I John 1:3.

[13] II Cor. 13:11, I. Thess. 5:13.

[14] I Thess. 5:14.

[15] Gal. 5:25,26.

[16] Harold R. Cook, *Missionary Life and Work* (Chicago: Moody Press, 1968). p. 117.

Intimate involvement with others is perhaps the most spontaneous and natural means of developing a personality that is Christlike in its relationship to others. One's experiences with others can, at least, provide data as to his ability to develop satisfactory in-depth inter-personal relationships, provided he can be both objective and perceptive as he analyses himself.

Beyond this there is a wealth of helpful information in any number of well written books.[17] Even more dynamic in impact would be participation in some form of group-dynamics experience under the guidance of a qualified Christian group leader. Study and experience in this area can not only increase one's sensitivity to others but also reveal one's own personal barriers which mitigate against satisfactory relationships with others.

Perhaps the greatest value of a study into interpersonal relationships is the insight gained about oneself. Such self study might help the prospective missionary in numerous ways. For example, if he determines that he is especially resourceful and self reliant with a talent for inspiring others to follow his lead, then he may look to a pioneer field where there are few structured programs, little supervision, and a need for effective leadership. On the other hand, if the prospective missionary finds himself to be an excellent follower, group oriented, and generally more comfortable when there are others around to help make major decisions, then he might be wise to seek a mission field where a good program has already been initiated and there is adequate supervision and direction.

This is just one example of a multitude of personal factors that can mean a great deal to the missionary. Does the work he visualizes demand more time than his family responsibilities will allow? Are there more responsibilities than he feels capable of assuming? Is there more or less freedom than his own personality needs? These and similar questions must

---

[17] See the "Interpersonal Relationships" section of the bibliography at the end of this chapter.

be asked and then forthrightly answered. Then the prospective missionary can point himself toward a ministry that more nearly meets the demands of his own unique personality, through prayer and study modify his personality to take up any slack that might remain, and enter the work with his own feet solidly planted and thus be in a position to interact successfully with others.

The prospective missionary who maintains an exemplary devotional life, is a true Bible scholar, and behaves with maturity and selflessness toward his fellow men, may not avoid all the dangers inherent in mission work but he certainly has a great deal working in his favor. Such an individual has obviously worked diligently to prepare himself and will likely be adding to that preparation daily.

INTELLECTUAL DEVELOPMENT

It may be impossible to truly separate spiritual development from intellectual development because each may contribute significantly to the other. However, at least analytically, a distinction is not only possible but essential for systematic study and evaluation. The following intellectual pursuits may influence spirituality but they are also ends in themselves which may prove invaluable to the missionary.

1. Training Programs.

The word "mission" comes from the Latin word *missio* and simply means *to send*. However, the full scope of the implications of "mission" is much more complex than this redundant definition might indicate. Why? When? Where? How should one be sent? These are the questions that every missionary in every age must ponder and attempt to answer. And woe to the missionary who takes it for granted that he knows the answers and never applies himself to a systematic search for the truth.

There is nothing more discouraging than to realize after many years of missionary labor that much of that labor was in vain due to distorted or erroneous ideas of the nature of "mission." And if, perhaps, there are irreconcilable differences of opinion concerning what constitutes true mission work, the individual missionary should at least be aware of the different ideas and thus in a better position to accurately determine his own views.

Perhaps, all too soon, this look into proper preparation will now meet with some challenges that may seem virtually insurmountable. This is due to the fact that a thorough understanding of mission will involve a lifetime of study and participation. There seems to be no honest way of telling the prospective missionary that he can first thoroughly prepare himself and then go into a mission field fully equipped.

The best preparation seems to be a combination of study and personal experience. Reading books and studying courses is good but after spending a few months or years on a mission field missionaries who re-read the books and re-examine the courses find that they really had not grasped all the implications until faced with the real situation. Does this mean that experience should precede study? God forbid! The prospective missionary should study as much as he can before going but he must realize that he cannot fully understand all that there is to know just by engaging in either formal or informal study.

Perhaps a realistic approach to this lifetime of preparation would involve the necessary formal study interspersed with any number of simulated and actual field experiences. Such a program could include (a) informal reading and study, (b) formal study (undergraduate level), (3) local experiences in personal evangelism, (d) seminars or summer study programs where field experiences are simulated, (e) an apprenticeship on a mission field, (f) additional formal study (graduate level), (g) and finally on the field training followed by full participation in a missionary enterprise.

Circumstances, personal needs, or any number of factors might mitigate against this exact sequence but, in general, it provides for that balance between theory and practice that can make both of these much more meaningful. Whatever plan one may choose to follow, remember that it must be a continuing process and that each step should be allowed to exert its influence upon performance and thinking whether it supports or calls for modification.

(a) Initial informal study might include a program of reading drawn from a wealth of material on the subject of mission. Most teachers of mission will be happy to supply book lists upon request or note can be made of the selected reading list that forms a part of the bibliography at the end of this chapter. However, at best, the reading of books on mission work will do little more than whet the appetite, provide an introduction to the many facets of mission study, and pave the way for more serious involvement. The serious student of mission will want to dig more deeply into the subject under the guidance of qualified teachers and this, of course, leads to formal study.

(b) Formal study is available to the prospective missionary through the course offerings of numerous schools and colleges. Glenn Schwartz has edited a directory containing mission course information on some 134 schools and colleges in the United States and Puerto Rico.[18] Two hundred and ninety-seven schools and colleges are listed in the 10th edition of the *Mission Handbook*, Edward Dayton, editor.[19]

Course work affords a great deal more to the student than he can usually gain by reading alone. Most teachers of mission courses have been missionaries and they can bring valuable personal experiences to their classes. In bringing these experiences to the student, the teacher not only has good illustrative material but also becomes a living bridge between the idea and the reality of mission work. But even an intimate association with good literature and successful

---

[18] Glenn Schwartz (ed.), *An American Directory of Schools and Colleges Offering Missionary Courses* (South Pasadena, California: William Carey Library, 1973), 221 pages.

[19] Edward R. Dayton (ed.), *Mission Handbook: North American Protestant Ministries Overseas* (Monrovia, California: MARC, 1973), pp. 603ff.

missionaries who have actually been there cannot replace first hand experience. Thus the next step is to begin getting that experience even while engaged in formal or informal study.

(c) Local experiences in personal evangelism can compliment one's academic approach and give valuable experience in leading others to Christ. Whether personal evangelism is a part of a school's curriculum, sponsored by a local church, initiated by some student group, or a purely personal project, it involves real contact with real people and duplicates many of the elements that will be found in foreign evangelism. However, in spite of its value in preparation of the prospective evangelist it is usually a domestic intra-cultural experience and lacks the cross cultural elements found in a foreign field.

(d) Special seminars or summer study programs are held by various agencies for the purpose of providing simulated or actual cross-cultural experiences. It may be that in these type programs the prospective missionary will make his first real contact with his own ethnocentricism and will experience the trauma of that discovery.

This initial self discovery does not come automatically upon contact with alien cultures but through a combination of contact and study. The literature can tell him that he views others through his own cultural bias but he cannot really understand the implications of this fact until he has had the experience. On the other hand, he can have the experience but never realize his bias unless someone reveals it to him.

In the contrived experience programs, every effort is made to stimulate ethnocentric behavior, challenge it, and then subject it to thorough analysis. Though the end result is usually deeply satisfying, the process itself can be rather startling.

Such experiences are very enlightening and extremely helpful but they are, by nature, short term experiments that "just touch the hem of the garment." Such programs play an important role in missionary training but they do not produce instant experts.

(e) Apprenticeship programs are being used by many schools and churches to give prospective missionaries "on-the-field experience" under the supervision of trained personnel. The apprentice missionary is a missionary in the full sense of the term. He may study language and culture and function under the constraints imposed on any new missionary but he generally has his share of the work to do and is considered by his fellow workers as a full fledged member of the mission team.

The apprentice has the advantage of supervision during his initial period on the field plus the freedom to change his mind about staying in that field or even about becoming a full time missionary. The apprentice can return home after his year or two and decide that he can serve better in another ministry without the stigma of failure. However, the retention rate of apprentice missionaries is very high and most of them go on to become full time career missionaries.

(f) Advanced study is frequently sought by the missionary on furlough and this later formal study can be one of the missionary's most rewarding study experiences. Against the background of a few years experience and maturity the classroom study can be especially meaningful.

2. General Areas of Study for All Missionaries.

Each training program (the informal study of books, or formal study in a school) will involve a certain selection of subjects determined by the ones who formulate the reading list or organize the curriculum. However, instead of blindly accepting whatever is available for consumption, the student would be well advised to select courses carefully. All courses have some value but there are areas that are so critical that they demand attention. It is this writer's opinion that a good introductory course a course on the Biblical basis for mission, cultural anthropology and linguistics rank very high on the priority list.

(a) An introduction to mission or principles and practices course is a *must* for all prospective missionaries. Such courses touch on many important areas and tend to alert the beginner to the total scope of responsibilities, liabilities, and possibilities inherent in mission work. Most courses of this type attempt to impress upon the student the seriousness of the missionary endeavor. He is brought face to face with many of the unique problems associated with cross cultural evangelism and then introduced to the tools that can help overcome those problems and lead to a successful ministry. Such tools might include (a) Biblical principles of world evangelism, (b) practical approaches that have succeeded in the theories past, (c) theories and models based upon experience and research, and (d) critiques of actual field situations.

As the name indicates, the introductory course is not an end in itself, even though it may be one of the most significant courses a missionary can study. If carefully designed, this course will be far more than a series of how-to-do-it lectures. It will honestly explore the limitations of methodologies as well as their merits, indicate the weaknesses as well as the strengths of each strategy, and, in a very forth-right manner, dispel the illusion that mission work is all fun and games.

The properly motivated student should complete the introductory course with a thirst for more knowledge and more information in a number of different areas. Then he is in a position to press on more enthusiastically into the following courses:

(b) The Biblical basis for mission (or theology of mission) is a course that should be designed to focus the prospective missionary's attention on the concept of mission as it is revealed in God's word. Such a course forces the student to come face to face with his own personal motive for wanting to do mission work, with the strengths or weak-nesses of his own predetermined concepts concerning the place of mission in God's plan for man, and with new insights that can add measurably to his own spiritual growth.

Very closely associated with the study of mission theology is the study of mission philosophy. Not all missionaries nor all sponsoring churches agree as to the real meaning of mission. Some include all Christian activity under the umbrella of mission while others define it somewhat more narrowly as the purposeful persuasion of men to become reconciled to God through Christ.

Currently, one of the most significant contributions to mission practice is the philosophy or theory of *church growth.*[20]   Church growth has become one of the most dynamic forces to influence mission work in the last fifty years. Courses are being taught in many schools and the prospective missionary would be well advised to keep himself abreast of this important influence.

(c) Cultural anthropology is regarded as an essential area of study by most mission teachers, missionary sending societies, and successful missionaries. Just as the apostle Paul was keenly aware of significant elements within the culture of the people he was trying to teach[21] and did his best to identify with the different people of his world,[22] today's missionary also ought to take advantage of every means of gaining insights into the cultures of the present world so that he, too, can become all things to all men. In light of this demand the prospective missionary should take advantage of the vast store of scholarly material that is being compiled by anthropologists.

It will be obvious to anyone who is aware of the complexity and depth of anthropological study that one or two courses cannot exhaust the field or make one an expert. However, one or two basic courses can alert the student to the nature of culture, train him to know what to observe when he visits another culture, introduce him to especially

---

[20] See Donald McGavran, *How Churches Grow* (New York: Friendship Press, 1957), 188 pages.

[21] Titus 1:12, 13 and Acts 17:28.

[22] I Cor. 9:19-23.

critical human behavior, and sensitize him to important human relationships.[23] Cuthbert suggests that four requisites of a basic course in anthropology should include (1) the basic principles of anthropology, (2) simulated practice of these principles through books, films, and discussion, (3) a close examination of one's own culture, and (4) a clear understanding that completion of the course does not indicate that the student knows all about culture and people.[24]

Obviously, even a good course in cultural anthropology will not make one a professional anthropologist but the insights gained through such a course can alert the conscientious missionary to the importance of recognizing and intelligently responding to cultural differences. There are numerous anthropology courses which can be valuable for missionaries but at least one basic course is absolutely essential. Later on, to meet special needs, other courses can be added, i. e., Cross Cultural Communications, Anthropology and Mission, Christian Ethnotheology, Urban Anthropology, etc.

(d) Linguistics is the name given to the specific, disciplined, and informed study of the structure and functioning of human language.[25] Though it may not be necessary for the prospective missionary to become a linguist, an introduction to this approach to language learning can be a valuable aid to anyone who finds it necessary to learn a second language. The linguistic approach to language learning is important because it avoids some of the weakness[26] of the traditional approach and, at the same time, provides the learner with insights that render new languages less threatening and mysterious.

---

[23] M. Cuthbert, "Anthropology in Mission Training," *Practical Anthropology*, Vol. 12 (March, April, 1965), p. 120.

[24] *Ibid.*, pp. 120, 121.

[25] H. A. Gleason, Jr., "Linguistics in the Service of the Church," *Practical Anthropology*, Vol. 9, No. 5 (Sept.-Oct., 1962), p. 205.

[26] Traditional language courses involve the translation of a limited vocabulary, the conjugation of verbs, and similar exercises which contribute to one's knowledge about a given language but which do not necessarily contribute to rapid nor natural mastery of that language.

It is alarming to see missionaries, who have been working with people of a given nation for many years, who still know how to say little more than, "Hello," "Good by," and "Thank you," in the language of those people. The local population may use some English or the missionary may use interpreters but these are, at best, makeshift means of communication that severely handicap the preaching of the gospel.

One reason that many tongue-tied missionaries are in evidence centers around the American's resistance to language learning. There are exceptions but generally the American missionary (who speaks only one language and who has not had special training) is rather inept at learning another language. The reason does not likely involve any intellectual weakness but, rather, the typical American's unfamiliarity with languages and language learning.

Some years ago in Seoul, Korea, a very capable language teacher was trying to get his American students to develop a "feel" for the Korean phrases they were studying by accompanying their speech utterances with a very slight but significant bow. This body gesture was used to help the students articulate the proper intonation of the phrases. When used, the result was almost automatic and the intonation problem virtually eliminated. However, most of the students were embarrassed about speaking in a foreign language in the first place and doubly embarrassed at the thought of bowing while speaking. Thus, the exercise deteriorated into a giggling, snickering fiasco, much to the consternation of the puzzled teacher.

The reaction of this group was very similar to the reaction of a Korean farmer to his first automobile ride. He was a very intelligent and capable person, but he knew almost nothing about modern machinery. When it came time for him to leave the automobile he had no idea how to open the door. The driver told him exactly what to do but in his confusion and embarrassment he either pulled the right lever the wrong way or the wrong lever the right way.

Even the most sophisticated of us sometimes have difficulty with new car doors but due to our familiarity with automobiles and gadgets, in general, we usually get the door open with one or two false starts and no embarrassment whatsoever. In much the same manner the European or Oriental who already speaks two or more languages seems to be less ill at ease when studying another language.

A good introduction to linguistics can help a prospective missionary become familiar with the organs of articulation, the range of sounds the human voice can make, and how these sounds are organized to produce meaningful utterances. Once this foundation is laid, language study becomes nothing more than the mastery of a tool. No longer must the language student, like the farmer in the automobile, grope in embarrassed frustration for the unknown. Like the product of the modern technological age who has no trouble getting out of a strange automobile, the prepared language student can study with confidence any new language.

A course in linguistics will also help the prospective missionary avoid other problems associated with language study. Some people take language study too lightly while others consider it an impossible task. The former naively consider a foreign language something they will "get" after a few months of casual study while the latter give up before they ever start. The truth is that mastery of a second language requires a high degree of motivation and intensive study, but it can be accomplished by anyone who is willing to exercise self-discipline.

There are many factors that contribute to one's ability to learn a foreign language. Some serious students may make surprising progress while others seem to have to try harder and work longer. However, for all it is a serious business and there are no real shortcuts that bypass concentration and study. Language may well be the missionary's most difficult challenge. However, as Gleason points out, when they fail, as many do, they are deprived of their own opportunity to serve, their sponsoring church does not get its money's worth, and the mission field gets stones instead of bread.[28] Language study is a must for most missionaries and an introduction in linguistics can be the prospective missionary's greatest asset.

3. Specific Areas of Study for Individual Missionaries.

To this point the suggested preparation has been virtually the same for all missionaries; however, from this point on each prospective missionary should use discretion and select areas of study that bear most directly on the type mission work he expects to do.

(a) Bookkeeping and Administration: All too frequently the missionary finds that a significant portion of his time is taken up with administrative duties including bookkeeping. A little knowledge in these fields can be very helpful.

(b) Para-medical and Survival Training: Since many missionaries are going into technically primitive areas of the world, it can be very helpful for them to have training which gives them confidence as they leave civilization and rely more and more upon God and themselves.

(c) Area Studies: Before arrival on any given field the missionary should know as much about that field as possible. MARC's *Unreached People*,[29] numerous *Country Profiles*,[30] as well as an abundance of anthropological studies[31] represent a portion of the material of this nature that is currently available.

---

[28] H. A. Gleason, *op. cit.,* p. 207.

[29] MARC *Unreached Peoples* (Monrovia, California: MARC, 1974), 117 pp.

[30] Contact: MARC Publications, 919 N. Huntington Drive, Monrovia, California.

[31] George and Louise Spindler (eds.), *Case Studies in Cultural Anthropology,* Stanford University.

(d) Historical Studies: There are historical accounts of almost all past missionary programs. Some have become widely accepted[32] while others hold meaning only for members of a single religious group. These histories may be as old as Ezekiel who was sent to Judah among the Babylonians or as new as any one of the hundreds of mission reports that come from the mission fields today.

Such studies often include an emphasis on missionary biography and it is not unusual to find foreign workers who made their decision to go into foreign evangelism shortly after reading some inspirational biography. Such stories can be very inspirational but they can also be very practical as they relate real experiences and how they were handled by real people.

(e) Leadership Training: One of the newer areas of formal study involves concern for the training of converts on the mission field. Much of the institutional work which has been done over the past few decades has been the result of a desire to train local workers. Preacher or leadership training schools have been very popular as means to this end but, today, another option is gaining in popularity. This is "leadership training by extension" where the emphasis is on taking the training to the student rather than bringing him to a formal school setting.

Obviously one could continue to list specific courses indefinitely. College catalogues are filled with numerous mission courses and new ones are appearing every day. However these should be enough to give the prospective missionary a feel for the vast array of courses that are available to the interested student.

---

[32] Kenneth S. Latourette, *The Nineteenth Century in Europe* (New York: Harper and Brothers, Pub., 1958), 498 pages.

SUGGESTED READINGS

(*Indicates selected bibliography as an introduction to mission)

*Allen, Roland. *Missionary Methods: St. Paul's or Ours?* Grand Rapids: William B. Eerdmans, 1969.

*Cook, Harold R. *An Introduction to the Study of Christian Mission.* Chicago: Moody Press, 1967.

Cuthbert, M. "Anthropology in Mission Training." *Practical Anthropology.* Vol. 12 (March, April, 1965).

Dayton, Edward R. (ed.). *Mission Handbook: North American Protestant Missionaries Overseas.* Monrovia, California: MARC, 1973.

Gleason, H. A., Jr. "Linguistics in the Service of the Church." *Practical Anthropology.* Vol. 9, No. 5 (September, October, 1962).

*Hodges, Melvin L. *The Indigenous Church.* Springfield, Mo.: Gospel Publishing House, 1971.

Kane, J. Herbert. *Missionary Candidates: How to Breed the Best.* Monrovia, California: MARC, 1961.

Latourette, Kenneth S. *The Nineteenth Century in Europe.* New York: Harper and Brothers Pub., 1958.

Lewis, Jack P. "Shall I Speak Falsely For God." Mimeographed speech delivered to the Summer Seminar, Abilene Christian College, Abilene, Texas, no date.

*Lindsell, Harold. *Missionary Principles and Practices.* New Jersey: Fleming H. Revell Co., 1955.

*McGavran, Donald. *How Churches Grow.* New York: Friendship Press, 1957.

Soltau, T. Stanley. *Facing the Field.* Grand Rapids, Michigan: Baker Book House, 1965.

Schwartz, Glenn (ed.). *An American Directory of Schools and Colleges Offering Mission Courses.* Pasadena, California: William Carey Library, 1973.

Unreached Peoples. Monrovia, California: MARC, 1974.

Interpersonal Relationship Section

Back, Kurt W. *Beyond Words: The Story of Sensitivity Training and the Encounter Movement.* New York: Russell Sage Foundation, 1972.

Bradford, et. al. *T-Group Theory and Laboratory Method.* New York: John Wiley and Sons, Inc., 1964.

Coulson, William B. *Groups, Gimmicks, and Instant Gurus: An Examination of Encounter Groups and Their Distortion.* New York: Harper and Row, Pub., 1972.

Goldburg, Carl. *Encounter: Group Sensitivity Training Experience.* New York: Science House Inc., 1970.

Rogers, Carl R. *Carl Rogers on Encounter Groups.* New York: Harper and Row, Pub., 1970.

Smith, Peter B. (ed.). *Group Processes.* Baltimore: Penguin Books Inc., 1970.

THE HOME CHURCH AND MISSIONS

Bob Douglas

The church of Jesus Christ has existed in the world for nearly 2,000 years. Its existence was the immediate outgrowth of the death, burial and resurrection of Christ in fulfillment of Old Testament prophecy. As Christ ascended to heaven, He charged His followers with the responsibility of continuing His mission, and thus of carrying God's eternal scheme to its ultimate conclusion. They were to do this by proclaiming the gospel throughout the world in such a way as to teach men of every tribe, tongue and nation.[1] In view of this, "Missions is Christianity in earnest."[2]

From the first century till now, churches have been faced with the responsibility of deciding the exact nature of the church's role in the world and with outlining the priorities necessary for fulfilling Jesus' expectations. Every congregation must arrange the following priorities in some scale of descending importance: self-perpetuation, individual edification, social service, and outreach—both local and world-wide.

According to the New Testament, the church finds its true identity as the people of God who serve as an extension of Jesus Christ, and are therefore called His body, having as their primary responsibility the preaching of the gospel.[3] The local congregation is the chief functioning unit in carrying out God's purpose. Missions start in the local church. Without congregations there would be no missions. The local church is the womb in which the missionary instinct ought to be created. It is the source of supply for recruits and

---

[1] Matthew 28:18-20; Acts 1:8.

[2] Brown, Wm. A. *The Why and How of Missions in the Sunday School.* (New York, Fleming H. Revell Co., 1916). p. 10.

[3] I Peter 2:4-9; Ephesians 3:10.

resources. A steady stream of missionaries flowing to the field is possible only where congregations are faithfully discharging their duties. The congregation, with its variety of talents, abilities, opportunities and vision, plays a role of tremendous importance as the home church, giving the missionary on the field a sense of physical and spiritual well-being. Its role cannot be minimized.

There is no room for chance or haphazard activity if Christ's mission is to be successful. For a church to be an effective home church, there must be considerable planning, proper organization, and thorough education of every member of the congregation in terms of the nature of mission, and the task of the home church. Only with effective preparation can an effective job be done. "Fundamentally, however, the study of Missions, . . . is a new discipline which has assumed independent existence in this century only."[4]

Even this is an exaggeration. More to the point, both in terms of college courses and congregation awareness, is the following statement. ". . . up to 1950 the study of Mission had been admitted, not to the temple . . . itself, but only to what may not inappropriately be described as the Court of the Gentiles."[5]

For a productive approach to the problem of world missions to be made by the home church, an attempt will have to be made to deal with such matters as the theology and philosophy of missions, mission methods both past and present, questions of selecting an appropriate field, choosing a qualified man to serve as a missionary, developing a practical system of support, and creating realistic oversight and communication. Permeating all of these there will have to be a fraternal atmosphere that will lead both the home

---

[4]Myklebust, O. G. *The Study of Missions in Theological Education.* (Oslo: Forlagel Land og Kirke. 1957). p. 286.

[5]*Ibid.*, p. 287.

church and the missionary to realize that a deep tie of brotherly love exists between them. For a congregation to fulfill its role as a home church, proper organization (keeping in mind its size and potentialities) and thorough education of the membership must be carried out. These two, namely organization and education, are mutually dependent. One fails without the other. For a congregation to have the proper organizational structure to function as a home church, while lacking an awareness of the need of continuing education and dissemination of information, is bound to fail.

No information, no inspiration! Without a doubt, the greatest barrier to the missionary propaganda of the church is lack of information. If there could be placed before the churches today a living demonstration of the methods, value, and benefits of missionary work in foreign lands, there would be no shortage of money nor of volunteers with which to carry it on. The churches that know most about missions are the churches that do the most—the chief reason, doubtless, for the lack of interest in missions, is that the membership of the church were not, in their youth, given a missionary vision."[6]

THE MISSIONS COMMITTEE

Churches which are successful in building and maintaining strong missions programs have inevitably given special attention to the matter of a missions committee. The missions committee is the hub of local coordination and direction. Where the missions committee is non-existent or half-hearted in carrying out its duties, missions is largely non-existent or half-hearted.

Every missions committee needs its members to be appointed for long terms. Behind such a statement is the assumption that a missions committee (certainly its chairman) ought to develop real missiological expertise. Such requires interest, time and commitment to study so as to be

---

[6]Brown, W. A., *op. cit.*, p. 5.

missiologically well informed. A number of excellent books, periodicals and articles are available as well as college courses, seminars and workshops. In view of the time invested educating a missions committee it would be ruinous to appoint the entire committee for only a short term of service.

One of the chief responsibilities of the mission committee is missions *policy*. Such policy would deal with a variety of issues. Examples are, missions goals, selection of missionaries, support levels, involvement with national workers and churches, support levels, involvement with national workers and churches, allocation of time, funds and personal missions education within the local church, policies of oversight, etc.

All these matters need to be well thought through on the basis of sound missions insights. They must be tailor-made to the local church scene. Ultimately they must be committed into writing, to insure continuity from year to year. They should be regularly reviewed and evaluated in the light of changing circumstances and adjusted.

SELECTION

The whole issues of who exercises the initiative in missions must be worked out. Initially God acted in sending His Son. The Son acted in selecting disciples and in endowing them with His Spirit. Today in the local church context initiative is usually left solely with prospective missionaries. That is, for whatever reasons, they decide to go, often with little encouragement from friends and church community. They seek out a supporting church, propose a specific work, secure cooperation and support, and set their own style.

There is no denying that God has initiated in these cases, as He has prompted this concern for going. His word has touched the heart of goers. But on the human level, should basic initiative be left with the individual? We think not. Local church leadership has a call to also exercise initiative. Leaders ought to be promoting missions within the local congregation. Such requires the creation of a whole congrega-tional-atmosphere. Leaders must actually lead the way in world wide awareness, concern and commitment to the lost.

Specific regular emphasis on missions must be part of the educative process in the congregation. Elders and preachers need to be actively tapping godly people on the shoulder to discuss missionary duty. For too long, the local church has stood back waiting for someone to woo her into cross cultural involvement, when she ought to have been doing the initiating.

The process of congregational initiative directed at recruiting from its own membership ought also to be emphasized.

As a local church thinks about missions it must take a long hard look at potential missionaries within its midst. Missionaries are both born and made. The process of making requires special skills. Young men and women need exposure to the whole mission enterprise in such a way as to offer them the option of roles—short term workers, career missionaries, at home Christians, living a lifestyle which involves commitment to missions morally and financially.

Preachers and elders are responsible for seeing that a climate is created where missions becomes a viable option with an adequate data base for a solid informed response. A great deal of teaching and counseling is necessary in such a process. Elders need to realize the mighty role college students have played in earlier missionary movements. Awareness needs to issue in encouragement of young adults to consider choosing missions. The place and contribution of vocational missionaries and retirees needs to be fully explored. Options of these kinds require publicity and healthy positive encouragement. Local church leadership must take the lead in recruiting from within the flock they shepherd. To leave such solely to returning missionaries, Christian colleges, or just to chance, ought to be unthinkable.

Likewise, a congregation ought to be willing to recruit missionaries from elsewhere, but never at the expense of bypassing local talent. Local leadership should likewise seize initiative in field selection. Again, such usually goes by default to the aspiring missionary who may be making his selection on woefully inadequate grounds. For a missions committee to act in these ways will require time, study, prayer and real courage. And yet is anything less real stewardship of God's resources, people and opportunities?

Selection of prospective missionaries demands the development of criteria for evaluating one's missionary aptitude. Useful procedures have been worked out using a variety of different important considerations. Direction in this area is available to concerned mission committees.

MISSIONS SUPPORT

Since missions is not an option for the Lord's church, and since going requires sending, missions support is a basic part of local church life. For a congregation to continuously focus its primary attention on itself is unbiblical. For it to consume the larger portion of its budget on itself year after year is also unbiblical. Money plays a vital role in missions today. One of the things diligent leadership will seek to do is raise the percentage of the local budget going into missions. The New Testament offers no magical figure. However, a poll of churches indicated they felt at least fifty per cent of the church budget ought to go into missions.

The amount allocated to missions is a partial reflection of a congregation's priorities, goals and self-understanding. Close to the heart of God is the task of reaching those who have never heard of Christ. Basic to budgetary increases for missions is a well thought out theology and philosophy of missions. A corollary of selfless giving to missions is selfless living—the adoption of a lifestyle that reflects Biblical priorities.

Missions money is usually included as a regular item in an annual budget. Some congregations have adopted a faith-promise approach to the missions budget. In the majority of cases the dollar amount received by missions went up substantially, without in any way cutting into local needs. Churches would do well to thoroughly explore "faith-promise" to determine if it could add a new dimension to their life. A variety of materials are available outlining faith-promise as adopted and adapted by a number of local churches.

MORAL AND SPIRITUAL SUPPORT

A local congregation's involvement with its missionaries must never be limited to an occasional check. Provisions need to be written into the missions policy covering the following areas.

1) Time together before the field is entered. A missionary family needs the opportunity of spending time with the local church. This is in a large measure solved if the missionary is recruited from the congregation's membership. Such however, is not often the case. Time with the home church ought to be of such duration and so structured as to allow missionary and supporters to come to know each other and feel a real sense of moral and spiritual accountability to each other before the Lord.

2) Prayer support. The best laid plans coupled with the finest financial arrangements are a travesty without God's blessing. Money alone won't solve many of the problems missionaries face on the field. Tensions within themselves, within their families and with fellow workers inevitably arise. Many things are needed for successful resolution of these with regular, specific personal prayer support being a major ingredient. Careful provisions need to be made for daily prayer for every missionary and each member of his family.

3) Communication. Keeping in touch with those sent out, especially after they have been away for a while, is a real challenge. Few things tax practical Christian concern more! Missionaries ought to be expected to regularly communicate with the home church. Business correspondence about field problems addressed to the mission committee must be supplemented by some sort of structure for getting a monthly communication into every household within the supporting churches. Within the congregation there must be a regular information flow concerning those supported. Like-wise, a structure providing a steady flow of notes, cards and letters (which do not expect specific answers) going to the field must be arranged and faithfully maintained. Where congregation and missionary are strangers to each other such an information flow is almost impossible.

4) Visit the work. Responsible oversight involves more than long distance involvement. Long distance involvement usually amounts to no real "involvement." The mission committee should arrange for regular annual visits by one or more members to the field. Such will be a great morale booster to the missionary while allowing first hand consultation and direct re-injection of enthusiasm in the home church. While the cost in terms of time and money can be considerable, responsible stewardship and oversight demands it.

5) Furlough. Missions policy needs to come to grips with the matter of the missionary's furlough. Different sponsoring churches have widely differing views regarding purpose, frequency, and length of furlough. Great care must be taken before a missionary ever goes to the field to work these matters out. Even then flexibility in view of developing needs must be granted. Where a furlough is for a rather extended stay specific provisions, including finances, ought to be made so the missionary can study somewhere to further sharpen his capabilities.

6) Re-entry. When a missionary comes back to America to stay some sort of provision needs to be arranged in advance to aid him in his re-entry process. He and his family will have changed as will his home church and his home land. The shock of re-entry will be as severe as the shock of coping with a different culture was on going to the field. Time, love and patience in abundance may be necessary. Some sort of special financial provisions are in order to facilitate setting up shop American style once again.

7) Training. A congregation ought to feel a real sense of obligation to assist its prospective missionaries get the best pre-field training available. Many opportunities for such now exist. The effectiveness of one's missionaries will be greatly enhanced through study. In today's complex world zeal alone is not enough. Even a basic Bible knowledge is less than effective where one is not prepared for communicating that knowledge cross-culturally. Where a home church does not insist on (and thus pay for) some pre-field training, it may be insuring failure and in turn its own demoralization.

8) Send Off. God always made a "big thing" of the new beginnings by his people. Local churches need to do the same with regard to a missionary's departure. Special services of mutual commitment ought to occur. Specific days of prayer and celebration are appropriate. Too often a missionary is simply allowed to leave and in the process is left empty and unfulfilled. The impact on the local church can also be profound. It can serve as a historic event to be regularly remembered, allowing for re-commitment.

MISSION EDUCATION

The second major area which the home church must consider is its responsibility for educating its own membership. Education for missions must be church-wide, and thus reach every member of every family. This is so because Christian mission is essential for everyone.

> . . . If there is no hope for our world comparable to the hope that lies in missions, if there is no cause that promises greater good for humankind than the missionary movement, if there is no fellowship with possibilities for peace and brotherhood and good will among men like that of the world-wide church, can there remain any doubt in our minds as to the imperative demand upon us to set up in every congregation the most effective program of missionary education which it is possible for us to devise?"[7]

When we talk of mission education, what are we discussing? An oft repeated definition is:

> the sum of all our efforts to cultivate in children, young people, and adults a Christlike concern for people of every class, race, and nation; an intimate knowledge of how the Christian fellowship is being extended both at home and abroad; and a hearty participation in all endeavors to enlarge this fellowship of Christian faith and brotherhood until it covers the earth.[8]

---

[7]Harner, Nevin C., and Baker, David D., *Missionary Education in Your Church.* (New York: Missionary Education Movement of U. S. and Canada, 1942), p. 16.

[8]Ranck, J. Allan, *Education For Mission.* (New York: Friendship Press, 1961), pp. 48-49.

Put another way, mission education aims at discovering 1) the missionary character of the Bible; 2) the missionary nature of Christianity; 3) that the missionary element is essential to Christian living; and 4) that mission effort is the highest form of Christian service. When Christianity ceases to be missionary, it ceases to be Christian.

> How then is education for mission to be related to the total task of Christian education? How is it to be kept from fencing itself off as a separate activity? If education for mission were distinct and separate, could it then be added or detached at will? . . . To ask these questions is to imply their answers. Christian education and education for mission are not two competing or conflicting interests. Education for mission is one element in the total spectrum of Christian education, and in the total life of the church, lifted up so that it may receive proper attention.[9]

Mission education should encompass two general areas. 1) There is the need for educating the congregation as to the role the church is to play in God's plan for history as well as educating it in terms of mission philosophy, methods, and the history of missions. 2) The home church must also be fully informed regarding the specific works in which it is involved both as to place, personnel, extent of involvement, reasons for involvement in these particular areas, results, problems and opportunities.

A number of avenues are available for accomplishing this work of educating the home church. These will be considered under four headings—the pulpit, the Bible school program, general publicity, and direct involvement. In general, we may say there should be a blending of the specific with the general in mission education. That is, while there should be some missionary sermons, all sermons should reflect the missionary spirit. While there should be special seasons of missionary emphasis, all the year should be permeated with missions. While there should be special

---

[9] *Ibid., p. 52.*

missionary lessons in Bible classes, all classes should embody mission emphasis.

It would doubtless come as quite a revelation to discover the exact attitudes of church members to missions. Such information could be obtained by means of a questionnaire handed out to all members. Sample questionnaires are included at the end of Ranck's book, *Education for Mission.* Only with a knowledge of where a church is, can leaders begin to determine specific steps to take the congregation to where it ought to be in mission awareness. When congregational leaders can run through a list of the sort that follows, and conscientiously state that these items are true, only then may they feel satisfied with their efforts.

1) An unmistakable missionary spirit running through the Sunday worship services.

2) A pronounced missionary emphasis in each congregational age unit—young people's work, ladies' class, etc.

3) A consistent program of missionary education in the Bible school.

4) Extensive missionary budget and service activities.

5) Full use of vacation and weekday Bible schools for the purposes of missionary education.

6) Frequent first-hand contacts with missions at home and abroad—the people, the work, the missionaries.

7) Abundant second-hand contacts through visual aids, reading, stories and displays.

8) Proper periods of special missionary emphasis.

9) A continuous program of training leaders in missionary education.

10 A broad, congregation-wide utilization of any special missionary papers, printed reports, etc.[10]

THE PULPIT

The use of the pulpit in educating the home church in its role is primarily the work of the preacher. In a secondary way the pulpit offers potential and returning missionaries an avenue of informing the congregation. The principal advantage of the pulpit as an educational tool is to be found in that it offers about the only avenue whereby the entire congregation in assembly can be instructed at one and the same time. The disadvantage comes as a consequence of the routine place a sermon occupies in the life of the average church member. Most sermons are little retained by even an attentive audience. Through long years of exposure to even the best sermons, people have become accustomed to only half listen, and thus the efficiency level of what is at best an inefficient process declines more. The sheer distance between speaker and audience works against a deep personal involvement on the part of the people.

This whole approach assumes that the preacher is keenly sensitive to the sweep of missions. This assumption is not always valid! Since the preacher does play a leading role in the spiritual life of the congregation, any tendency on his part to lack mission sensitivity will surely cause the congregation's zeal to flag. Unfortunately, the program of studies some preachers follow in preparing to preach does not automatically ensure a missionary outlook. Often quite the reverse! Thus, wide awake elders may have to assist the minister in overcoming this deficiency. Appropriate reading, mission seminars, overseas travel and association with missionaries may help enrich the preacher.

The minister needs this mission concern not only for his own spiritual growth, but for his adequate ministry to his congregation. He himself must be an agent of motivation to bring others into leadership in this essential aspect of the congregation's life.[11]

[10] Harner and Baker, *op. cit.,* p. 37.

[11] Ranck, *op. cit.,* p. 88.

THE BIBLE SCHOOL

The second major avenue available for educating the home church is the regular Bible school program. Sunday and Wednesday Bible classes offer one of the most effective mechanisms for indoctrinating people of all ages in any given subject.

> Missionary efforts, according to the Master, must begin at Jerusalem. It is as impossible to think of a successful Bible school without missionary effort in every department as to think of a successful automobile without a motor.[12]

Too much attention cannot be given to the role the Bible school plays in mission education.

> Despite all its shortcomings, it still reaches more people of more ages for more minutes than any other agency in the average church. If it is shot through with missions from top to bottom, a great advantage has been won; if not, a great opportunity has been lost.[13]

William Brown hardly overstated the case some fifty years ago. "The evangelization of the world waits alone upon the willingness of the workers in the Sunday School.[14] (1906:13). And yet another says,

> Sustained missionary interest and endeavor in a church are not the result of devices, but of a carefully planned and faithfully executed educational program. It is not enough for a church to have a strong missionary history. Education in missions and Christian world relations is part of the total program of Christian education, for it is based on the Bible and is fundamental to the building of complete Christian experience. Englightenment and enlistment in the field of missions are part of the process of Christian growth. So

---

[12]Craig, J. Brad, *Bible School Teacher's Handbook,* (Nashville: Cokesbury Press, 1928). p. 205.

[13] Harner and Baker, *op. cit.,* p. 48.

[14] Brown, *op. cit.,* p. 13.

they have a place in the curriculum of Christian education. Promotion on behalf of missions finds natural response when the meaning of Christian stewardship is taught and practiced as part of this same educational program.[15] (Stevens, 1953:20-21.)

Only in recent years has care and planning been applied to the Bible school program of churches of Christ. For many years the concepts of trained teachers, capable overseers and a balanced curriculum were ignored. It is vital that mission materials be carefully integrated into the total Bible school curriculum. Even where a curriculum now exists, this phase of Christian education often goes begging. This is demonstrated by the sheer lack of materials of this kind being published by Christian publishing houses.

> Curriculum is an important element in Christian education. It is, in essence, a plan to ensure that the growing experiences of children, youth, and adults over a period of years of consecutive study will lead them to a mature Christian faith. Curriculum provides for learning situations and resources.[16]

There are many churches where facilities are ideal, where teachers are well trained, but where missionary zeal and vision are absent. This is due to Bible school leadership which is either unaware of unconcerned about mission education in the Bible school program. To develop an effective program certain persons must assume mission education as their chief responsibility. In a large congregation there may be the need of an assistant to the educational director, charged with formulating and implementing and directing a program of mission education. This would need to be done in cooperation with the educational director and the education committee.

---

[15]Stevens, Dorothy A., *Missionary Education in a Baptist Church,* (Philadelphia: Judson Press, 1953). pp. 20, 21.

[16] Ranck, *op. cit.,* p. 59.

What qualities constitute a good mission education director? 1) He must know mission work well enough to interpret it convincingly to others. 2) He must have had a rich Christian experience and be so deeply concerned about other people that he cannot rest while they are without Christ. 3) He needs to have reached some proficiency in the techniques of Christian education in general and mission education in particular.

> To envelop the whole school in such an effective atmosphere of missions as shall most surely encourage the finer growths of missionary interest and more quickly kindle the fires of missionary enthusiasm is the essential task in missionary leadership. It is as true in missions as it is in everything else: atmosphere conditions life and growth. The personal bearing of the leaders is the greatest factor in creating missionary atmosphere in the school.[17]

On the grass roots level of the Bible class program, the Bible school teacher is in undisputed control of the situation so far as effectiveness of the program of missionary education is concerned. The mission response of students depends almost entirely on the teacher's attitude. Thus the education committee in cooperation with the mission committee must seek:

> ... to lead all Sunday school workers to have a favoring personal bearing towards missions, and to cultivate in them those encouraging missionary attitudes which will enable them to heartily support all missionary endeavors.[18]

The most logical time to begin instruction concerning world evangelism is in the early years of a child's life. Such instruction to have its full impact must be continued throughout the entire period the youngster is growing to adulthood. It is during the junior years that greatest impres-

---

[17] Brown, *op. cit.*, p. 15.

[18] *Ibid.*, p. 64.

sions can be made on young lives. Churches of the American Baptist Convention require that each child receive a minimum of ten hours training per year in missions.[19] Adult classes must not be neglected either in terms of materials that teach mission principles or materials that relate directly to this church's role as a home church.

EDUCATION THROUGH PUBLICITY

The third principal avenue for educating the congregation to its role as home church is through the various avenues of publicity which are available. A committee for public relations should be one of the regular committees of a congregation. It would be the responsibility of this committee to oversee the dissemination of information to the congregation regarding all phases of its program, as well as dealing with information directed to the general public. It would be exceedingly helpful if at least one member of this committee was also a member of the mission committee, and was specifically charged with seeing that regular reports of major mission points are carried by the Bulletin.

EDUCATION THROUGH INVOLVEMENT

The fourth principal avenue by which a congregation can be educated to its role as a home church is through involvement.

A growing number of church schools have learned that teaching is not synonymous with telling; that the function of the pupil is not merely to be a good listener; that the teaching process does not consist of a series of 'lessons' with a story as the central part of each one. When the teacher teaches, what do the pupils do? If they do nothing, the teacher is probably not teaching, however much talking there may be. The pupils, as well as the teacher, must be active, with a sense of purpose and of participation.[20]

---

[19] Stevens, *op. cit.*, p. 129.

[20] Lobingier, John Leslie. *The Better Church School.* (Boston: The Pilgrim Press, 1952), p. 33.

Though this avenue may overlap with some activity carried on in the Bible school program of the congregation, there are, nevertheless, many opportunities for involving people in mission experiences. The use of appropriate motion pictures, slides and tape presentations would be one avenue. This audiovisual contact can do much to condition the heart to greater sympathy toward missions. Any person who is exposed to such devices certainly becomes involved in what he sees and hears, unless he is a most passive kind of individual.

There is great educational value in the involvement that comes by Christians visiting actual mission points. While it is customary for members of the mission committee, elders, and other persons serving in official capacity, to visit mission points periodically, there is a great deal to be gained by encouraging the average Christian to visit such sites. A wise body of elders can select people who have unique influence in given circles within the congregation, and ask them to visit specific sites. Not only will they be stirred and influenced, but because of the respect they have in the eyes of their peers, they will do a worthwhile job of infecting others with their new knowledge. Such visits can be encouraged as a part of one's vacation trips. Visits of this kind could also be specifically planned and funded by the congregation.

A slightly different approach would be a trip en masse by a group from the home church to a given mission area. This would certainly present an ideal opportunity for a campaign, though the side effect of multitudes seeing a given mission point at work could possibly outstrip the value of the campaign itself. Another avenue of involvement would be making a greater use of the missionary's presence when on furlough, by arranging visits in appropriate homes, classes and church gatherings. Such could be far more than mere social occasions. At the present time, involvement of the above kinds is rather infrequent at most churches. Members of the mission committee do make periodic visits. However, the other avenues mentioned are largely unexplored.

Missionary education through involvement also includes acts of Christian service.

> Active participation in the life of the church is important especially in expressional groups. Here the pupil will learn to speak in public, discuss religious and social problems, and think with others about the application of Christian principles to life situations. There will be participation in such practical tasks as visiting the sick, helping the weak and needy, giving guidance to the perplexed and winning men to Christ as Lord and Savior.[21]

Many types of projects may be carried on in the churches. Here, the emphasis is upon missionary education projects. These have a distinctly educational purpose, education for Christian world brotherhood and Christian world-mindedness. "Learning by doing" is true. Often it is exciting to have the experience of doing things with people because a bond of fellowship is developed in that fashion. It is the purpose of missionary education to increase these bonds through learning to know more about our world neighbors and through sharing Christ with them. What mission service does for a congregation: 1) Quickens the life of the church. 2) Discovers workers. 3) Enriches spiritual life. 4) Makes prayer a greater reality. 5) Develops right attitudes. 6) Lifts life's horizons. 7) Makes for Christian certainty. 8) Makes for a satisfying Christian experience. 9) Completes Christian living.

> It is only a half-truth to say that good missionary education results in Christian service and helpfulness to those in need; that first our hearts are touched, and then we serve; that first we learn, and then we give and do. The other half of the truth is that Christian service is good missionary education; that the experience of serving has power in and of itself to touch our hearts; that we learn by giving and doing. The rendering of Christian service to those at hand as well as to those at a distance is an indispensable part of any church program of missionary education.[22]

---

[21]Murch, James DeForest, *Teach or Perish.* (Grand Rapids: Eerdmans, 1961), p. 101.

[22] Harner and Baker, *op. cit.,* p. 63.

While many projects of a benevolent or other kind might be undertaken, Christians must never overlook service through teaching others. The personal work program of the local congregation provides a great avenue of education through involvement. Though this is somewhat removed from missions as they are generally conceived, it nevertheless has a vital role to play. People who are not interested in saving the lost at home generally have little interest in saving the lost away from home.

EVALUATION

The question that continually haunts the worker in missionary education is whether he is doing all that he can and accomplishing all that he should. By and large there are only three places at which to look for an answer to this question. The first is the program of missionary education itself to see if it is all it ought to be. The second is the congregation to see if there are any evidences of steady growth in missionary intelligence and passion. The third is individual boys and girls, men and women, to see how their hearts and minds stand with regard to the Christian missionary enterprise.

Perhaps, as in all spiritual matters, hope and faith are the essential words. Christian attitudes and virtues can be demonstrated, but they cannot be weighed on an apothecary's balance or analyzed in the chemist's test tube. After we have done our best, we trust God's Holy Spirit to complete the work in our lives and in the lives of our friends. Yet with a little imagination, we can find some clues that indicate what spiritual growth has occurred.

Perhaps the following five questions will serve as a simple yardstick with which to measure its adequacy in our program: Are we using all the available avenues of missions education in our church? Are we giving balanced attention to all phases of the missionary enterprise? Are we reaching all ages equally well? Are we reaching both sexes equally well? Are we reaching an ever-increasing proportion of our constituency? A committee or an individual, concerned for the adequacy of a local church program of education for mission, might use a check list like the above to assess the merits of the program of missionary education that is being planned.

Possibly the words of James DeForest Murch—words written of Christian education in general—and applied by the present writer to the specific problem of mission education, form a suitable conclusion for us:

> Christian education for today and tomorrow must completely recapture the characteristics of Christian education in the early Church. It must be primarily a local church responsibility; it must be a major concern in all the churches; it must be for the whole membership and for as many others outside the communion as can be induced to take instruction; it must be intensely evangelistic; it must be synonymous with life itself and, in close association with the leadership of the Church, it must be responsible for the nurture and discipline of those who look to it for protection and guidance. Because of the extreme exigencies of the hour the Church must through all its local congregations mount this kind of an educational program. It must teach or perish![23]

SUGGESTED READINGS

Brown, William A., *The Why and How of Missions in the Sunday School.* New York, Fleming H. Revell Co., 1916.

Collins, Marjorie A., *Manual for Missionaries on Furlough.* Pasadena, California: William Carey Library, 1972.

Manual for Accepted Missionary Candidates. Pasadena, California: William Carey Library, 1972.

Who Cares About the Missionary? Chicago Moody Press, 1974. 1974.

Craig, J. Brad, *Bible School Teacher's Handbook.* Nashville, Cokesbury Press, 1928.

---

[23]Murch, *op. cit.,* p. 72.

Elkins, Phillip W., *Church Sponsored Missions,* Austin, Texas, Firm Foundation Publishing House, 1974.

Elkjer, Charles B., *The Launching Pad: The Local Church Can Evangelize the World.* Pasadena, California: The Association of Church Mission Committees, 1975.

Harner, Nevin C. and Baker, David D., *Missionary Education in Your Church.* New York, Missionary Education Movement of U. S. and Canada, 1942.

Lobingier, John Leslie, *The Better Church School.* Boston, The Pilgrim Press, 1952.

Murch, James DeForest, *Teach or Perish.* Grand Rapids, Eerdman's 1961.

Myklebust, Olav Guttorm, *The Study of Missions in Theological Education.* Oslo, Forlagel Land Og Kirke. 1957.

Norton, Howard W., *The Eldership and the Missionary,* Oklahoma City, Oklahoma, the OCC Education Associates, 1971.

Ranck, J. Allan, *Education for Mission.* New York, Friendship Press, 1961.

Stevens, Dorothy A., *Missionary Education in a Baptist Church.* Philadelphia, Judson Press, 1953.

Vieth, Paul H., *The Church School.* Philadelphia, Christian Education Press.

PERSONALIA

WENDELL W. BROOM, SR.
Assistant Professor of Missions
Abilene Christian University
M. A., Missions, School of World Missions, Fuller Theological
Seminary
Mission experience in Ghana and Nigeria.

DAN C. COKER
Associate Professor of Missions
Abilene Christian University
PhD., International Education and Anthropology, University of
Florida
Mission experience in Guatemala, Honduras, and Mexico

B. EDWARD DAVIS
Professor of Communications
Abilene Christian University
PhD., Cross-Cultural Communications, Michigan State University
Missions experience: Consultant in research in mass media
evangelism and Bible translations.

BOB DOUGLAS
PhD. candidate, School of World Missions, Fuller Theological
Seminary
Mission experience in Libya, Egypt and Lebanon

GEORGE P. GURGANUS
Professor of Missions and Director of Seminar in Missions
Abilene Christian University
PhD., Cross-Cultural Communications, Penn State University
Mission experience in Japan

DANIEL C. HARDIN
Professor of Bible and Missions
Lubbock Christian College
EdD., Oklahoma State University
Mission experience in Korea, Past President of Korea Christian
College

JOYCE HARDIN
Associate Professor of Education
Lubbock Christian College
Ed.S., Oklahoma State University
Mission experience in Korea. Authored Missions textbook for
women

EDWARD F. MATHEWS
    Assistant Professor of Missions and Specialist in Leadership Train-
        ing by Extension
    Abilene Christian University
    S. T. B., ACU; and M. A. in Missions, School of World
    Missions, Fuller Theological Seminary
    Mission experience in Guatemala

STAN SHEWMAKER
    Resident Missionary
    Abilene Christian University
    M.A., School of World Missions, Fuller Theological Seminary
    Mission experience in Zambia

GLOVER SHIPP
    Missionary in Brazil
    M.A., Cross-Cultural Communications, Pepperdine University
    Mission experience in Belo Horizonte, Brazil

C. PHILIP SLATE
    Assistant Professor of Missions
    Harding Graduate School of Religion
    D. Miss., School of World Missions, Fuller Theological Seminary
    Mission experience in Europe